East Beach Press

presents

Prophet—The Hatmaker's Son

The Life of Robert Muller

Author: Douglas Gillies

ISBN: 0-9702705-3-4

Size: 6 X 9 inches

Pages: 288

Format: Hardcover, 4-color cover, Index, References, Bibliography, Photos

Category: Nonfiction, Biography, World War (1939-1945), United Nations

Price: $24.95

First Printing: 5,000

Publication Date: March 11, 2003

East Beach Press
P.O. Box 6890   (805) 965-0200
Santa Barbara, CA 93160   (805) 563-9690 fax

info@eastbeach.org   www.eastbeach.org

Early acclaim for

Prophet—The Hatmaker's Son
The Life of Robert Muller

"Prophet - The Hatmaker's Son is the inspiring, true story of Robert Muller, a man who lived through the atrocities of World War II and then dedicated his life to peace. Gillies brings to vivid life the remarkable achievements and astounding story of this great global citizen. *Prophet* is a reminder to every reader why war does not work—and offers a path to a better way."
> **—Mary Manin Morrissey,** author of *Building Your Field of Dreams* and *No Less Than Greatness*

"Robert Muller's biography is a testimony to a man who has dedicated his life to peace, vividly showing the development of his passionate commitment working for the greater good of all." **—Riane Eisler**, author of *The Chalice & The Blade*,
> *The Power of Partnership*, and *Tomorrow's Children.*

"Robert Muller is one of our greatest voices for world peace and for a new international politics based on spiritual principles. His commitment to global citizenship embodies the truth revealed by quantum physics that we are all one at the most fundamental level of existence. His biography should be read by everyone who cares about global unity and the spiritual well-being of humanity."
—John Hagelin Ph.D., author of *Manual for a Perfect Gov't*

"Robert Muller has been an inspiration to countless people around the world. What a joy it is now to read the story of this remarkable life."
> **—Peter Russell**, author *From Science to God*

Robert Muller has seen our species at our worst and still ebulliently believes in our best. In his presence, you want to rise and rise and rise again to whatever occasion is before you. He is a global treasure—and so will you be if you let his spirit enter your life. I did... and look what happened!"
> **—Vicki Robin**, coauthor of *Your Money or Your Life*

"An extraordinary saga of an extraordinary man—one of the first truly global minds of the 20th century, with the prophetic insight we so desperately need in the 21st!"
—**Ervin Laszlo**, Founder of the Club of Budapest; author of *Macroshift*

"This is a great book, a powerful piece of work."
—**Frank Kelly**, author

"Breathtaking! It is brilliant because Robert Muller's contribution to world peace is brilliant! Gripping style by Gillies. I've been a professional writer-editor for 60 years and my first clipping through it jumps up and says *Great!*"
—**Nada-Yolanda**, Exec. Director Mark-Age/I Am Nation

This is the story of an optimist who worked at the UN from its founding. The writing is very good and the story is fascinating."
—**Dan Poynter**, author of *The Self-Publishing Manual*

"Robert Muller's life is dramatic, inspiring, and has historic significance, simultaneously. Everyone who reads *Prophet* will have a new perspective on war, and an intimate grasp of why peace should be the foremost motivation in human relationships. I couldn't put it down!"
—**Gloria Crook**, Founder, Robert Muller Schools

"Robert Muller has a pulse on the planet. He understands the global trend lines. His biography is worthy of being read by teachers, historians, business leaders, professors, clergy, writers, elected officials, and international civil servants."
—**Sanford Hinden**, Founder, Director Peace Museums

The author has a remarkable ability to correlate facts and tell them in a way that makes you feel you are participating to those events. —**Sergio Tripi, Ph. D.**, Good News Agency

"*Tour de force.* Gillies nailed it. This true story of personal bravery and moral courage is better reading than any fictional hero." —**Lois Clark McCoy**, President, NIUSR

PROPHET

THE HATMAKER'S SON
THE LIFE OF ROBERT MULLER

PROPHET
The Hatmaker's Son
By Douglas Gillies

Published by:
East Beach Press
P. O. Box 6890
Santa Barbara, CA 93160-6890

(800) 942-7617
www.eastbeach.org
orders@eastbeach.org

ISBN, print ed. Hardcover   0-9702705-3-4
ISBN, print ed. Paperback   0-9702705-4-2
ISBN, PDF ed.   0-9702705-5-0
First Printing 2003
Printed in the United States of America

Publisher's Cataloging-in-Publication Data
Gillies, Douglas
Prophet: the hatmaker's son/Douglas Gillies
1st ed.
288 p. cm.
Includes bibliographical references and index.
ISBN 0-9702705-3-4
1. Muller, Robert, 1923 —.
2. United Nations—Biography.
3. World War, 1939 – 1945—France.
4. United States—History—20th Century.

Cover Design: Lynda Rae, Image Graphics
Cover Photograph: "Sun on the Horizon" by Nathaniel Gillies

For LeeAnn

Contents

Acknowledgments

Alphabetical order is an approach to acknowledging the good people who have contributed to this work that suits the man whose story is told in this book. Robert Muller sees every human being as an equal, whether they are running the biggest country on Earth or walking the smallest dog in the park.

I am deeply grateful to all of the optimistic, loving, funny, and caring souls who educated, supported, and encouraged me to write a book big enough to tell Robert Muller's story:

Desmond Berghofer, Honorable Rodrigo Carazo, Larry Carp, Center for ReUniting Families, Linda Crawford, June Denton, Ron Dexter, Joanne Dufour, Cathy Feldman, Foundation for the Future, Marie Elaine Gabriel, Jay Gary, Barbara Gaughen-Muller, Don George, Nathaniel Gillies, Bill Gladstone, Stephanie Glatt, Michael Gosney, Carol Hawkins, Didier Hemmert, Peter Huber, Marcelle Muller Hubert, Frank Kelly, LeeAnn Kendall, Helga Kollar, Lola Kristof, La Casa de Maria, Margery Layton, Bill Levis, Chris and Inge Mair, Sandra Martin, Avon Mattison, Joanie Misrack, Dr. Gisèle Muller-Parker, Philippe and Mari-téré Muller, Solange Muller, François Muller, Gene Nash, Barclay Palmer, Howard H. and Alice K. Parker, Michael B. Parker, Pathways to Peace, Dan Poynter, Lynda Rae, Alan Reich, Gay Reich, Nancy Rivard, Airline Ambassadors, Auguste Rivet, Vicki Robin, Anita Routh, Dyanne Routh, Santa Barbara Public Library, Shane Saxon, Bruce Schuman, Geraldine Schwartz, Greg Siadal, Susan Sostman, Steve Ternoey, Duane Unkefer, Rhona Walter, Ramona Winner, World Community on Disability, and Lucia Van Ruiten.

Preface

Bogsch was the name of the Director General of the World Intellectual Property Organization in Geneva. During one of Robert Muller's visits, Dr. Arpad Bogsch held up a dog-eared copy of Robert's first book, *Most of All They Taught Me Happiness*.

"Muller, your book is a turning point," he said. "In our society, it is fashionable to be pessimistic. Very few people speak optimistically about the future. You have the courage to come out bluntly for life, progress, hope, ethics, morality, and spirituality. I ordered copies for all my directors."

"I'm surprised it aroused such interest," Robert said.

"Together with Hammarskjöld, you are probably the only one at the UN who will live in the memory of humankind."

"But I can't even write a consistent book from beginning to end. All I do is write little stories and anecdotes."

Pointing his finger, Bogsch said, "Don't you realize what you're doing? You express yourself like the prophets!"

Prophets come in different shapes and sizes. There are prophets who speak for God and prophets who foretell future events, prophets of hope and prophets of doom. All of them test our limits and challenge our beliefs.

When I first met Robert Muller, I asked him, "How can an ordinary person like me think like a global citizen?"

He said, "It's pretty easy. You just take everything you do and multiply it by six billion."

Six billion—that's a sobering idea. Choose between six billion paper or plastic grocery bags at the market, drink coffee from six billion Styrofoam cups, leave six billion light bulbs burning in the kitchen while I'm reading in the living room. This was my first taste of Robert Muller's 5,000 ideas for a better world.

When we met in 1994, I was producing an event called *The Big Picture Summit*. Participants met for five days at La Casa de Maria in Santa Barbara to look for answers to one question: "How can we speed up the shift to wholistic thinking from linear, reductionist, compartmentalized thinking?" In other words, *how can we get people to see the big picture?*

They had written 70 strategies when Barbara Gaughen said, "On July 11, there will be 2000 days to the year 2000. Let's put our heads together and come up with one idea per day for a better world."

Everyone just sat there. Two thousand ideas is a lot of ideas. Then Robert Muller stood up and said, "I'll do it!"

I practiced law for twenty years, and trial lawyers work on problems from the past. Each trial asks the same question: "Who are we going to blame and what's it going to cost them?" When I retired from law, I had an uneasy feeling that the world was getting worse and it didn't matter whose fault it was. We had made it this far. Let's just let bygones be bygones and look for a plausible, positive course into the future—before it's too late! My trials were over, judgments were final, appeals were exhausted, and every case was closed. But every day, despite all the good intentions in the world, the world was getting worse.

On July 11, 1994, Robert wrote his first idea for a better world. He wrote the second idea on July 12. He completed 365 ideas on July 11, 1995, 730 ideas a year later, 1,095 the year after that. Most of us would be lucky to write a good idea once or twice a month. By the end of 1999, Robert Muller had published *2,000 Ideas and Dreams for a Better World* and then, when anyone else would have taken a day off, he changed the title to *3,000 Ideas and Dreams.*

There was something about Robert Muller that I didn't understand. As a lawyer, I had a feeling for where the Common Law stood and where it was headed. That was my job. But with Muller's ideas, it was as if he was discerning an emerging common agreement that will allow our civilization to continue for another thousand years.

I knew there had to be a good story in there somewhere. I visited Robert's cottage in Costa Rica. I followed him to New York, San Francisco, and The Hague. In February 2000, my dear friend LeeAnn said, "I found this quote by Robert Muller in the workbook from a seminar."

> Use every letter you write
> Every conversation you have
> Every meeting you attend

To express your fundamental beliefs and dreams.
Affirm to others the vision of the world you want
Network through thought
Network through action
Network through love
Network through spirit
You are the center of the network
You are the center of the world
You are free, a powerful source of life and goodness.
Affirm it.
Spread it.
·Radiate it.
Think day and night about it
And you will see a miracle happen.

I had interviewed Robert Muller a dozen times during the previous five years, recording his talks and catching glimpses of his conversations with people who were making the world a better place. At the Hague Appeal for Peace, I watched him light up audience after audience with his audacious humor and his energetic, creative mind. He was almost 80 years old and he still inspired hope and courage everywhere he spoke.

He's more than a man, I realized. Muller had worked for enlightened world governance so long that he embodied the spirit of public service, but his lifelong commitment to peace had lifted him another notch. Robert Muller was a prophet.

If there is to be a civilized world in another hundred years, Muller's words will ring out like a clarion. His ideas, his spiritual fortitude, and his passion for life will leave an indelible impression on future generations. He will be remembered as a visionary whose message during a time of transition laid the foundation for humanity's shift of allegiance from too many quarrelling nations to one great love for the world.

Robert Muller's life makes sense of the 20th Century. The more time that passes, the brighter his light will shine.

Chapter 1 – A Crack in the Wall

"C an you meet me in Paris?"
Robert Muller studied the telegram for some clue. Something was missing. It could not be Waldheim's idea. Muller sat down on the front steps of his farmhouse and read the telegram again:

Arriving Paris Thursday 10 August 1972 Hotel Hilton. Will be accompanied to China by Mrs. Waldheim, Tang Ming-chao, and Robert Muller. Can you meet me in Paris?

It was more of a summons than a request, but there was no explanation. *Why would Kurt Waldheim want me to go?* Robert wondered.

His ten-year-old son sat down next to him on the step.

"Do you have to go to work, Daddy?" Philippe asked.

"I'm going to China."

"Right now?" his son asked, tugging his sleeve.

"No, not until tomorrow. But I'll be back in a week."

"Why do you have to go, Daddy?"

"Well, it's what I do. It's part of my job."

Philippe trudged back inside the house.

How do you explain to a ten-year-old that China is very important to the UN, and it's a big honor to be invited, even if it means cutting short your summer vacation? How could his son possibly understand?

He put the telegram in his pocket and tried to focus on the problem at hand, giving himself a little time to sort things out.

The problem was, there was a road in his front yard. Via Strada was a fine old road that ran along the foothills west of Geneva. The Romans had built it there so that they could keep an eye on the Swiss as the Legionnaires marched north towards Belgium. The road had endured for 2,000 years because the stones had been set with such skill and precision. Robert liked the road; he just didn't want it in his front yard.

Four years before, the Mullers had finished restoring the farmhouse. Robert and Margarita and the children had driven up to St. Gix from Geneva every weekend to work on the old place. They hauled away junk left behind by the shepherds, scraped dung off the floors, patched holes in the roof, plastered, painted, put up shutters and shingles, and planted fruit trees that were finally bearing fruit.

It was one of the finest original farmhouses around Divonne. They had even restored a horse-drawn sleigh and placed it on display in the open loft of the barn. Children from Divonne and neighboring French villages were making special trips to see the sleigh. They called the Muller's farmhouse *La Maison du Père Noël*—The House of Santa Claus.

The only project that had not been completed was the stone wall. For five years, Robert's contractor in Divonne had collected stones and constructed elaborate excuses for postponing the work. Now that Robert was living in New York, the wall was put off year after year. Robert was standing in his front yard thinking about the wall when Waldheim's message arrived.

"What's this I hear about China?" Margarita said from the living room window.

Robert held up the telegram. "Waldheim wants me to go with him to China. I'm supposed to meet him in Paris tomorrow."

"That's odd," she said. "Who's he taking?"

"His wife, two aides, Tang, and me."

"That doesn't make sense. Why would he invite you?"

"I don't know."

"Well, you'd better start packing," she said.

Margarita had resigned herself to the demands on her husband's time. Ever since Robert had been assigned to the Secretary General's office, his job had consumed almost every waking minute. Summer vacations were the only time they could get away to their hideaway and relax with the children.

Robert's mind was buzzing with ideas about China. After he packed, he read the telegram again. Waldheim was departing from New York later that day. He would meet his wife in Paris, where she would arrive from Vienna. On Friday, the Secretary General's party would fly to Peking on Air France. Three full days in China. It was just enough time, if they got right down to business.

Margarita brought him a cup of tea.

"What are we going to tell your mother?" she asked.

Robert sighed. They had put off visiting Sarreguemines until the end of summer. Although Robert had grown up in Sarreguemines, his family preferred to stay in St. Gix during summer vacations. Robert could relax and unwind in the tiny hamlet—five Celtic farmhouses at the end of a little road in the foothills of the Jura Mountains. Geneva was only ten miles away, where Margarita and the children could visit their friends.

Robert's mother wouldn't understand. His parents had always lived in Alsace-Lorraine, and their parents, and their parents, and everybody on both sides of Robert's family all the way back to the days of the Huns. Robert didn't even want to think about what his mother would say if they skipped the annual visit.

"This trip to Peking will only take a week. If we close up the house in a day, we'll have time for Sarreguemines."

"I'll take care of that. You'll be tired when you get back."

After dinner, Robert sat with Margarita and the boys at the kitchen while Gisèle and Solange cleared the dishes. Margarita had been a member of Chile's delegation when she met Robert Muller at the UN and she had remained his closest advisor for twenty years.

"Why would Waldheim want me to go to China?" Robert asked. "Tang is the Under-Secretary General for Political

Affairs, so he has to go, and Mrs. Waldheim, of course. But why take me, the director of his office? Shouldn't it be Brian Urquhart, or somebody else in political affairs?"

"There was no hint that this was coming?" she asked.

"Nothing, just this telegram. He must have known for weeks that he was going to China."

"I don't understand this Kurt Waldheim," Margarita said. "The first time I heard him speak was last January, and I was appalled. He is not a good man."

"He's only been in office a few months. He may still need some time to get his footing."

"You shouldn't stay with a man like that!"

"The big powers must have had a reason to elect him. And it's quite an honor for me to be invited to China. This trip will be one of the high points in Waldheim's career."

"He did absolutely nothing to deserve it. U Thant opened the door for China."

"Still, the veil is finally lifting. Waldheim's trip means that the world is changing."

On the way to the airport the next day, Robert purchased several cartons of Meccarillos. The little Swiss cigars would be a novelty to the Chinese, who had lived in isolation for 25 years.

Margarita kissed him goodbye at the airport. "Be careful with that man," she said.

The Waldheims sat in first class with Tang Ming-chao; Robert was seated in coach, which gave him time to organize his thoughts. Robert tried to recall every event that might explain why he was on this trip.

Kurt Waldheim was only halfway through the first year as Secretary General, so his administration was still in transition. Most of his senior staff had been inherited from U Thant and he was not yet certain whom he could count on. Among Waldheim's top advisors, Robert Muller was one of the most popular with UN staff, but he had the least experience in political affairs. Robert's career had been devoted to economic and social programs.

Waldheim didn't seem to understand Muller. There were

common elements in their backgrounds, but the differences outweighed the similarities. Waldheim had been born in Austria in 1918, so he was five years older than Muller. Both of them grew up during the interval between two wars. Their childhood homes were less than 400 miles apart, with Germany between them. Muller had been raised in Sarreguemines on the French side of Germany and Waldheim was from a town near Vienna on the east. Both were teenagers when Hitler took control of their countries.

Kurt Waldheim graduated from the University of Vienna with a Doctor of Jurisprudence in 1944, during German occupation. Robert Muller earned his J.D. at the University of Strasbourg after the war. They each chose a career in international relations. First Waldheim entered the Austrian diplomatic service in 1945, and then Muller joined the United Nations in 1948.

Waldheim was a career diplomat. He was ambitious and calculating, and he had a reputation for ingratiating himself to leaders of major powers, or anyone he considered his superior.[1] Muller was a public servant committed to world peace, a pragmatic economist who had transformed into a spiritual idealist during his two years with U Thant. He was beginning to be recognized in the UN as a visionary. Robert's style was more informal and relaxed, and he was comfortable with people regardless of rank.

Robert followed his instincts in making decisions, and tended to do whatever he felt was best. Such an intuitive personality was incomprehensible to Waldheim, who obsessed over the smallest details before making a decision. Waldheim could infuriate his staff by insisting in the middle of a discussion that they go back to the beginning and start over.

Robert recalled an incident a few weeks after they started working together. Waldheim was in a hurry to talk with Muller; an aide reported that Muller was taking a UN class in Chinese. When Robert returned to the office, Waldheim confronted him.

"Why are you taking this course?" Waldheim demanded. "You already speak seven languages. Why do you need another?"

"I have a feeling I'm going to need it," Muller replied.

Could that be the reason I'm going to China? Robert thought. *Is it because I took that class in Chinese?*

It didn't make sense.

This can't be Waldheim's idea. The Chinese must have insisted that I come. But why?

Robert pieced together every event that might connect him to China. It had started two and a half years earlier with the memo from U Thant, the previous Secretary General. Robert was in Prague at a planning session for the UN Budget when U Thant's memo arrived. U Thant wanted his Budget Director to comment on a letter from The Big Four—the United States, France, Germany, and Great Britain were proposing a 3-year freeze on their dues to the UN.

Robert sent back a terse note to U Thant: *Ask them to compare the UN budget with their military expenditures. You could recommend they freeze the latter.* He attached a detailed analysis comparing the UN budget to routine government allocations.

Muller was instructed to return immediately to New York to meet with the Secretary General.

U Thant began the meeting without formalities. "I understand you have been telling people that our UN budget is smaller than the State of Colorado."

"Yes, I sent you an analysis. In fact, our budget is the same as the fire department in Tokyo or New York," Robert said.

"Or the U.S. Army budget for military bands," U Thant said.

"*Voilà!*" How can anybody ever accuse the UN of being wasteful?"

U Thant sized up the Director of the Budget. Robert Muller was strong-willed. He was a skillful administrator, but he was certainly not afraid of confrontation. It was obvious that he had enormous energy. Robert was like a freight train. He was strong, but perhaps he was a little too hard after dealing with the frustrations of the UN for 21 years. But there was something about Robert Muller that appealed to U Thant. There didn't seem to be any selfish motives driving him, no self-consciousness in his manner. He wasn't holding anything back.

"I want you to come to work for me," U Thant said softly.

To his surprise, Robert felt a mixture of excitement and hesitation. He had dreamed of working in the Secretary General's office, but when the opportunity was presented, he had doubts. He asked for a little time to think it over.

Two of U Thant's top aides, Ralph Bunche and Brian Urquhart, cautioned Robert to weigh his decision carefully.

"He's a very nice man," Ralph Bunche said, "but he's not really very active."

"He's not energetic," Brian Urquhart added. "These are his two last years, and it might be a waste of your time."

"But two years is a long time," Robert said. "I'll have to think it over."

Early the next morning, Robert sat at his wooden desk in the living room of their small family home in Ardsley-on-Hudson. He stared out the window at the intricate patterns of ice on the bare branches in his orchard as he wrote in his journal:

> Tuesday 27 January 1970
> I still cannot believe it. Some mediocre individual will put an obstacle to it. It is not possible that such an occasion is offered to me—to become the Director of the Executive Office of the Secretary General of the United Nations, one of his main, direct collaborators. My life was an incomplete circle. All of a sudden, my ascension to the highest floor of the House of Hope, whatever situation I will find there, makes it a novel, a magic story.

Robert notified the Secretary General's office that he would accept the assignment. Robert's stint as the head of the Budget was so brief, UN staff called it, "The Spring of Prague." [2]

Robert remembered February 3, 1970, as the happiest day of his life. He boarded his 8:35 train at Ardsley-on-Hudson. After passing Yankee Stadium, the train crossed the Harlem River and slipped into the familiar black tunnel. He felt like he was floating as he walked out of Grand Central Station and headed down 42nd Street, moving against the morning tide of office workers. The United Nations Building looked more majestic than usual. He stepped into an elevator, pushed the top button, and rode to the 38th floor.

Muller slipped into his new office unnoticed. From his briefcase he retrieved a framed photograph of an emaciated young man dressed in a mismatched khaki uniform with a revolver on his hip. Robert placed the photograph on his desk. Before anyone could interrupt him, he made a note in his journal:

God did not grant me the gift of art. I had to express myself in my own life, in my thoughts, in my feelings, in my dreams and ideas, and in my love for all humanity and the Earth. I feel human, totally ecstatically human. I will help this planet, with all my abilities and love, to become what it was always meant to be: the planet of God, a true miracle in the universe, inhabited by a happy, fulfilled, peaceful, loving humanity, thankful for the miraculous gift of life.

The next day, Robert had a bowl of Alsatian sauerkraut in the UN cafeteria with his former boss, Philippe de Seynes, the Under-Secretary General for Economic and Social Affairs.

"Congratulations on your appointment," de Seynes said. "I have already talked to U Thant about you. I told him that he is getting someone of the highest character. I said it would be unforgivable not to utilize you fully."

"It's not my person that matters," Robert said.

"Yes, I know, you said that at Father de Breuvery's funeral. You said, 'All that counts is the common, collective effort.' But Robert, it is much more than that! There is also the contribution of your person, of your experience, of your past."

"What did U Thant say when you told him that?"

"He said, 'I will be enchanted, because I barely see my Chef de Cabinet anymore. Narasimhan spends almost all his time at the UN Development Program.' "

"So my main role will be to replace Narasimhan during his absences," Robert said. "Since I'm an economist, you'd think he would rather keep me in the Budget Division."

Robert met U Thant the following night for the first time in his new position. U Thant was standing under the large UN flag when Robert entered his office, and because of his diminutive stature, or perhaps it was U Thant's tranquility, the pale blue United Nations flag seemed enlarged.

"I think you will be happier here than in the Budget Division," U Thant said with a smile. With this, Robert guessed the reason for his assignment. There were rumors the Americans wanted him out of the Budget Division.

A few days later, Robert asked the Secretary General, "Do you have any unfulfilled dreams?"

U Thant looked at Muller with the barest hint of a smile. "Yes, I have three," he answered. "I always listen to political and economic speeches. I never hear a spiritual voice in the United Nations, even though I am a spiritual person above everything else." The word *spiritual* rocketed through Muller's mind. "Secondly, I was once the headmaster at the National High School in Burma. I am convinced that the world will not change unless we have a new education. But most important, the UN doesn't make any sense without a representative from China. I want to see China take a seat."

Robert said, "Okay, let's work on all three."

U Thant nodded impassively.

"The Vatican is a state," Robert said, "The Holy See is a very tiny state, but they maintain permanent observer status here. You can invite the Pope to address the General Assembly, just like you would invite any other visiting head of state."

This brought another smile to U Thant.

"Ever since Napoleon," Robert continued, "there have been schools that teach soldiers how to fight wars. You never hear about a university that teaches peace. No one wants to pay for that. It will be up to the UN to build the first university for peace. But that may take some time.

"As for China, I'm aware that a resolution has been introduced in the General Assembly every year since 1950, and still they refuse to budge. Peking is adamant that there can only be one China in the UN. Taiwan insists they will never give up their seat. There is only one thing you can do. You must take a stand. Maybe then they will find a way."

"My views are known," U Thant said. "See what you can do."

Robert sat down at a typewriter and started working on a speech for the Secretary General. It was a familiar topic. The Nationalist government in Taiwan, headed by Chiang Kai-shek, had been a founding member of the United Nations. Nationalist China had worked with the Soviet Union, the United Kingdom and the United States to write the first proposal for a UN charter in 1944. China was one of the five permanent members of the Security Council when the UN Charter was drafted in San Francisco at the Fairmont Hotel, but nobody anticipated that Chiang Kai-shek's government would be defeated by a Communist revolution. When the Nationalists fled to Taiwan in 1949, the People's Republic of China, led by Mao Tse-tung, set up a new Communist government in Peking and found itself diplomatically isolated from the rest of the world. Twenty years later, the government in Taiwan still held itself out to be the legal representative of the Chinese people—one fifth of the world's population.

Starting in 1950, a resolution had been introduced every year in the General Assembly proposing UN membership for the People's Republic of China. Every year, the General Assembly had voted against the Communist regime. When Muller started working in U Thant's office, the American delegation was leading the opposition.

Robert handed the speech to U Thant a few days later. The Chief of Cabinet, C. V. Narasimhan, cautioned U Thant against taking the initiative on such a vital question without clear direction from the General Assembly. A fellow Hindu, Narasimhan had considerable influence over the decisions of the Burmese Secretary General. It was understood on the 38th floor that if Narasimhan opposed an action, U Thant would not go forward against his advice. But Robert continued to encourage U Thant to push the China debate to the foreground. With uncharacteristic boldness, U Thant started speaking out.

On April 11, 1970, U Thant addressed an assembly in Manila. "The participation of the People's Republic of China in activities of the international community is increasingly desirable." [3] At the Fairmont Hotel on June 26, celebrating the 25th Anniversary of the United Nations, he said, "I recommend that the United Nations be made universal. The absence of the People's Republic of China has given to the United Nations a great deal of artificiality." [4] On September 14, he concluded his remarks at the New York Hilton by saying, "It is high time that the People's Republic of China be involved in international affairs and that the idea of the universality of the United Nations be given priority in this year's agenda."[5]

The repetition of U Thant's position generated intense discussion in the General Assembly, giving new impetus to a weary controversy. In October 1970, the question of China's entry into the United Nations was debated on the floor of the General Assembly for the 21st consecutive year. For the first time, a majority of the delegates voted in favor of China's admission, but before the celebrations could begin, the United States made a procedural motion declaring that China's representation was an *important question* which required a two-thirds majority. The motion was approved retroactively, blocking China's admission.

On April 10, 1971, nine American table tennis players flew to Peking, the first Americans allowed into China since the Communist takeover. Ten journalists were invited to cover the team's visit, ending an information blockade that had isolated the People's Republic since 1949. Reporters called it "Ping-Pong Diplomacy."

Three months later, Henry Kissinger feigned illness during a visit to Pakistan and took a 4:00 a.m. flight to China. After two days of secret talks with Kissinger, Premier Chou En-Lai invited President Nixon to visit China. On July 15, Nixon made a surprise announcement on television that he would visit Peking in 1972. By coincidence, the Albanian delegation happened to introduce Resolution 2758 on the same day.

For eight consecutive years, the Albanians had introduced a resolution in September, at the start of each new session of the General Assembly, calling for the Peking government to replace Taipei in the UN. Eight times it was defeated. But U Thant's remarks had stirred up powerful forces in the UN. Giving itself more time to build support, Albania introduced its China resolution on July 15, 1971, three months earlier than usual.

Resolution 2758.

Recalling the principles of the Charter of the United Nations,

Considering that the restoration of the lawful rights of the People's Republic of China is essential both for the protection of the Charter of the United Nations and for the cause that the United Nations must serve under the Charter,

Recognizing that the representatives of the Government of the People's Republic of China are the only lawful representatives of China to the United Nations and that the People's Republic of China is one of the five permanent members of the Security Council,

Decides to restore all its rights to the People's Republic of China and to recognize the representatives of its Government as the only legitimate representatives of China to the United Nations, and to expel forthwith the representatives of Chiang Kai-shek from the place which they unlawfully occupy at the United Nations and in all the organizations related to it.

On August 2, United States Secretary of State William P. Rogers announced that the U.S. was suspending its 20-year policy opposing Communist China's admission to the UN, but would not vote to expel Taiwan. The next day, Peking's foreign minister denounced America's two-China policy as a "gross insult to the UN charter."

In September, President Nixon said the U.S. would support seating the People's Republic on the UN Security Council because "it reflects the realities of the situation." He added, "We will vote against the expulsion of Taiwan."

A few days later, U Thant spoke at the Waldorf Astoria. "The government of an ancient and populous nation may soon be taking its place at the United Nations. This may have come ten years too late. Nevertheless, I deeply believe that this event will signify a fundamental turn for the better in world affairs."[6]

The Albanians and the Americans lobbied vigorously. After weeks of arm-twisting by American delegates at the UN and private pressure in foreign capitals, it was widely anticipated that Resolution 2758 would fail. The delegates from smaller countries were not well enough organized to fend off the American campaign, which was described by *The New York Times* as, "the most vigorous diplomatic campaign ever waged by the United States."

On Monday, October 25, 1971, the day before the vote was to be taken, *The New York Times* reported that the outcome was so uncertain that it would hinge on last-minute decisions by a handful of small countries. It was Veteran's Day, a holiday in the United States. Government offices were closed. A heavy rain fell in Washington and senior officials went home early.

Sensing an upsurge in support, the Albanians acted swiftly and called for a vote one day sooner than expected. Leaders in the White House and Congress were not aware that a vote was being taken. On the opposite side of the world, Henry Kissinger, the most vocal critic of the resolution, boarded a plane to Washington from Peking as the roll call started. He had just concluded a second round of meetings with Chou En-Lai to finalize arrangements for President Nixon's visit.

At 9:47 p.m. the General Assembly finished the roll call. The resolution passed by an overwhelming margin of 76 to 35, with 17 abstentions.

Salim Ahmed Salim, a flamboyant delegate from Tanzania, jumped to his feet and led his delegation in a victory dance across the front of the General Assembly. In a black tunic, Salim danced with wild abandon, as if it were his custom to lead tribal dances in the vaulted auditorium.

Also sitting in the front row, America's UN Ambassador George Bush slumped in his chair. For long minutes, the packed hall rang with applause and cheers. The Albanian delegates laughed and hugged everyone in sight. As Salim's dance evaporated, a turbulent scene rocked the hall. An American delegate quietly walked across the front of the room and approached the exuberant Tanzanian.

United Nations General Assembly Auditorium, New York City. UN photo.

"You just made the most expensive vote you will ever make, Mr. Salim," the American said. "The United States is cutting off all foreign aid to your country."

The Americans quietly retreated. George Bush met with newsmen shortly before midnight at the U.S. Mission across the street. He said he hoped the UN would never again "relive this moment of infamy. The United Nations crossed a very dangerous bridge tonight." Bush later complained that Henry Kissinger's presence in Peking during the vote undermined his efforts to save Taiwan's seat.[7]

The following morning, *The New York Times* reported "a crushing American defeat" and "a distinct public setback for the Nixon Administration." Six different stories about China appeared on the front page. "With the vote at the United Nations tonight," the *Times* proclaimed, "China burst fully and finally from the isolation first imposed on her by the United States a generation ago, and periodically preferred by her own Communist Government."

The Peking government was caught off guard. Reporters flocked to the Chinese Embassy in Ottawa on the morning following the vote. Embassy officials said they had no instructions from Peking. Four days after the vote, the United States Senate signaled its displeasure by defeating the 1972 Foreign Aid Bill, which included $141 million in dues to the United Nations.

In its twenty-sixth year, United Nations membership finally represented a cross-section of the world's population. Peking automatically became a permanent member of the Security Council on the day it replaced Taipei. A month later, the People's Republic participated for the first time in the selection of a Secretary General. China repeatedly vetoed the nomination of Kurt Waldheim from Austria. After many failed efforts, the Chinese changed their position without explanation and Kurt Waldheim was elected Secretary General.

Robert had his answer. The Chinese must have heard that he was behind U Thant's decision to speak out in favor of China. *It must have leaked out. It's the only possible explanation. But why would they insist that I come to China with Waldheim? I'm not a big shot at the UN.*

Robert drifted off to sleep over the Himalayas.

· · ·

As soon as they landed in Peking, Robert approached Waldheim. "When is Mao Tse-tung going to see you?"

"Nothing was said about a meeting with Mao," Waldheim replied.

"You came to China without any assurances that you will see the leader of the Chinese people?"

"Well, they said Chou En-Lai would see me."

"Who sent you the invitation?"

"Chi Peng-fei, the Foreign Minister."

"That is not enough! You should never have accepted."

Foreign Minister Chi Peng-fei and Chiao Kuan-hua, an aging Vice Foreign Minister, greeted them at the airport. Chiao escorted them to a private residence in a limousine. When Muller asked about the itinerary, he received only polite assurances that meetings would take place after the guests were afforded every opportunity to relax and get acquainted with China. Robert typed a speech for Waldheim that he had drafted on the plane.

At a banquet the following evening hosted by the Foreign Minister in the People's Hall, Waldheim read Robert's text:

> I am very happy to be in China and I wish to thank the government of the People's Republic for its kind invitation, which gives me an opportunity to have personal contacts with the leaders of your country. The arrival of the People's Republic of China at the United Nations was an event of great historical importance, which brought the Organization close to universality.

On the third day, Chiao Kuan-hua escorted them around the city to meet minor officials in the Chinese government. A veteran of Mao Tse-tung's revolutionary army, the aging Vice Foreign Minister complained to Robert about the long hours he worked under Chou En-Lai.

After Chiao excused himself, Waldheim grew increasingly nervous as his party was shunted from one minor official to the next. With exaggerated smiles, he tried to show interest in the mundane details furnished by the interpreter, but he glanced at Muller with growing alarm. In the afternoon they visited the former Imperial Summer Palace and a hospital clinic. Despite the heat, the UN visitors wore business suits while the Chinese officials dressed in plain, open-collared shirts.

Robert was beginning to notice a feeling of equality in the people he was meeting, regardless of profession or rank. He overheard a nurse and doctor speaking to each other with a tone of mutual respect about a surgical procedure. A high-ranking Minister arrived by car in the morning and paused to listen attentively to a night watchman who was going off duty. A cleaning woman stopped to listen to a conversation between officials in a hallway, and then she joined in. Eye-to-eye contact was universal, evidence of a shared sense of dignity. Muller did not see anyone bow to an official.

Robert was comfortable with the displays of equality. He had written in his journal: *A head of state or a Minister sitting opposite me is first of all a human and I am his complete equal, fascinated only by the kind of human he is.*

Chinese values were consistent with the ideals practiced in the UN. The United Nations had promoted human rights everywhere in the world. The General Assembly offered visible proof that an African head of state was equal to a European; an Asian delegate was just as important as the American in the next chair. But the Chinese experiment seemed to be taking the principle of equality a step further.

If this were coupled with the UN's emphasis on human rights, Robert thought, China's experience could point the way to evolution.

Robert offered packs of Meccarillos to his servants at the house, but they politely refused. Wherever he went, people took only one or two cigarillos. They were not acquisitive. The streets and alleys seemed safe and peaceful. There were no billboards encouraging shoppers to buy things, no advertising in shop windows. His bathroom did not have any little "complimentary" bottles of soap.

Robert was flustered at the end of the third day.

"You should not be left waiting," he said to Waldheim.

"Call them," Waldheim pleaded.

"You should not have to call to find out when you will be received," Robert said.

After a quiet dinner, a message was delivered to the house. At ten o'clock, the Foreign Minister would arrive to escort them to the People's Hall.

Premier Chou En-Lai greeted them with enthusiasm. He looked refreshed and rested. "I apologize that I work in the evening and I must receive you too late," he said. "I cannot be asleep while they are awake at the Pentagon in the United States."

The Premier then apologized to Waldheim for opposing his nomination for Secretary General. "It was not you, personally. It was a matter of politics."

Waldheim relaxed. "What was your objection?"

"Asia has the largest population, and yet the United Nations does not have even one agency in Asia. Everything is in New York, Washington D.C., and Geneva. The first Secretary General was Trygve Lie from Norway. Then came Dag Hammarskjöld from Sweden. U Thant was Burmese, of course, but now you are from Austria. We must have geographical rotation of the Secretary General. You are the last Westerner. We will probably vote for an African in the next election."

"Why did you change your mind?" Waldheim asked.

"We did not want to give the appearance that we were starting out by obstructing the United Nations."

"You know, the Secretary General doesn't really have a very important role."

Chou's eyes widened. "On the contrary, your role is vital! Leaders do not talk to each other. We do not trust each other. As an intermediary, you can do what we cannot do."

"What is China's position on the Middle East conflict?" Waldheim asked.

"Why are you interested in the Middle East?"

"Well, because it's important."

"You will still have it in a hundred years," the Premier said. "I have nothing else to offer as an opinion."

Robert listened intently, taking notes as the two men talked about history, politics, and China's role in the UN.

"Europe is a big family with many brothers," Chou said, "as we were in feudal China. China was backward because it was so tranquil. China has the longest recorded history of feudalism. The class struggle has been slow to develop. But we have no foreign debts, no internal debts, no income tax."

This is a very simple man, Robert thought. I would never have guessed he is an intellectual and a head of state. He does not give the impression that he is one of the most powerful men in the world.

Glancing around the room, Robert noticed a big world map on the wall, where Chinese leaders kept track of enemy troops and equipment. Muller suddenly realized that the leaders of the superpowers could not telephone each other at the first sign of trouble. They spoke through diplomats and couriers, coming face-to-face only at elaborately staged official summits.

He thought, *how idiotic can these guys be?* If there is an incident in Korea, Chou En-Lai should be able to pick up the phone and call Nixon. Robert made a note that direct phones should be installed in the offices of every head of state.

"China was not prepared to join the United Nations," the Premier said. "We had not reviewed anything because we were certain the vote would be against our country, or the Americans would find some other way to prevent our arrival at the UN. Recognition in the UN came earlier than we expected. China will go slow and prepare itself."

"It was really just the U.S. that was in the way," Waldheim said. "Almost everyone else was in favor of it, but so many of our member states are dependent upon assistance from the U.S."

Chou En-Lai smiled. "I accompanied Dr. Kissinger to the airport at the end of his second visit. He was about to step into the airplane when he turned and shouted at me over the sound of the engine"—the Premier cupped his hands around his mouth—"'And China will *never* get into the United Nations without Taiwan!' "

With this, Chou En-Lai looked directly into Robert's eyes and nodded. His eyes were filled with gratitude and respect.

The Premier escorted them to the exit.

As they shook hands, Robert thanked him in Chinese. The Premier raised his eyebrows in surprise. "I didn't know you could speak Chinese!"

"*Hen shao*—very little," Robert hastened to add.

Chinese Premier Chou En-Lai speaks Chinese with Robert Muller in the Imperial Palace, Peking, on August 14, 1972. UN photo.

The Premier spoke flawless French, sparing Robert the embarrassment of showing the limits to his comprehension.

"Where did you learn to speak French?" Robert asked.

"I worked in a Renault automobile factory in France."

The Premier extended his hand to Robert with a warm smile. Robert felt a deep sense of respect and appreciation from Chou En-Lai when he looked into the Premier's eyes. There was no barrier between them based on differences in rank. They were just two men meeting on their journey through life.

On the fourth day, the Vice Foreign Minister accompanied them on a sightseeing visit to the Great Wall of China. Near the steps leading up the enormous structure, a crack in the Wall revealed a loose patch of mortar and bricks lay strewn on the ground—a sign that tourism was not flourishing in China. They climbed to the top of the Great Wall and strolled at a leisurely pace. Robert walked next to Vice Foreign Minister Chiao Kuan-hua.

"We often work all night," he muttered. "Soon I will quit."

It was a gray, wet morning. The party posed for a photograph on top of the Great Wall. The Vice Foreign Minister stood next to Kurt Waldheim, Mrs. Waldheim, and their two personal aides. Robert Muller stood on the far right, smiling gamely into the camera. Everyone in the photo was protected from the rain by large umbrellas, everyone except Muller, who stared straight ahead with his jaw firmly set as the rain drenched his hair.

The party headed back to the waiting cars. Robert walked slowly until the others were ahead of him. Then he ran back to the entrance, picked up one of the loose bricks, and slipped it into his briefcase.

Through the car window while they waited for a ride to the airport, Robert saw the servants run out of the house with their arms loaded with cartons of Meccarillos.

Robert watched helplessly as they opened the door and carefully stacked the cartons on his lap. He blushed, unable to think of anything to say. Waldheim stared at him with confusion.

Secretary General Kurt Waldheim poses at China's Great Wall with Mrs. Waldheim, Tang Ming-chao and Robert Muller. UN photo.

.   .   .

On the Boeing, a stewardess offered a selection of liquor in miniature bottles. Lost in thought, Robert declined. The simplicity of life in China had given him a new measure of freedom. As the plane followed the sun to Paris, Robert wrote:

> I saw a society organized on the principle of mutual help. Perhaps the West has gone too far—rewarding people for greed, acquisitiveness, exploitation, and outfoxing each other. I see a time when all humans will be equal guests at the great banquet of life.

Robert rode his bicycle into town on the morning after he returned to the farmhouse from China. His contractor rose to greet him with the familiar apologetic smile. Robert placed a brick on his cluttered desk.

"This stone is from the Great Wall of China on the other side of the Earth, Monsieur Gery. It is to remind you of a little wall you are to build for Mr. Muller."

The wall was completed within a month.

When children ride their bicycles up Caesar's Via Strada from the villages to visit *La Maison du Père Noël*, they take turns touching a special brick for good luck, a brick prominently set in the wall at the entrance to the restored farmhouse. They say touching the brick will make their dreams come true, and the brick was brought all the way from the Great Wall of China by Robert Muller, who worked in the Palace of Nations.

Chapter 2 – Children of War

Sarreguemines, 1929

Dirty smoke trailed from the chimney of the iron locomotive. White steam panted out the sides. Two boys, barely six years old, watched the freight train pull out of the station. It was gaining speed as it reached the switch and veered towards them. The smoke filled the sky and the ground trembled as the train disappeared into the tunnel under their feet.

The boys clenched their teeth and grabbed each other. Then something caught their eye. An old truck rattled down the street on the uneven cobblestones. It was a war surplus truck from the United States left over from the War and it still had the American liberty badge bolted to the rusty grill.

"Watch this," Robert said to his friend. He held out his half-eaten apple. "Watch me get it in the back of the truck."

Robert threw the apple as hard as he could. It flew through the open window and splattered inside the cab.

Wheels screeched and the truck skidded to a stop. Robert watched his friend disappear down the embankment leading to the tracks. The truck door flew open and an old man stepped out. He was at least as old as Robert's grandfather, but his face was unshaven and it was deeply scarred. His narrow eyes locked on the terrified boy. Robert's feet froze to the ground as he helplessly gasped for air.

The truck driver picked wet pieces of apple out of his hair as he approached the boy. The man was muttering in French—only the old people could swear like that in French—and then he slapped Robert across the back of the head.

"What the hell are you trying to do, boy, kill me?" he roared. The man yanked Robert up to his face. "Show me where your father works!"

He deposited Robert on the narrow buckboard seat. Robert held on to the greasy plank with both hands when the man released the brake. The truck rolled forward and heaved as the engine roared to life. The man pumped the brakes, locking and releasing the rear wheels until the truck, whining in low gear, reached the bottom of the hill.

Robert tried to find the right words to explain—but his voice didn't work! He moved his lips but nothing came out. He pointed out the turns as the truck negotiated through the crowded market district of Sarreguemines.

"You live in the Goldstrasse, eh?" the man growled.

Everyone still called it the Goldstrasse. It didn't matter that the French had changed the name to Rue d'Or after the War. It had always been the Goldstrasse, ever since the Middle Ages, and it was still the poorest section of town. Little shops lined both sides of the street, except for a large building that blocked the far end where a pedestrian tunnel led to Goethe Plaza on the other side, where Robert could see children playing in the fountain—that's where he wanted to run.

He cringed at the thought of bringing this man home. He smelled worse than the dogs in the alley behind the butcher shop and he kept shifting his eyes as if everything around him was moving. What if Robert's mother was helping a customer when they came in and the man started yelling? Robert was never supposed to bring anybody home without telling his mother.

The man shoved Robert inside the little shop, jangling the bell over the door. His mother wasn't anywhere in sight. The man's eyes darted uncomfortably from one mannequin head to the next. There were rows of plaster heads evenly spaced on wooden shelves, zombie-like faces adorned with fashionable hats. The man grew more agitated, as if he expected the mannequins to come to life.

"Where is the father of this boy?" he shouted.

"And who might you be?" Robert's mother demanded, filling the room with her voice. She was standing in the kitchen door.

The man hesitated. Léonie Muller was a formidable woman, she was only half his age, and she was holding a black iron skillet. A thumping sound echoed somewhere behind the wall. The man eyed the skillet while they all stood in strained silence listening to the heavy clod-clump of wooden shoes descending the wooden stairs.

Clod-clump! Clod-clump! The man bared his yellow teeth when Robert's father came into the room. He was holding a woman's hat on the tips of his thick fingers. Robert's father smiled with pride over his newest creation—a blue felt cloche hat with an upturned brim, one of the newest styles from Paris. His face froze in a lopsided grin as he glanced from his wife to the stranger...to his son.

"Hello, son," he said, guessing the reason for the visit.

"Your boy tried to kill me!" the man shouted.

"My son...Robert?" Robert's father placed the hat on a mannequin. "How could he possibly do that?"

"He hit me on the head with an apple! I almost crashed my truck!"

"This boy here, Robert, he hit you in the head—"

"Yes!"

"—with an apple?"

"Exactly!"

"Well, there you go! He must have been trying to hit something else."

"Oh yeah," the man growled. "How would you know?"

"Robert can never hit anything. Every time he tries to throw me the ball, it goes somewhere else."

"I *wasn't* trying to hit him," Robert said.

"If you don't teach this boy a lesson—"

"Oh, I'll teach him a lesson," Robert's father said, looking at his son sternly. He spanked him once, a hard whack that stung. "You wait for me upstairs!"

Robert retreated to his room. Nobody believed him.

He listened to the muffled voices until finally he heard

the bell tingle on the front door, followed by a thud. His father climbed the stairs and paused at the door to his room.

"I wouldn't waste any more apples on that old goat if I were you," his father said.

Robert started to speak, but his father held up his hand.

"No! There's no excuse for throwing things at people."

"I'm sorry." Robert's body sagged as his father returned to his workshop in the attic.

"Robert Muller!" his mother shouted.

Léonie was standing at the bottom of the stairs. She pointed to the step in front of her, but before he was halfway down, a customer came in. Robert reached the landing and waited by the open door.

"I didn't mean to hit him," he whispered. "It was just—"

She glared at him.

"*De Schwede wäre disch frässe!*" she snarled in German. The Swedes will devour you!

That was all she said. Then she turned to the customer. "*Bonjour, Madame.*"

It was as if she was saying that the matter was out of her hands now, that the forces Robert had turned loose were so horrible that she could do nothing to contain them. Robert trudged back up the stairs.

His sister watched him from the door to her room. "The Swedes will devour you," Marcelle whispered. She looked at her big brother as if he were a lost cause.

"You don't even know what happened," Robert said, and closed his bedroom door.

Dark images flooded the boy's head. Robert remembered everything his mother had ever told him about the Swedes—how they sounded like thunder when they rode into town on their huge black horses and they stole everything in sight before they burned down the village. And if any little boy got in their way, they would pick him up like a sardine and swallow him whole!

The worst part was their banners. The Swedes carried banners bearing a map of Alsace-Lorraine cut in the shape of a woman, but she was cleaved down the middle, from head to toe, and she was flanked by the Swedes, who were stabbing her with spears and burning her with torches.

The Swedes! Robert had never actually seen a Swede, but he wasn't going to let any Swedes get their big, ugly hands on him!

He tiptoed to his parents' room in the back and scanned the trees across the river. Sometimes he could see Germans walking on the trail, but that day, everything was quiet.

If the Swedes were coming, they must be coming through the town down Rue de la Montagne, or maybe they were sneaking around the side of the hill through the fields.

Robert found his father at the workbench in the attic. His broad forehead was creased with concentration as he pressed a gray sheet of steaming felt into a wooden mold and fastened the forms together.

"Mama told me the Swedes are coming!" Robert said.

"Oh? You don't see that many Swedes around here."

His father tightened the clasps and set the mold on a shelf.

"How are you supposed to know which way they're coming?" Robert asked.

His father studied the boy for a moment. "Does this have anything to do with that man in the truck?"

"I wasn't trying to hit him."

"Uh huh. Well, I don't think you have to worry too much about Swedes."

"I just want to know when they're coming so I can get to the caves," Robert blurted out.

"The caves by the river?" his father asked. He took off his gloves. "Yes, I suppose that would be a good place to hide, as long as you always take me with you, or else your mother. People can get lost in those caves. But the Swedes, they haven't made any trouble around here in quite a long time."

"About how long?" the boy asked.

His father stepped away from the worktable and hung his white apron on a hook.

"Well, let me see, when were the Swedes here? I guess that would be the Thirty Years War, wouldn't it? Hmmm. Yes, that was about 300 years ago."

Robert gave it some thought.

"How much is that?"

. . .

Forces that would set the coordinates for the opening and closing chapters of Robert Muller's life began to materialize 8,000 miles away from Alsace-Lorraine in the 1870's when California gold prospectors fanned out to distant parts of the Americas in search of richer veins. Some of them headed to Costa Rica. They crossed Panama by train, boarded a boat in the Caribbean and disembarked on Costa Rica's eastern shore at Puerto Limón. They bounced up a steep, rutted trail through a rain forest until they reached San Jose. Then they continued for another 30 miles to Mt. Rasur.

Mount Rasur was sacred. The Indians told stories about a secret place in the tropical forest where the elders purified their spirits in a hundred pools of water strung up the side of the mountain like a necklace of sparkling pearls. An Indian prophecy said there would be peace on Earth when the eagle and the condor were reunited on Mt. Rasur.

The prospectors weren't interested in Indian stories, but they were passionate about the gold. Cavities appeared in the green forest on the south face of sacred Mt. Rasur. They hauled away all the gold they could carry and headed back to California. During the ride across Panama, the prospectors purchased hand-woven white straw hats from Ecuadorian women who sold crafts through the train windows at whistle stops. When their boat docked in Los Angeles, the gallant white hats afforded the prospectors a peculiar air of distinction. Photographs of sensational gun-toting miners in "Panama" hats appeared in newspapers from Los Angeles to New York City. The pictures inspired a Broadway play, and when "The Panama Hat" went on the road and toured Germany, it was a hit.

By the end of the 19th Century, the demand for Panama hats outpaced the supply. A German company opened a Panama hat factory in the frontier territory of Eupen-Malmédy, where labor was cheap. As demand for the hats grew, the company opened another factory in Sarralbe, 100 miles to the south in the German territory of Alsace-Lorraine. The Sarralbe factory was managed by a tall, distinguished hatmaker—Laurent Muller.

Women manufacture Panama hats in Sarralbe at the factory of Laurent Muller, Robert's grandfather.

· · ·

Robert's mother, Léonie Schneider, grew up in Haguenau, a city about 50 miles southeast of Sarreguemines in Alsace. Although French culture was strong and varied in the Lorraine region where Sarreguemines was located, Alsace was more uniformly German than French. Quaint wood-framed Alsatian houses were decorated with window boxes filled with bright geraniums. Blonde children played in the streets.

A large forest separated Haguenau from the picturesque village of Schweighouse where Léonie's father, Emile Schneider, was raised. Schweighouse's long history dated back to Roman times. The town was destroyed when the Swedes went on a rampage during the Thirty Years War after the King of Sweden ran out of money and couldn't pay his troops.[8] Schweighouse was so completely demolished that it was abandoned for two generations, despite a widespread shortage of housing in the region. It was finally re-settled in 1666 by Swiss immigrants.

Emile Schneider married Marie Rose, who gave birth to five children—four girls and a boy. Léonie was their third child, born in 1902. Léonie grew up to be proud of her father, who was the stationmaster at the railroad yard. On weekends, Emile took his family to his brother's bakery in Schweighouse. The towns were linked by the Moder River, which was lined with giant stork nests and meandered through vineyards, dairy farms, and fields of hops—the special ingredient that brought out the rich flavor in the famous local Alsatian beer. Families in the surrounding villages turned out to harvest the green hops flowers, bringing the children, the grandparents, and even the village priest—to give the harvest his blessing. It was Léonie's favorite event of the year.

They were as comfortable as any family in Haguenau until Marie Rose went to bed with a hacking cough when Léonie was twelve years old and the doctor came by the house one night and he said it was tuberculosis.

Wars were brewing all over Europe in 1914 when Léonie dropped out of school to take care of her mother. France wanted to recover the lost provinces of Alsace and Lorraine, which had been taken away by Bismarck as spoils of the Franco-Prussian War of 1870. Russia was making advances on Romania as a hedge against Germany, which was taking over the Turkish army. Bosnian Serbs were plotting to break away from Bosnia and unite with Serbia[9] to create a new nation of Yugoslavia, so Austria threatened war against Serbia, but Germany restrained her.[10] All over Europe, people were saying that only a war could relieve the tension.

Archduke Franz Ferdinand, heir to the long-reigning Hapsburg throne, was next in line to be Emperor of Austria and King of Hungary. He was a brutal, obstinate man who had no patience for opposition, an unfortunate disposition for such a man at a time when democracy was on the rise.[11] Ferdinand had his own visions of a renewed Austrian empire where neighboring countries could join together in voluntary fellowship.

Serbian nationalists, calling themselves The Black Hand, targeted the Hapsburgs in general, and Ferdinand in particular, calling them oppressors who had robbed Serbs of their national destiny. The Black Hand furnished guns to a half-dozen schoolboys in Sarajevo who volunteered to take a shot at Archduke Ferdinand when he visited Bosnia's capital on June 28, 1914. The royal car took a wrong turn and the chauffeur stopped the car. One of the schoolboys walked out of a store and found the royal car stopped directly in front of him. He stepped onto the running board, shot Ferdinand in the head, then shot his wife Sophie.

Léonie couldn't tell a Serb from a Croat or a Slovak. She had studied enough history to know that the King of France had hired the Swedes during the Thirty Years War, after the King of Sweden lost control of his army, then sent them to Bavaria to make trouble for the Hapsburgs. Léonie had only a vague idea why any Serb would want to kill a Hapsburg in 1914. She had no idea that the assassination was supposed to provoke Austria into declaring war against Serbia so that the Serbs could rally around the banner of national unity. Even Serbian militants were surprised when the murder of Archduke Ferdinand and his wife Sophie sparked a furious exchange of diplomatic blunders that ignited into World War I.

Austria launched an investigation to prove that Serbia

was behind the killings. When they came up empty-handed, Austria declared war against Serbia anyway. It was more of a diplomatic ploy than an act of military aggression,[12] but on July 31, a reluctant Czar, prodded by his generals, mobilized the Russian army while processions paraded in the streets of St. Petersburg and strangers embraced with patriotic zeal. Emperor Francis Joseph mobilized Austria's army, followed by Holland's Queen Wilhelmina, then Switzerland.[13] Germany demanded that Belgium permit passage of the Kaiser's troops to the French border, and when King Albert called upon every Belgian to resist a violation of Belgian soil, Germany declared war against Belgium. On August 6, Great Britain entered the fray and declared war against Germany to protect the neutrality of "little Belgium" and "to make the world safe for democracy."

Crowds cheered in St. Petersburg, London, and Paris during the first days of August. Soldiers marched through Berlin singing the national anthem as cheering crowds threw flowers. Men all over Europe bragged that they would win the war and be home for Christmas. Léonie knew they couldn't all be right. A deep skepticism crept into her heart so far as political groups were concerned.

Austria invaded Serbia on August 11, 1914 and Europe toppled into chaos. Germany attacked through the lowlands of Belgium and advanced so rapidly towards Paris that they outran their supply lines. Their plan was flawless as far as it went, which got the Germans within thirty miles of Paris. Six million soldiers poured into the conflict during the first battles, men who had no experience of war. French and British troops retreated until the Germans ran out of steam and stopped.[14] The Germans pulled back, dug holes in the ground, set up their modern "machine" guns, and waited.

The battle lines were drawn. Trenches were dug in the mud across France from the English Channel to Switzerland, a distance of 400 miles. During the next four years, the lines grew wider and the trenches were dug deeper, growing into an enormous network of reinforced concrete battlements, but the lines changed position only slightly. Léonie watched conscripts from Alsace and Lorraine as they were loaded into freight trains at her father's yard and hauled away to the front.

Germany was confident that it could feed its population without imports, given its monopoly on artificial fertilizer and gunpowder, but food became scarce after the men were taken from the land. They didn't come back for the harvest, not for Christmas, not even for the spring planting. When food prices shot up, everyone sent their pigs and cattle to market to make a quick profit and soon the supply was exhausted. [15]

Léonie and her sisters started fighting their own battle against starvation in the summer of 1915. Léonie turned thirteen on December 20, 1915. Six days later, her mother died of tuberculosis.

Emile Schneider had no time to mourn the loss of his wife. He had to take care of five children while working two shifts. The Haguenau yard was a hub on Germany's western front. Trains filled with soldiers and arms passed through Haguenau at all hours. Europe was at war and the trains had to run on time.

The children scrounged for food. Local merchants couldn't keep up with the demand after their customers starting hoarding food. Prices had already skyrocketed when the Kaiser's agents came around and reminded the farmers that the German army would have to be fed.

The girls made a pact to stick together as a family through the war. Berthe, the eldest, was only fifteen and she couldn't work and take care of five children, so Léonie stayed home from school to watch little Emile, her four-year-old brother. Uncle Alphonse dropped by as often as he could get away from the bakery to help out around the house. He would sit up late with his brother Emile as they tried to sort out the chaotic events that were driving civilized countries into barbarity.

Then Alphonse was drafted into the German army.

Were it not for two scientists, the Germans would have run out of food and ammunition in 1916 and everybody could have gone home. First, Wilhelm Ostwald, a Latvian chemist living in Germany at the turn of the century, developed a process for making nitric acid out of ammonia, for which he was awarded the Nobel Prize in Chemistry in 1909. Then German chemist Fritz Haber discovered a way to manufacture ammonia by combining nitrogen and hydrogen gasses under pressure, for which he won the Nobel Prize in Chemistry in 1919. Haber teamed up with industrialist Karl Bosch and they perfected the Haber-Bosch process for manufacturing fertilizer and gunpowder out of thin air using chemical reactions invented in the previous century by Sweden's legendary Alfred Nobel.

Before the Haber-Bosch process was invented, Germany imported its nitrogen from Chile. Most of the world's supply of nitrogen was derived from saltpeter mined in from Chile's Desert of Atacama, the driest place on Earth. The Kaiser knew he couldn't ship nitrogen all the way from Chile past the American and British navies, and Germany couldn't win a war without gunpowder and fertilizer. So when a nitrogen factory opened in Sarralbe to exploit the Haber-Bosch process, the balance of power shifted. The rest of the world was still dependent upon imported nitrogen from Chile, since the Haber-Bosch patents left out certain details about catalysts needed to complete the cycle. Ironically, German investors controlled the nitrogen cartel in Chile, so the price of Chile saltpeter went through the roof at the outset of World War I until gunboat diplomacy put the mines into the hands of Chilean families.

The Battle of Verdun started in February 1916, in the middle of a harsh winter. Alphonse returned home from Verdun in time for Christmas ten months later with a bullet hole in his right hand. He told Léonie about hiding in bomb craters, where rats foraged for corpses while soldiers mowed each other down with machine guns and bayonets. When his unit became too exhausted to fight, they were sent back to a secure area to get some sleep, but when they arrived they were ordered to sit up in a makeshift church and listen to a priest who praised them for killing the wicked French for God. Alphonse swore he would never go to church again.

Léonie's uncle wouldn't say much about his experience in the trenches, but he couldn't stop talking about all the other battles as the war dragged on. The newspapers were censored, but news traveled up and down the railroad.[16] Alphonse could go on for hours rattling off names of towns and rivers where battles were fought, the number of casualties and the names of generals.

Léonie listened to Alphonse's reports with growing bitterness. She had been raised in a town where people enjoyed close kinship. Now everybody was taking sides and turning against each other, civilians were starving, and the whole world was going insane. The meager harvest in 1916 was aggravated by a severe drought. The girls scrounged for turnips in the frozen fields between Haguenau and Schweighouse and foraged for roots and nuts.

Europe was still bogged down in the trenches in 1917 when the Americans arrived in ships filled with arms and supplies. The Germans changed tactics in 1918. Rows of infantry were broken down into small groups of skirmishers armed with light portable weapons. They probed enemy lines for weaknesses,[17] but wherever the German advance troops broke through Allied lines, they found supply tents piled to the roof with fresh provisions and modern American weapons. Germany could not feed her people—800,000 civilians died of starvation. Morale collapsed and rumors of defeat spread through the German army like a plague. The German lines cracked. Knowing he could not win, General Ludendorff sabotaged France's northern coalmines as his army retreated to Germany.[18] Ludendorff hoped to gain an edge over a future trade competitor, but it was a costly blunder.

The shooting stopped at 11:00 a.m. November 11, 1918, but the blockade continued through the winter and spring while statesmen and lawyers haggled over the terms of the peace treaty at the Palace of Versailles. President Woodrow Wilson sailed into Europe's steaming political waters brandishing his Fourteen Points for a new world order. The centerpiece of his plan was a proposal to form the League of Nations.[19] Wilson received a hero's welcome in Paris and was swarmed by adoring crowds. Prime Minister Poincaré urged him to visit the northern provinces and see the sabotaged mines with his own eyes, but Wilson refused. He said that such an expedition would make him "see red," and he didn't want to deal with matters of state in an angry mood.[20]

The Treaty of Versailles—76,000 words divided into 440

articles—was signed seven months after the armistice on June 28, 1919. The blockade was finally lifted. The Allies divided up Germany's colonies and France recovered the provinces of Alsace and Lorraine. Eupen-Malmédy, a disputed territory to the north near the border of Belgium and Germany, was consigned to Belgium until its status could be resolved by the League of Nations.

The Sarre Territory and the Rhineland—all of Germany's territory west of the Rhine—were placed under the administration of the League of Nations. Germany's army was reduced to 100,000 soldiers and she was forbidden to manufacture arms, tanks, poison gas, or military planes.[21] Disarming Germany, the Allies promised, was merely the first step in a worldwide disarmament. German coalmines west of the Rhine were awarded to France as compensation for the mines sabotaged by General Ludendorff. With legal precision, France also gained title to "all machinery, electric power plants, electric lines, water plants, land, buildings, offices, worker's dwellings, schools, hospitals, dispensaries, stocks, supplies, archives and plans" in connection with the mines.

The Treaty of Versailles was supposed to bring an end to eleven centuries of European wars, but U. S. participation in the League of Nations was a key. Having neglected to build bi-partisan support in Washington for the crown jewel of his presidency, Wilson went home to a changed political climate. The Senate refused to ratify the Treaty of Versailles, blocking the U.S. from joining the League of Nations.

The celebration of peace was short as Europe slumped into a post-war depression. France's industrial corridor on the Belgian border was depopulated and devastated.[22] Farmland had been carved into concrete canyons, laced with barbed wire and sown with explosives. Three quarters of all French soldiers sent into action were listed as casualties—two million were missing or killed; 4.3 million were wounded.[23] Across the English Channel, one million British soldiers did not return home and two million needed rehabilitation.[24] With a national debt of £7,000,000,000 Britain was one of the bankrupt winners of the war.

Germany was still the most populated country in Europe

with seventy million people, compared to forty million in France. Germany's industrial capacity was intact—the war was not fought on German soil. Despite Germany's loss of a million and a half men, the surrender of her colonies, the fall of her monarchy, and chaos in her political institutions, Germany emerged from the war with the most robust economy in Europe. While other European countries staggered to their feet, Germany enjoyed a rebound in the popularity of Panama hats.

The Schneider children were informed they were citizens of France in Léonie's sixteenth year. She was a determined, restless young woman with a deep-seated distrust of groups and politicians. Despite her keen intelligence, Léonie would never recapture her lost education or her adolescent years.

On May 20, 1921, Emile Schneider fell between railroad cars and was crushed to death. Haunted by her father's death and unable to find work in Haguenau, Léonie set out from home. She spoke only the dialect of Alsace, a peculiar mixture of German and French, so it was difficult for her to interview for jobs.[25] Thirty miles away in the Lorraine town of Sarralbe, she found that business was booming for two reasons—there was a demand for chemical fertilizer all over Europe, and a surging market in Germany for Panama hats.

Léonie found domestic work in the home of Laurent Muller, manager of Sarralbe's Panama hat factory. Away from home and free of family responsibilities, Léonie soon discovered that she was no longer just a small town girl. She was an independent 18-year-old woman who was optimistic, rebellious, and perhaps a little wild.

When Léonie Schneider married Robert Muller at the Mayor's office in Sarralbe on September 10, 1922, a few days before her twentieth birthday, she had two big secrets. One, she was in love with the town pharmacist, which she didn't tell a soul. Two, she was not exactly ready to marry Robert Muller. Nature made that decision for her.

Léonie could see that Robert Muller was a good man, even if he was not much of an intellectual. He was an apprentice hatmaker studying a profitable trade under his father, Laurent Muller, who had been trained by his father, who had been trained by his father. Robert Muller's father was in charge of the biggest Panama hat factory in Lorraine, so the young man had a promising future. Léonie anticipated that Robert would be a dependable husband and a good father. He was proud of his profession and loyal to his family, he was the most eligible bachelor in town, and it was obvious to anyone who saw them together that he was in love with Léonie Schneider.

His pride in the family business showed when he gave Léonie a special tour of the factory during his campaign to win her affection. The hats, he explained, were made with palm leaves imported from Namibia, formerly the German colony of Südwestafrika. He pointed out the long rows of racks where green palm leaves were spread out to bleach in the sun before they were sliced into strips and distributed to local farmers to be woven by hand. Since the sun rarely shone in the gloomy Lorraine climate, the bleaching process slowed down production.

So when the Panama hat factory in Eupen-Malmédy perfected a new chemical process for bleaching palm leaves, which eliminated the need to bleach the leaves in the sun, it made a certain amount of sense to send Laurent's apprentice son Robert to study the chemical process, along with his young bride Léonie—*before* anyone noticed she was pregnant.

It was the first time either Robert or Léonie had ventured out of Alsace-Lorraine. The newlyweds rode a train through Luxembourg to Belgium and rented a cottage in the village of Weismes. Robert reported for work at the Debrus Panama hat factory. Léonie started hunting for provisions to set up the cottage while she struggled to learn Walloon, the local dialect.

Walloon was a mixture of Latin and French that had been spoken in the Malmédy region of eastern Belgium for 2,000 years, ever since the Romans established their forts in the hills of Malmédy to repel Dutch horsemen. Walloon had outlasted the Roman Empire by 1,600 years.

Their first child was born at home in Weismes on Sunday, March 11, 1923. They named him Robert, after his father, with the middle name of Georges. Robert G. Muller was a robust baby boy with his father's firm jaw and his mother's strong disposition.

To ascertain Robert's nationality at birth would have cost his parents a small fortune. The Treaty of Versailles stated in Article 34 that Germany "renounced all rights and title to Eupen-Malmédy," but with one minor concession that called for the establishment of a register in which the inhabitants of Eupen-Malmédy would be entitled to:

> Record in writing a desire to see the whole or part of (Eupen-Malmédy) remain under German sovereignty. The results of this public expression of opinion will be communicated by the Belgian Government to the League of Nations, and Belgium undertakes to accept the decision of the League.

Since time was on Belgium's side, the register was still open collecting signatures and gathering dust five years later when Robert Muller was born. The sovereignty of the region had still not been settled and the nationality of Eupen-Malmédy's residents was a matter that remained to be officiated by the League.[26]

The infant Robert Muller, born in Eupen-Malmédy of French parents, was without question a citizen of France. But children born in Belgium could make an election to become citizens of the place where they were born after reaching the age of 18. Not being of Belgian or German origin, yet born in Eupen-Malmédy during the referendum, Robert Muller was a dual citizen—a citizen of France, and arguably the world's first global citizen.

The Mullers returned to Alsace-Lorraine to visit their families and show off the baby. When they returned to Eupen-Malmédy, where alcohol was banned, Léonie filled Robert's baby bottle with her husband's favorite schnapps, a homemade Alsatian brandy distilled from golden mirabelle plums. She plugged the nipple, wrapped the bottle in a diaper, and placed it in Robert's mouth when the customs officer inspected the train. Robert's father looked so guilty he was ordered to the back of the car for interrogation. Léonie sat blithely while Robert fussed with the bottle.

Léonie never talked about the pharmacist, never told him how she felt. But she kept one candle burning in her heart.

"When our son grows up," she declared to her husband after Robert was born, "he is going to be an *intellectual.*"

When Robert's father came home from work, Léonie was fuming while she nursed Robert's baby sister.

"Robert's gone," she said.

"Again?"

"I don't know what's gotten into him."

"I suppose a boy needs a bigger world than his backyard when he's four years old," Robert's father explained. "He likes to visit the farmers across the pasture."

"I can't be chasing after him while I'm nursing Marcelle!"

Robert's father crossed the field behind their house and knocked timidly at the back door of the farmer's cottage.

"Come in, Muller," said one of the men inside.

Three men were gathered around the kitchen table. Robert was sitting with them at the table, happily swinging his legs. He was barely able to see over the top of the table.

"I'm sorry that my son keeps coming over here," Robert's father started.

"No problem for us," the eldest farmer replied. "He's a fine boy."

"His mother sometimes gets busy," Robert's father explained. "You know how it is when you have a baby."

"I raised two sons!" the farmer said.

"Your boy can come here any time he wants," said another.

That was good news for Robert. The farmers smelled like alfalfa and bacon and they liked to tell stories. Sometimes they lowered their voices and talked quietly about their sons and how things would have been different if they had come back from the War.

Robert's father was uneasy with the farmers. As a factory worker, he felt a little out of place around people who grew food. But as far as the farmers were concerned, it was the way Robert's father *talked* that set him apart. He could speak Walloon well enough—he had lived in Weismes for four years—but he still had that German accent.

Robert, of course, spoke Walloon like a native.

"Thanks again," Robert's father said as he nudged his son out the door. "I appreciate your hospitality. Very nice of you."

His father relaxed when they were alone. "You worry your mother every time you wander over here. You must tell her where you're going. I shouldn't have to come home after work and find your mother all upset like that."

A stray dog sniffed at Robert's feet. "*Va al mahon machi chen,*" Robert said in Walloon as he shooed the dog away. "Go home, you dirty dog."

"Let's stop and watch the sunset," his father said. "It looks like God took out his best box of colors tonight, son."

The western sky was thatched with patterns of crimson and copper streaks, which were giving way to storm clouds from the north. They stood there for several minutes, father and son lulled into a trance by the majestic beauty and power of creation. An old man approached them on the road without paying them any attention. Robert removed his cap until the man passed.

"Why do you always take off your hat when you see an old person?" his father asked.

"Because they have lived so long, father, and they know so much! I want to learn everything they know."

As the bright colors faded into gray cauliflower puffs, Robert tugged at his father's sleeve. A storm was brewing. They got home just before a tremendous thunderclap announced the first sheet of rain.

As they were eating dinner, a round ball of fire entered through the window and moved slowly toward the lamp hanging from the ceiling in the middle of the room. The ball hovered under the lamp, then exploded. Everyone shrieked, but nobody was hurt.

"Have you ever heard of such a thing?" Léonie whispered.

Robert and his father shook their heads.

"I'll ask around, that's for sure," Robert's father said.

Robert kept staring at the lamp, waiting for another fireball to appear.

"That does it!" Léonie said. "I've had enough of this place. We're going home."

Robert had trouble getting to sleep that night while his parents talked in the next room.

"Still no jobs at your father's factory?" his mother said.

"I haven't heard back, yet. But you know how it is. Things are a little slow."

"Yes, I think I do know," she said. "It's been four years now."

"Anyway, our life is not so bad here," his father said.

"I'm not raising our children to be Belgian farmers. Our son starts school next year!"

"He's not going to be a farmer," his father said, laughing. "He's going to make hats, like me."

"Everyone at home is speaking French now, but you and I are still using German, and our children speak *Walloon*."

"Walloon is French. It's just the way they talk here."

"It makes a big difference if you can't speak properly. I don't want our children to grow up sounding like peasants. We're not waiting another year. It's time to go home."

"All right, I'll see what my father—"

"No, not Sarralbe," Léonie said.

"What do you mean? Why not Sarralbe? Where else would we go?" Robert could hear panic creeping into his father's voice.

"Sarreguemines has plenty of jobs, and it's not far from Sarralbe. I talked to an acquaintance from Schweighouse. He's the school librarian in Sarreguemines, and he said they have a good school."

"But...but there's no hat factory in that town!"

"Then you'll have to find something else."

"Not make hats? That's crazy," he said, raising his voice.

"Four years we've been stranded here by your father," she said. "I won't go back to Sarralbe."

"Mama!" Robert called out. "I can't sleep."

His mother came into the room carrying her worn-out copy of the Grimm Brothers fairy tales.

"Just one story, tonight," she said.

"Okay."

Léonie sat in a rocking chair and opened the book.

"Next to a big forest lived a poor wood-cutter and his second wife and his two children. The boy was called Hansel—"

"I'm Hansel," Robert said.

"—and the girl's name was Grethel, and they had very little to eat."

Chapter 3 – The Miracle of Life

E ven the pubs were empty by the time the Mullers arrived at their new house in Sarreguemines. The children were sound asleep when their father carried them up the stairs.

Robert was already gone the next morning when his father checked the room. He found him outside in his pajamas. Robert had found the garden, where fruit trees bordered rows of vegetables, and the trees were just beginning to show little nubs of green fruit. There was even a chicken coop in the back and a rabbit hutch.

Robert was holding something cupped in his hands.

"What do you have there?" his father asked.

Robert parted his fingers slightly to reveal a tuft of yellow down. "This is Grethel!" he said with a big grin.

"Grethel, huh? That's nice. Maybe you can feed that little chick and she'll think you're her mommy, or, her daddy."

"I'm Hansel," Robert corrected him.

"Oh? Well then, you two should get along very well. Maybe your mother won't mind if you keep Grethel in the house for a few days until she's big enough to stay in the chicken coop."

The house was located in Cité des Faïenceries, an area four blocks long filled with identical workers' houses. It was adjacent to the chinaware factory, where Robert's father had found a job. They shared the house with Gabriel, a worker in the factory who was a volunteer fireman. Robert soon found Gabriel's uniform in the hall closet and the polished brass helmet on the shelf dazzled him.

After a whistle sounded and all the men went to work, Léonie took her children by the hand and led them to the Sarre River a block away. A thick forest of black chimneys towered over the brick factories. The sky was cloudy with soot from the kilns. Robert squeezed his mother's hand as he vacillated between curiosity and disappointment. It was not how he had pictured the Sarre Valley, the home of his ancestors.

Earthenware made in Sarreguemines was decorated with brightly colored metallic glazes in intricate designs of floral patterns, romantic figures, and pastoral scenes. Robert's father started out as a tunker. All day, he dipped the completed ceramic pieces into the glaze before they were fired in the oven. When Robert's father came home from work, he was often sullen and withdrawn.

As Grethel grew into a black hen, Robert's world blossomed. When Robert called Grethel's name, she flew across the yard and landed in his arms. They sat together by a brook in the garden, where a trickle of water wandered through tender grasses and spring flowers, shaded by a blossoming cherry tree. Robert marveled that a tree could grow bright pink flowers and then the flowers would turn into fruit. The garden was carpeted with treasures—seeds for Grethel, pebbles for Robert, sprouting vegetables, earthworms in the soil, bugs, ants, caterpillars, and rabbits.

On holidays, soldiers paraded in formation on the road along the west bank of the Sarre River. Robert felt a rush of excitement when the French soldiers approached in their crisp uniforms, although he secretly preferred the outfits worn by Belgian soldiers. They had polished helmets with pom-poms dancing from their peaks and he suspected the French soldiers were not quite as good as the Belgians. Everything glorious seemed to be connected to the soldiers, who wore smart uniforms instead of the dull clothes worn by workingmen. Soldiers pressed their shoulders back and marched with glorious precision to trumpets and drums. Shiny medals and braids danced on their chests.

Children led the procession, lifting their arms as high

as they could and taking giant steps to the rhythm of the drums. Robert marched with the rest of the children, but his mother didn't stand at the curb with the other mothers to wave and cheer. Léonie stood alone in the back and watched them pass with an air of suspicion.

The nearest city was Saarbrücken, the capital of the Sarre Territory, ten miles down the Sarre River. Robert wondered why so many soldiers were stationed on the streets. He stared at the intricate, unfamiliar decorations on their uniforms. There were Africans, Muslims, Indochinese, and even Malgaches from Madagascar,[27] all recruited from French colonies to patrol the Sarre Territory and the Rhineland on behalf of the League of Nations. German children were tight-lipped around the foreign soldiers and glared at them with contempt.

"I'm not getting anywhere in this factory," Robert's father said to his wife a few months later. "Let me be a hatmaker!"

Robert's father talked incessantly about hats at the dinner table. One night, Léonie said, "I've heard enough talk about hats. It is time you started looking for a building in town where you can make your hats. I can sell them while I keep an eye on the children."

One year after their arrival in Sarreguemines, Robert's father returned home late for dinner. He had the old sparkle in his eyes.

"I found a place. The store is on the street. It has an apartment on the second floor, and I can make hats in the attic. It's three doors from the corner on the Goldstrasse."

"But what about the children?" Léonie said.

"They'll find friends to play with, and they can each have their own room. It's not very far from the river. Anyway, it's just a place to get started. Then we can look for a house." He looked sadly at Robert. "But I'm afraid there's no place to keep a hen, son. There's no back yard and they don't have any gardens in that neighborhood."

"I can keep Grethel in my room," Robert said quickly.

"She wouldn't like that because Grethel belongs outside. We'll have to find her a new home."

.   .   .

The Goldstrasse had been a Jewish quarter in the Middle Ages where jewelry, gold, and silver were traded. Every building in the Goldstrasse was similar—they all had a door and two windows on the sidewalk and two or three windows on the two upper floors. The Mullers rented an ancient three-story structure with windows that were framed with heavy iron shutters and walls as thick as a fort. Robert's father borrowed money to buy used hatmaking machines from a company that had closed its doors in Saarbrücken.[28]

A local farmer adopted Grethel. Robert's mother agreed to let Robert accompany her in the rain to the farmer's house. Robert held Grethel close to his chest tucked under his black and white raincoat. He kissed her head and beak and talked to her softly all the way to the farm.

"You'll be okay," Robert said. "They're going to take good care of you. You're the best hen in the world and I love you."

It was the saddest thing he had ever done. Grethel stayed by his feet until his mother said it was time to go home. She could not see his tears as they walked back in the rain.

As Robert lay in bed that night thinking about Grethel with an aching feeling of helplessness, he heard a man in the next building shouting and cursing so loudly his voice cracked. A woman screamed for help. There was a loud crash as a chair or table smashed against the wall, followed by more screams. It was their first Saturday night in the Goldstrasse. On Saturdays, men went to the pubs at noon and stayed until night. They worked long hours and they had not earned decent wages since the War.

With the demands of starting a business and setting up a new home, Robert's parents didn't notice that their son was spending more time in his room. Robert didn't like living in the Goldstrasse. There were no trees or flowers—nothing grew at all. He sometimes wandered down to the river to watch the *Schiffnickel* keeper's boat cross the Sarre River to Germany, where passengers bought cheap tobacco. One time, he got too close to the water and came back with mud on his pants.

Robert Muller with his parents in Sarreguemines under
his favorite cherry tree.

His mother scolded him. *"Oh! Du loosh wie a Schlowak!* You look like a Slovak!"

In June, after the hatmaking machines were set up and the store was open for business, Robert and Marcelle followed their father to an orchard on the outskirts of town. "This cherry tree is for you," he said. "I bought the entire crop! You can come here as often as you like and pick cherries."

At first, all they could do was stare. Then Robert clambered up the tree, where he found thousands of sweet cherries. Plucking one, he polished it on his shirt, popped it in his mouth and spit the pit on the ground. Then he looked at his father to see if he was in trouble.

His father stood under the tree with a big smile. "Yes! Yes! There you go, good! Eat as many as you want."

Robert started spending more time exploring the town. Early one morning, he slipped away from home while his parents were asleep and wandered past the farmers' market as they were setting up tables. Three blocks from the house, he heard organ music coming from the Church of St. Nicholas, patron saint of Sarreguemines. He pulled open the heavy wooden doors and went inside. Music filled the church and stained glass windows sparkled with sunlight, spilling fractured rainbows across the benches where elderly parishioners prayed. Robert started down the aisle, stopping every few steps. The priest was celebrating the Eucharist when Robert's voice echoed through the church.

"Das leben ist göttlich!" he shouted.

Everybody stared at the five-year-old boy with his arms lifted high. To a woman kneeling next to him, Robert said it again. *"Das leben ist göttlich."* Life is divine.

Robert's father bought himself a new bicycle as soon as the hat business began to pick up. He was happy as a kid riding the new bicycle through town. He offered Robert a ride on his fifth birthday and they took off through the center of town. Robert's father pedaled faster and faster, howling like a train while Robert balanced precariously on the crossbar shouting at the top of his lungs. People on the sidewalk smiled and waved, and soon they started yelling and pointing.

Robert's father finally realized that his son wasn't smiling. The bicycle made a loud pinging sound as soon as he stopped making train noises. They skidded to a stop. His son's right foot was wedged between the fork and the spokes. Robert's shoe was shaved away and his ankle was planed to the bone.

His face sagging with guilt, Robert's father carried him into the big Victorian hospital at the top of the hill. It was several months before Robert could walk to school, and he always would walk with his right foot turned out.

When Louis XVI was beheaded in 1793, separation of church and state became a cornerstone of French culture. From that time forward, religious education was forbidden in public schools.

At the end of World War I, French officials traveled to Alsace-Lorraine to meet with the people in the recovered provinces. They asked if there was anything about German culture they wanted to keep. The people said they wanted to preserve the German practice of offering religious classes in public schools. French officials reluctantly agreed, but only on condition that the classes would be voluntary and non-denominational, and they had to be taught by a rotating faculty of Protestants, Catholics and Jews.

Freemasons taught the required subjects in Robert's school, and they had plenty to say about religion.

"The priests are stupid."

"Organized religion is a system of lies."

"Going to church is a waste of time."

"When I find a student talking to a priest, I see a child who has too much time on his hands."

Ridicule was stronger medicine than religion. Miracles could be found in nature, Robert decided, but not church. He looked forward to the arrival of the first bananas and oranges at the farmers' market in the spring and he loved taking walks in the forest with his father. As he grew older, he spent many long hours wandering alone through the

Forest of Welferding, which stretched from the Caves of Welferding by the river all the way past town and across the hills towards Sarralbe. He learned the pleasure of feeling cool moisture from the trees on his skin, and he discovered that the moss along the banks of the brook smelled like musk when his nose almost touched it. But Robert's enthusiasm for the miracle of life was diminished by the monotony of school.

The Freemasons taught French history, geography and philosophy. Geography covered the area from Belgium in the north—an ally of France—to the Pyrenees in the south—which kept the Spaniards out of France, and from the Rhine in the east—which kept Germany in its place, to the Atlantic coast in the west. In history, Robert learned that the French people were the world's champions of liberty and equality. France had won the Great War, with help from the Allies. Students memorized the words of André Maginot, a politician whose family was from Lorraine, who declared in 1919 during the protracted negotiations for the Treaty of Versailles, "We are always the invaded. We are always the ones who suffer. We are always the ones to be sacrificed. Fifteen invasions in less than six centuries gives France the right to insist on a victor's treaty."[29]

When Robert recited the speech at home, his mother said, "I wonder if André Maginot ever heard of Napoleon."

Léonie never talked about her experiences during the war, except when it might give her leverage over the children. "I would have given anything to have cucumbers like that on my plate," she said. "All we had for dinner during the war was dandelion soup and, if we were lucky, a slice of stale bread. It is always the soldiers who are fed. Now finish your meal before you study."

Lunch was usually a heavy soup. A typical dinner was boiled potatoes, onions and cottage cheese. They ate meat every week—on Sunday.[30] If Robert didn't finish every bite, he would find the leftovers on his plate the next day.

Léonie refused to let him join any clubs or play on any teams. "Those groups will capture you and limit you. Even before you were born, I dreamed you would become a great intellectual. Now go upstairs and study."

He was not allowed to take music lessons. "Don't waste

your time on that," his mother said. "You must cultivate your mind."

Léonie expected Robert to study every day after school and again after dinner. The penalty for bringing home poor grades was a beating and a night without dinner. Although discipline at home was extremely strict, there was never any doubt that Léonie Muller loved her children and cherished her family above all else.

On special occasions, the family album came out and they pored through photographs of the first Christmas tree, toys, gifts, family outings, and finally—soldiers in uniform. In one picture, Robert's father wore a German uniform. He looked aggressive and threatening. His helmet was heavy and foreboding. In the next, he was a French soldier. His helmet was light and elegant, his face looked gentle, and he was smiling.

"Why do you wear two uniforms?" Robert asked.

His father shrugged. "When I was seventeen, the Germans were our masters. They put me in a uniform and sent me to Schwerin, a city in the north of Germany. When the French came, they put me in a different uniform and sent me to a French city called Toul."

"But why did you fight on both sides?" Robert asked.

His father threw up his hands in exasperation. "In Alsace-Lorraine, it is our fate to be tossed from one side to the other and to be ordered to shoot in opposite directions. I can't explain it."

"In school," Robert said, "the teacher asked us where we were born. I said Belgium. The other kids said that was far away so I must not be French."

"You are French and you are Belgian. When you were born, the people in Eupen-Malmédy had not yet decided whether they would be Belgians or Germans. Now it is settled; they are Belgians. When you are 18, you can decide whether you want be French or Belgian. Right now you are both."

Robert's parents bought new hat molds in Paris every spring. The shop carried the latest fashions. Robert learned how to make hats in the attic with his father. He helped when it was time to release the new aluminum press that held seven steaming cones in a row.

Above: Robert Muller Sr. was a third generation hatmaker.

Below: The Muller family photo album showed Robert's father, on the left, wearing a WWI German army uniform in one picture and a French uniform in the next.

All year long, Robert looked forward to summer visits at his grandfather's Panama hat factory in Sarralbe. The factory was bustling with people, and Robert loved the exotic grassy smell of palm leaves that arrived by boat from Africa. First the leaves were stored in the attic. Then workers dipped them in big kettles of boiling water before bleaching them. The leaves were hung on poles in sheds where sulfur was burned to make them mold-resistant in the damp European climate. Then the leaves were pulled through a rack of razor blades and bundled into thin strips. Horse-drawn wagons delivered the bundles to farm workers who lived along the crooked border between Alsace and Lorraine. In the evenings and all day long during the winter, farm workers wove Panama hats by hand. Finally, the hats were pressed before they were shipped all over Europe.

Robert and his sister slid down mountains of palm leaves stored in the attic above the enormous kitchen, where workers' meals were prepared. Their tall grandfather closely supervised every step of the process, strolling through the factory in a clean, white lab coat with a Kaiser Wilhelm mustache carefully curled and waxed to a delicate point.[31] Laurent Muller commanded respect, but he could always get the workers laughing when he played the harmonica.

Robert sensed the presence of ghosts when he was alone in the big courtyard behind the factory. His grandfather told him that Germans had imprisoned British soldiers in the yard during the war. Laurent's daughter Eulalie had to walk through the yard every day to feed the pigs. The prisoners would stretch their arms through the barbed wire and beg her for handfuls of slop.

Robert studied the details of a dark oil painting hanging over the mantle in his grandfather's living room. It was the only picture of Benoit Muller, Robert's great-grandfather. He had a triangular forehead and thick lips, and he looked directly out from the painting with a candid expression, intensified by his bushy eyebrows.

"You can see by that painting of my father that the Mullers are descended from the Huns," Laurent said with a smile.

Although Robert felt bored and restless in school, he sat for hours in his grandfather's living room poring over his

18-volume German encyclopedia, the *Meyers Konversations-Lexicon*. He found hundreds of pictures of men in uniform. All the European wars melted together in the boy's mind into a colorful parade of uniforms. Each country came out with a new uniform for every war.

"When I was born in 1863, we were French," his grandfather said. "I was five years old when Bismarck made a speech in Germany and he said, 'The weak were made to be devoured by the strong.' How do you like that? Then he sent his army to France and bombed Paris until they surrendered." [32]

He showed Robert an old photo of his four brothers wearing French army uniforms. "My older brothers served in the French army, but I guess the Germans were better fighters. After the French surrendered, Bismarck went to the Hall of Mirrors in Versailles and announced that France would have to pay Germany one million pounds. He wanted to teach them a lesson for losing the war—a war that he started! After that, I had to speak German." When Robert's grandfather talked about the Germans, he faced east, and when he talked about the French, he faced west.

"But that's enough about war." He handed Robert a small box. "Go ahead, open it."

Tucked inside, wrapped in a red silk cloth, was a shiny new harmonica. Robert's eyes almost fell on the floor. He held it tightly for a moment, then he handed it back.

"Mama says I'm not allowed to play music."

"Your mother is afraid you'll drop out of school and be a poor musician. Don't worry about your mother. I'll tell her that nobody ever left school to play the harmonica in a band. Here, all you have to do is blow through the little holes and music will come out."

Robert's mother went along with the harmonica, but she wasn't so keen about hearing him practice above the store.

"It's time we found a house," she said when Robert was nine years old. "We've been here long enough."

On October 31, 1932, they rented a house at 84 Rue de la Montagne, halfway to the top of the prominent hill in Sarreguemines. It seemed like a palace compared to the apartment. There was space for a garden in the backyard, a little park across the street, and the best park in town was only a block away.

In the spring, Robert turned ten years old. He was sure that everyone had forgotten his birthday by the time his father sent him out to the backyard to get some firewood. There, at the bottom of the steps, he found a shiny new bicycle.

His father came outside, followed by his mother and sister. Robert was holding the handlebars with his mouth hanging open.

"Is this for me?"

"Happy birthday, son," his father said.

"But it's a girl's bike!" Robert muttered.

"So what?" his father said. "It works just the same, and when you get too big for it, your sister can ride it."

The boys at school thought it was funny, but after a few hours they got tired of repeating the same old jokes. All they could get out of Robert was a shrug or a shake of the head. As he pushed the bike back up Rue de la Montagne, which was too steep to ride, he realized it would make more sense to walk to school. No boy wanted to be seen pushing his bike.

His mother was at the shop when he got home, so he took off on his shiny new bike towards the country. In a few minutes, he was in the rolling hills where nobody could see him, riding past farms and patches of forest, turning left or right on a whim at every fork in the road until he was so completely lost, only the setting sun gave him any idea which way was home. He chased his lengthening shadow to Sarreguemines, pedaling as hard as he could to get home before dark.

"Sorry, Mama," he said when he got in. Everybody was eating dinner at the kitchen table.

"Your father buys you a nice new bicycle—I don't know what has gotten into you!" she said. "We're in the busiest month and you come waltzing in here after dinner."

"I'm sorry."

"You can feel sorry all you like, but do it in your room. We're having dinner, so go on, now. Your father will teach you a lesson about being late after we finish eating."

Robert's father and sister kept eating without looking up, hunched over their bowls.

. . .

A strong pacifist current spread across France during the 1920's. Many French officials believed that the Treaty of Versailles made war obsolete, but military leaders warned that Germany had twice as many people as France, a higher birthrate, greater steel-making capacity, and a burning resentment over their humiliation at Versailles.

When the French government wanted a soldier's opinion about creating a new defense strategy in 1923, they called upon General Henri-Philippe Pétain, Inspector General of the French Army, Commander-in-Chief in the Event of Hostilities, and a man hailed as the savior of Western Civilization. Pétain was the champion of the defensive war. He had learned at Verdun that forts could withstand the impact of shells if they were constructed properly—two layers of concrete and a layer of sand between.[33] The fortifications at Verdun stopped the Germans, he argued, and every new military invention since 1918 favored the defense. He lectured the politicians about "battlefields prepared in peacetime" and recommended the construction of a line of forts from the North Sea to the Alps, modeled on the trenches of the Great War.

André Maginot, President of the Parliamentary Army Committee, lobbied hard for funding. He raised most of the money by selling surplus defense properties. Maginot died in 1932, but for all his trouble his name was attached to the project by the press three years later. Newspapers and politicians started calling the Maginot Line "an impregnable wall of steel and concrete,"[34] thus assuring André Maginot an enduring place in history, if not an enviable one.

In the summer of 1933, Robert's family traveled to Trier, Germany, to see the exhibition of the Lord's Holy Robe. Nazi troops marched provocatively in front of the pilgrims, who lined up at the cathedral for a glimpse of the cloak believed to have been worn by Jesus Christ. Robert took out his harmonica on the steps of the cathedral during the long

wait and played the French national anthem, "Marseillaise."
It was the only song he knew.

A firm hand squeezed his shoulder. Robert saw only the
fingers of a black leather glove.

"You will come with us," a man ordered. He was wearing
a brown uniform with a red swastika armband and his face
was tight. Robert's parents were in line some distance away.
The Nazis whisked Robert into a truck and drove off, but
they stopped and let him out a few blocks away. Robert ran
back to the cathedral, where he found his father wandering
around looking for him while his mother and sister stood in
line.

"Where did you go?" his father asked.

"Some Nazis gave me a ride."

His father looked baffled. The church bells rang and the
crowd surged towards the door.

Marshal Pétain met with the Senate Army Commission in
1934 to answer questions about defenses on the Belgian
frontier. Asked about the Ardennes, a hilly, forested area
along the Luxembourg border, he replied, "It is
impenetrable if one makes some special dispositions
there...This sector is not dangerous." He predicted that
France's enemies would come the way they had always
come—over the top through Belgium, across the middle
through Alsace-Lorraine, or up the Rhône Valley from the
south.

The Maginot Line was the longest permanent fortification
built since the Great Wall of China. In terms of depth,
complexity, cost, and firepower, the Maginot Line had no
equal. Teachers described it in Robert's school as a miracle
in engineering. The estimated cost was a whopping three
billion francs. Local contractors were hired to do the
construction and materials were stockpiled all over town.
Every child in Sarreguemines knew someone whose father
or uncle or brother worked on the Maginot Line.

Trenches were excavated 30 stories deep in the farmland
east of Sarreguemines, where Fort Simserhof grew into one
of the largest forts on the Maginot Line. The trenches were

lined with cement, shaped into tunnels, fitted with miles of underground railroads, and covered up with dirt.[35]

On Armistice Day in Robert's eleventh year, November 11, 1934, the Mullers moved into their own house, a sturdy three-story residence built on a lot they picked up for a good price. It was the first house built on the crest of the highest hill in Sarreguemines

The property was on the corner of Rue de la Montagne and Rue de la Prison, four blocks up from the house they had rented for two years. Out of the living room window on the side facing Rue de la Montagne, they saw the big Victorian hospital through the trees. Across the street from the front door was a gloomy, red-stone prison bordered by a ten-foot high gray wall. An outer fence made of cast iron on a stone base ran along the edge of the sidewalk. Several times a week, prisoners were escorted through the armored door and led down Rue de la Prison past the Mullers' front door to Rue de la Montagne, then around the corner past the living room window towards the courthouse.

Robert moved into the attic on the third floor. From his window, he could see across the river past the German border to hills far away—a commanding view of the region. Over the years, more houses were built on the hill, but Robert's view remained unobstructed. When he retreated to his room, he was in a world to himself. The only interruption was announced by a thumping sound when his father brought home a new masterpiece and climbed the stairs. He paused at Robert's door with his eyes sparkling as he twirled the hat on the tips of his fingers.

"I have the most beautiful profession in the world," he said. "I hope I will always be able to make hats."

In the spring and autumn, when demand was high, Robert's father made 20 to 30 hats a week. Robert helped out at the shop after school. Léonie continued to run the store, but with the arrival of autumn she went home early to can preserves with Marcelle and knit warm clothes for the winter. After dinner, when the chores were done and the dishes were put away, they all gathered around the kitchen

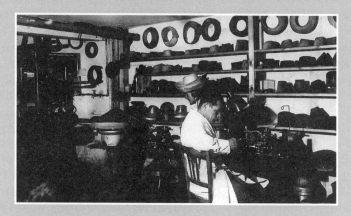

Robert Muller Sr. called it "the most beautiful profession in the world" as he taught his son Robert to make hats.

stove to save fuel and electricity. While the children finished their schoolwork, Robert's mother painted portraits.

"I want to try painting," Robert said one evening.

"Your studies are more important," she replied. "When my work is done for the day, I can relax. But you don't have the time to fool around like that. Do you want to be a poor artist when you grow up? Have you forgotten you want to be a doctor? You have to work hard to be self reliant."

Léonie brought home a Rottweiller puppy named Bella to cheer Robert up as he drew further away from the activities of his schoolmates. He forced himself to read the textbooks assigned in school, but nothing in the texts inspired him or pointed to the limitless possibilities that percolated in his mind. The more he tried in school, the less hopeful he felt.

In his twelfth year, Robert pressed his mother to let him paint a copy of the portrait of his great-grandfather hanging in his grandfather's living room. She cautiously gave her approval. Based on his observations of her technique in the kitchen, Robert painted a copy of the Renaissance portrait of Benoit Muller during his summer vacation in Sarralbe.

While Robert was staying with his grandfather, the Petit family from Lyon moved into an apartment on the first floor. Marcel Petit was hired as a teacher for Robert's seventh grade; his wife taught at the girl's school. Their son Jojo was Robert's age. Jojo had a thin, angular face and he shared Robert's aversion to competitive sports and groups. They became friends as they went for long walks in the woods with Bella and worked together in the garden.

When Robert was not with Jojo, he spent as much time as possible in his room, where the world faded away as his mind wandered. On his twelfth birthday, his grandfather gave him the 18-volume German encyclopedia. As soon as Robert finished reading one volume, the next one was presented. This arrangement encouraged him to plunge into a universe of topics alphabetically. Robert delved into the meanings of words and traced their origins as he read the entire encyclopedia from cover to cover, volume by volume.

Four months after they moved into their new house, the Sarre Territory voted to join the Third Reich in the spring of 1935. The French government reacted with alarm, but the residents of Alsace-Lorraine were not surprised by the tally.

*Robert Muller's first Communion at the age of twelve in
St. Nicholas Church. March 11, 1935.*

They knew that the people across the river were different. They had always been Prussians and there was no reason to expect they would distance themselves from Berlin. Every evening when they sat in the kitchen, Robert's mother rummaged through the *Courier de la Sarre*. Robert noticed a scowl on his mother's face whenever she read the newspaper. Her eyes darted from one headline to the next and she held the paper at a distance with suspicion, as if it were poison.

"What are you looking for?" Robert asked.

"Lies," she said.

"Is that why you hold the paper so far away?"

"Son, as long as I live, through war and peace, French, German, prosperity, depression, there is always the same amount of bad news in the papers. It must be some basic human law that the world will never be happy. I have my own house and family to care for and that's all I can do. If the world were about to perish, people would only care about their own families."[36]

"So why do you bother to read it?" he persisted.

"To know if a disaster will come too close to my family."

"What kind of disaster?"

"War."

Léonie never talked about The War, but Robert learned about it during history class in school. God and heaven were forbidden subjects, but war was a central theme.

Robert's uncle had been wounded at Verdun. In school, Robert read that the fighting in Verdun started in February 1916, soon after Uncle Alphonse was drafted. During the next ten months, France and Germany suffered 600,000 casualties[37] fighting for control of five miles that had no strategic significance. The French held the line and General Henri-Philippe Pétain became a hero for winning the Battle of Verdun.

While Pétain was defending Verdun, British General Douglas Haig suited up his British soldiers in bright red coats for the Battle of the Somme on July 1, 1916 and sent them marching shoulder-to-shoulder into German machine guns. By the end of the first day, 20,000 British soldiers were dead and 40,000 were wounded.[38] The battle lasted for four and a half months.[39] At a human cost of over a million casualties, the front moved less than five miles in a few places. The Germans held the line.

The United States joined the war against Germany on April 6, 1917, after Germany resumed U-boat attacks on American merchant vessels. A week later, General Nivelle, France's Commander in Chief, launched a new offensive against the Germans and ordered French infantry to march into another massacre. Fifty-four divisions refused to follow orders. Thousands of men deserted. By the end of April, Nivelle was out of a job and General Henri-Philippe Pétain was France's new Commander-in-Chief. Pétain court-martialed 100,000 deserters; 23,000 were found guilty.[40] Pétain doubled everyone's leave, improved the food, and pledged to fight a defensive war until the Americans arrived. Pétain's swift measures restored order and won him the respect of the French people.

When Robert read the history books, he recoiled from the carnage. He had nightmares about "Big Bertha," named after Bertha Krupp. Bertha's father had built a giant 420-mm howitzer in 1890 to defend Germany's coast. In World War I, it was hauled on a train to Flanders.[41] Firing every twelve minutes, "Big Bertha" lobbed one-ton mortars from six miles away into the medieval city of Ypres until the city was destroyed on April 20, 1915. The Germans then released canisters of chlorine gas and depopulated four miles of the French defense line. Robert tried to erase the images from his mind of one-ton shells blowing everything apart—the 12th Century Cloth Tower, the cathedral—while soldiers collapsed in a green fog a short distance away. The images faded in time, but not his apprehension.

One Friday afternoon in the summer of 1935, Robert's father climbed the stairs to the attic. "Now that you're 12 years old, it's time I showed you something. Tomorrow we're going to Verdun."

They left in the morning, changed trains in Metz, and reached Verdun before noon. As they walked across the legendary battlefield towards the Trench of Bayonets, Robert stumbled over something sticking out of the ground.

Robert Muller's schoolbooks showed the Cloth Hall in the Belgian town of Ypres before and after the town was destroyed in WWI by "Big Bertha."

He dug into the soil with his fingers and pulled out a rusty rifle that had been buried for almost twenty years. It was still in good condition. When Robert asked an attendant for permission to keep the rifle, the man merely shrugged. A little further, Robert saw the tips of bayonets sticking out of the ground where a French platoon had been buried alive.

They continued walking to the Ossuary of Douaumont, a building 600 feet long. Through the windows, Robert stared at a mountain of gray bones—the remains of 130,000 French and German soldiers.

"If another war is about to break out," he said to his father slowly, "the leaders should all be locked up in that cellar until they make peace."[42]

Betting that the Saarländers would not vote to be realigned with Germany, France postponed construction of the missing link in the Maginot Line near Sarreguemines. France had hoped to extend the fortress into the hills east of the Sarre River because the soil on the French side was unstable. When the Sarre Territory rejoined Germany, France rushed to fill in the gap. A network of dams was constructed near Laurent Muller's factory so that fields surrounding Sarralbe could be flooded to repel invaders. By the time the Maginot Line was completed, the final cost had climbed to six billion francs, twice the amount that André Maginot had predicted.[43]

French troops passed through Sarreguemines by train to participate in military exercises at Simserhof, the only fort with enough open space to practice firing machine guns, mortars, anti-tank guns, and howitzers. French engineers visited Czechoslovakia to supervise construction of fortifications that were identical to the Maginot Line.

In March 1936, Hitler defied the League of Nations and sent troops into the Rhineland and the Sarre Territory. It was just a bluff. Hitler later admitted that his troops would have fled if even one shot had been fired, but the French merely responded by sending soldiers to the Maginot Line. The Allies had no desire to fight a war over territory that had always been part of Germany.

The first crack in Pétain's fortress appeared in 1936 when Belgium issued a declaration of neutrality. With the loss of its ally, France was undefended in the north, but it had no money to extend the Maginot Line along the industrial border to the North Sea.

Saarländers started wearing Nazi uniforms—girls, boys, men and women—except old and disabled Germans were forbidden to wear them. Hitler started drafting teenagers to serve in the youth corps—*Arbeitsdienst*—after they completed a period of manual labor. Emotions in Alsace-Lorraine were stirred up by the rising militancy in Germany. Some of the boys in Robert's school started marching defiantly in the streets, shouting Nazi slogans.

Along the border, Nazis held noisy parades on the German side of the Blies River, only a stone's throw away from Sarreguemines' soccer field on the riverbank. Fans traditionally sang the "Marseillaise" at the start of every game. The Nazis retaliated by staging political rallies directly across the river at the start of every soccer game, drowning out the French voices with blaring music and shouting as they counted off and practiced the goose-step march. Robert and Jojo attended one game, and vowed never again.[44]

While France hoped for the best, massive public works projects and a rapid buildup of arms in Germany slashed unemployment from six million in 1930 to one million in 1936. Roads were built to carry tanks and factories sprang up which could easily be converted to manufacture arms. Germany emerged as an industrial giant, second only to the United States.

To avoid a flagrant violation of the Treaty of Versailles, the German army made a secret deal with Joseph Stalin to train German soldiers on Russian soil. After Francisco Franco came to power in Spain, with Hitler's backing, Germany built airplane factories in Spain. The Luftwaffe practiced aerial dive-bombing in the Basque city of Guernica in 1937, where 2,500 civilians were killed. Pablo Picasso started painting *Guernica* two days later.

· · ·

After visiting Verdun, Robert retreated deep into his books, avoiding the angry demonstrations in town. Despite all the hours he studied, his heart wasn't in his schoolwork. He couldn't seem to please his mother and the lessons seemed pointless. With each semester, Robert felt more lethargic.

One night on his way down for dinner, he heard his father muttering in the hall as he hung his coat in the closet after work.

"Is anything wrong?" Léonie asked.

"Why are the French so gullible?" his father said. "I saw Erwin Raiffenrat today. God, what a crazy mess."

"What did he do now?" she asked.

"You know I don't trust that man. His heart is German, and he will never fit into a French officer's uniform."

"They made Erwin Raiffenrat an officer?" Léonie said. "Why would they do that?"

"Because the French are divided and they're so stupid. They don't know what to think!"

"Who is Erwin Raiffenrat?" Robert asked.

"I went to school with him," Robert's father said. "His mother was French, and his father, I don't know, he may have been a fine man, but he was from Germany. To become a French citizen, he needed an endorsement from a local resident. My father was on the city council and he vouched for Erwin's father. Fine, that was his decision, but I grew up with Erwin. I saw him every day at school."

"What's the problem?" Robert asked.

"Erwin is no good. I have a bad feeling about this."

Chapter 4 – The Exodus

From his attic window, Robert watched the ancient forests on the German side of the river cleared away to make way for corn and wheat fields. A new village materialized on the banks of the Sarre River—Adolph Hitler Dorf. German newspapers praised construction of Hitler's Siegfried Line in Germany, a fortification parallel to the Maginot Line, which they claimed would protect the Fatherland from French aggression. They called it the most formidable system of defenses ever built, much sturdier than the "old fashioned" Maginot Line, but they neglected to report that it was built entirely above ground with no connecting tunnels. It was a sham compared to the Maginot Line.

School was a diversion, at best, until Robert's teacher of German literature failed to show up for class one morning in the spring of 1938 and they couldn't find a teacher to replace him. Mr. Hehn, the school librarian, was sent in to fill the gap. Hehn was from Schweighouse and he had grown up with Robert's mother. His studies had stopped during the war and he was never able to obtain a French teaching certificate.

"How many of you have heard of Friedrich Schiller?" Hehn asked as he handed out a stack of green books. He was tall and confident, and with his forceful manner he quickly took control of the classroom. Robert read the curious title of the green book, *On the Aesthetic Education of Man,* which he had seen on his grandfather's bookshelf.

Several hands went up.

"Ah, Muller! Can you tell us anything about Schiller?"

"He said that life imitates art," Robert answered shyly.

"Very good. And what do you suppose he meant by that?"

"I don't know, a lot of people would say it's the other way around. Maybe what he means is that people get new ideas by looking at art and reading books."

"That's good," Hehn responded. "And that's why we come to school, isn't it? To wrestle with ideas! Friedrich Schiller was the leading dramatist of his time. You may have heard of *Don Carlos,* his most famous play, which he completed in 1787." Heads nodded. "Six years after *Don Carlos,* Schiller wrote a series of letters to his patron and spelled out his ideas about aesthetics. He wrote, 'Art is an expression of values. Life imitates art because art is a voice preparing the shape of things to come. Man not only imitates art; he transforms himself into what he imitates.' "

Robert was twitching uncomfortably. The way Hehn prowled around the room while he talked, the way he seemed to be hunting for ideas, his restless energy pulled Robert out of his lethargy. *How can a guy like this be a school librarian?* Robert wondered.

"Schiller wrote that artists are mankind's true shapers. Therefore, the artist must not bend—*must not bend*—to public opinion. The artist's job is not to entertain. It is to elevate, to free us from our animal nature!

"Would you agree with that, Mr. Muller?"

"I, I don't know...I have to think about it, but...yes, I suppose so. Art must be something more than just a record of what people are thinking."

"Good!" Hehn said. His eyes flared with enthusiasm, and Robert could feel the infectious energy spreading inside him.

"But the bell is about to ring and soon you will go out to play, so I leave you with one more thought. Schiller wrote that play is an activity for its own sake. It is done as an end in itself without any secondary motive of profit. Therefore,

Schiller suggest that play is a state of being that constitutes wholeness.'"

The bell rang.

"All right, go out and play! Play like artists!"

Robert was scarcely aware of his surroundings as he left school. Hehn had lit a fire. Robert was burning with the idea that art could point people in new directions. At home, he whistled happily while he studied.

"What's gotten into you?" his mother asked at dinner.

"We have a new teacher—Mr. Hehn."

"Hehn, yes, I know him. He teaches German."

"German literature," Robert said. "He's teaching us about Schiller, but he's more like a general than a teacher."

"A German general?" she asked coolly.

"Umm, yes, he's definitely more German than French. I have to study now."

Robert sat up late reading Schiller's green book:

Only play makes the man whole and unfolds both sides of his nature at once. Man only plays when he is in the fullest sense of the word a human being, and he is only a human being when he plays.[45]

Robert could see that the best moments in his life had been spent in nature—climbing trees, taking walks with his father and Jojo in the forest, or sitting by a brook. He felt joyful when he played harmonica, especially with his grandfather. It was fun, and yet it was fulfilling.

The next day, Hehn was at the door, waving them into the room as if they were about to embark on a journey.

"Let's see if anybody read the assignment. Schiller wrote, 'If beauty brings the senses nearer to reason and beauty brings reason nearer the senses, there must be a state midway between matter and form, somewhere between passive and active. Beauty transports us to this middle state.'

"Question: what did Schiller call that middle state?"

Hands went up.

"Very well, everybody at once!"

"*The aesthetic state.*"

"You're doing very well. What does he mean by that?"[46]

More hands went up. Hehn had only a few weeks to leave a mark on his students, and he worked fast. The hours in his class were a race against time.

"How many of you have heard of Goethe?"

More hands.

"Then you probably know that Goethe studied law in Strasbourg. Who else from Alsace-Lorraine contributed to German literature?"

"Gutenberg invented the printing press in Strasbourg," said one student.

"Good, I'll accept that. How about Erckmann and Chatrian—they were both born in Phalsbourg."

"Joan of Arc!"

"Yes, though not a writer."

Hehn held Robert spellbound. Real life entered the classroom when he spoke—the people, the countryside, the dreams, and the secret passions of each student. Robert began to read Goethe and Schiller eagerly. There was now meaning to his schoolwork. The words in books came alive and they felt like they were connected to his world. Years later, Robert wrote about Hehn's class:

> His tools were Goethe and Schiller, a painting, a poem, an old clock, a legend, the etymology of a word, the Lord's Prayer in old high Germanic or an article in the newspaper. Through these tools he told us about life, he taught us life. Passion, enthusiasm, a deep belief in oneself, love for life, obsession with life—these are the great motors of learning and human happiness. I became a joyful student.[47]

Robert's enthusiasm spread to other subjects. Teachers began to classify him *exceptional*. At the end of the school year, Robert raced home to show his mother his report card. He had earned the highest grades in his class.

He found her in the kitchen preparing dinner. Léonie glanced at the report and handed it back to him. She returned to her cooking while Robert waited expectantly. Finally she noticed him again.

"Why should I be excited?" she said. "You didn't do that for me. You did it for yourself."

She turned back to her work. Robert retreated to his room. His fists pressed against the desk as anger simmered inside him. He took off to the woods with Bella and walked at a furious pace until his frustration diminished.

"I don't care what she thinks," he said, tears streaming down his cheeks. "I'll do even better."

Two days after Robert's fifteenth birthday, Hitler announced the unification of Germany and Austria on March 13, 1938. He was gambling that the Allies could not rally their people for war. The Allies stuck to a policy of appeasement, which had started on the day Germany seized the Rhineland.

"They're all Prussians anyway," people said.

The Petits announced that they would move back to Lyon at the end of the school year. "You can bend with the wind," Jojo's mother said to Léonie. "The Germans say the people who live in this region are German, and the French insist you are French. But we are French, no argument about it, and we're not safe here. If you have any trouble, you can come and stay at our summer home in Champdor. It's very nice in the Jura Mountains. You'd like it there."

In September 1938, Hitler amassed his troops on the border of Czechoslovakia. France threatened war and called up the reserves. Robert's father was sent to Fort Simserhof. Residents of Alsace-Lorraine who lived between the Maginot Line and the German border were encouraged to evacuate. Léonie took Robert and Marcelle to the Petits' summer cottage in the Jura Mountains.

Robert walked for hours every day in the Juras. He was relieved to be away from the hostility in Sarreguemines. Every morning, he set out to explore the paths through the woods and enjoy the autumn colors, carrying a book or two for the warm part of the day. His favorite was an essay written by Goethe in 1783:

Nature! We are surrounded and enveloped by her—incapable of stepping outside of her and incapable of penetrating deeper into her. Neither asked nor warned, we are received in the cycle of her dance and carried along until we drop, tired, out of her arms.

She creates ever-new shapes; what exists has never before existed; what has passed away will not return. Everything is new and yet always the same.

We live in her midst and are foreign to her. She constantly speaks to us, but never reveals her secret to us. We constantly affect her, but have no power over her.[48]

British Prime Minister Neville Chamberlain and French Prime Minister Édouard Daladier met with Hitler in Munich on September 30 and handed him Czechoslovakia without a fight. "After all," people said, "Czechoslovakia wasn't even a country until 1918."

Neville Chamberlain was cheered in London when he announced he had achieved, "Peace in our time." Winston Churchill stood up in the back of the House of Commons and protested that the Munich Agreement would lead to disaster. He was shouted down. French papers went along with the Munich Agreement and the French people sighed with relief.

After Hitler occupied Czechoslovakia, he ordered his best troops to simulate an attack against the Czech fortifications that were modeled after the Maginot Line.[49] They reported back that they did not have the firepower to break through. Czechoslovakia could have resisted the first wave of a German assault.

The Mullers returned to Sarreguemines hoping that war had been averted, but the town had changed. There was constant anxiety that violence would break out. Robert continued his studies, blocking out the mounting tension in the streets with his new passion for literature. With Jojo gone, he spent almost every free minute in his room.

Some of Robert's classmates were infected with their own strain of Nazi fever when a new political movement sprang up in France. "Blue-Shirts" marched in Sarreguemines every Sunday wearing blue shirts crossed with black leather straps, black Mounties' pants, which they imported from Canada, and matching boots. Awkwardly, the militants copied the Nazi goosestep, shouting slogans. Robert wrote:

There seems to be always in every human group a certain percentage of people who need public exhibition and who will join any movement that offers them a uniform. They are despised by the rest of the population. They usually know it and retaliate when they are in power.

Soldiers streamed into Alsace-Lorraine from the French colonies—Africans, Muslims, Malgaches, and Indochinese. The courtyard by the river at Laurent Muller's factory filled with soldiers housed in temporary barracks[50] during the winter of 1939. Many died of pneumonia and tuberculosis.

During a visit to his grandfather, Robert saw an African soldier, a sergeant, dancing playfully in the courtyard. He urged his men to get up and dance to tribal rhythms while others tapped on cans and pieces of wood. As the men began to dance low to the ground, he called out to Robert.

"Hey boy! Why do you stand like a rock on two feet? Can you hear the rhythm? The time for rock feet is gone."

"Who are you?" Robert asked, keeping his feet very still.

"My name Bou Sidi," he said in a singsong voice, "and I am here to dance with you."

"But I don't know how—"

"You don't know how you can say no to Bou Sidi? Take my hand."

Robert tried to imitate the steps of the Africans, and soon other children were dancing with the troops.

"Why do you dance?" Robert asked.

"If I keep my men dancing and laughing, they will not give up."

Robert spent as many hours as possible with Bou Sidi during the summer before the war.

On August 24, 1939, a telegram arrived at the Muller home. German troops were assembling on Poland's border. The reserves had been called up. Robert's father was ordered to report for duty at the Maginot Line. He came up to Robert's room after packing.

Robert Muller (2nd row, 2nd from right) poses with his high school class in front of the school in June 1939— two months before the start of World War II. Jojo Petit is 3rd row, far left. Most of Robert's friends did not survive the war.

"I'll be back in a few weeks, son. You know how these things are. The French will never go to war with Germany over Poland. Why would they fight over Poland when they've given up Austria and Czechoslovakia? I want you to keep an eye on your mother and your sister until I get back."

"I will, Papa."

"And stay away from those idiots in the blue shirts."

"Yes, sir."

With that, his father was gone. Notices were sent to every home spelling out a new evacuation plan. Everyone was to report to the train station within three hours of the order. Each person could take only 30 kilograms of luggage.

A few days later, Hitler gathered his generals for a pep talk. "Close your hearts to pity!" he told them. German tanks poured into Poland, while 2,000 Stuka dive-bombers attacked behind the lines.[51] Over 16,000 privately owned German cars and trucks were commandeered to move German soldiers to the front, although most troops invaded on foot or on horseback.[52] France ordered a general mobilization the next day.

Robert ignored the commotion and stayed in his room. He dreamed about American Indians as he read "With the Savages," an essay by Chateaubriand, a French Count who had visited America in 1790. Chateaubriand described an excursion to Florida, where he spent several days with the Seminole Indians:

> I felt as if I were living and vegetating with Nature in a kind of pantheism. I leant back against the trunk of a magnolia tree and fell asleep; my slumbers floated on a vague surface of hope.
>
> When I emerged from this lethe, I found myself between two women; the odalisques had returned; not wanting to awaken me, they had sat down silently by my side; then, either in a pretence of sleep or because they had really dozed off, their heads had fallen on my shoulders.
>
> A breeze flew through the grove and deluged us with a shower of magnolia petals. Then the younger of the Seminoles began to sing. No man who is not sure

of himself should ever expose himself to such temptation: one cannot tell what passions may enter with the melody into a man's breast.[53]

Robert heard his mother's sharp footsteps climbing the stairs. She walked into his room without knocking.

"Boy, get up this minute! We have to evacuate."

"I couldn't care less about war," Robert blurted out. His sudden anger took him by surprise. He whirled around and faced his mother, trembling with defiance.

"I hate war!" he shouted. "Why should some idiot like Hitler interfere with my life and stop me from studying?"

She looked at him silently. Her blue eyes flared and then they turned cold. Without warning, she slapped Robert so hard she almost knocked him down the stairs.

She left without another word. Robert stuffed his duffel bag with shirts, pants, socks, and underwear, cramming everything in and piling books on top. He twisted his rain jacket so it would fit around the books and tossed a sweater on top, then more books.

The clasps on the duffel bag were too far apart. He threw some clothes on the bed and forced the bag closed. It was only for a few weeks, maybe a month or even two—but no, even that was unthinkable! Why should they have to leave their house for even one day because of that idiot?

He heaved the bag against the door and glared out the window. That room was Robert's sanctuary, and now the house would be left open and thieves could just walk in. The Prussians—or anybody else for that matter—could take anything they want. Who was going to stop them? The French couldn't guard a whole town with just a handful of reservists. It was stupid. The whole thing was wrong.

War! The word was like a poison dart shooting out of everyone's mouth. Robert hated the sound of it. *War.*

Robert took his harmonica out of the desk drawer, carefully wrapped it in the red silk scarf, and tucked it into his pocket. He took the portrait of his great-grandfather down from the wall, covered it with a pillowcase and wrapped it in a blanket. He carried the painting downstairs, dragging the duffel bag, and set them by the front door.

His mother was in the kitchen pulling cans and jars out

of the cupboard and piling them on the counter. Marcelle was packing things in boxes. Red jam oozed down the side of a cupboard and formed a puddle on the floor. Neither of them looked up.

"Where can I find an empty box?" Robert asked.

Léonie pointed to a box full of canned goods.

"Take that to the car," she said.

"I need an empty one."

"What for?" she asked.

"The encyclopedia," he said.

"Forget it. There's no room for all those books!"

"But we can't leave them here!"

Robert's mother glared at him. "Take that to the car."

"I thought we were going by train."

"I will not allow my family to be packed into cattle cars *like animals!*"

"But they sent us a notice. We're supposed to give them the car if there's an evacuation."

"Jules Frank was assigned to confiscate the car, but he came rushing over here before he got his orders, so I talked him into driving us to Lutzelbourg. But we don't have much time."

"Where?"

"I rented an apartment in Lutzelbourg."

She shoved the heavy box into his arms.

In a blur, Robert carried the box down the front steps and around to the garage. The black Simca was parked in the driveway facing the street. Jules Frank sat motionless in the driver's seat with both hands on the wheel. He was staring across the street at the prison.

"Mr. Frank, could you give me a hand?" Robert said.

Frank glanced at Robert, then back to the prison. "I must be out of my mind. It's the first day of the war and I'm already disobeying my orders."

"Nobody has declared war yet," Robert said, "and you can't disobey an order if you haven't received it."

"That's what your mother said, but I don't know."

"Should I tell her you've changed your mind?"

"No, don't! What? Are you kidding? She wouldn't even give me the keys!"

"Then open the door, will you please? This box is heavy."

Frank reached around and opened the back door.

Robert set the box on the seat and hurried back up the steps. He recognized a family on the sidewalk in front of the house. Robert knew one of the boys from school, but when he called out his name, the boy just glanced up and kept walking. Each of the children was carrying a box. The parents were carrying suitcases, one in each hand. Further up the street, Robert saw more people walking towards town. Some were carrying bundles tied up in sheets and others were pulling wagons and carts.

Robert filled the car. Then he squeezed into the back seat with Marcelle. Bella climbed in between them, panting. They watched their mother close the door and place the key in the lock. She hesitated, shook her head and walked away, leaving the key in the door.

"We can get through in Sarralbe," she said, "but don't take the river road. The streets will be jammed. We have to go the long way through Puttelange. Thank you, Jules."

Their mother directed Frank down a side street behind the prison. As they rounded the corner, Robert said, "Stop! I left my painting by the door."

"Drive!" Léonie said.

After several blocks, they merged onto the highway and drove through miles of empty farmland. They crossed the river in Sarralbe and pulled up in front of the hat factory. Robert's grandfather met them in the courtyard.

"I don't have to go," he said. "This side of the river is not in the prohibited zone. If I lived over there"—he pointing across the water—"I'd have to evacuate. I guess Hitler can't swim."

"That little river won't protect you, Grandpère," Robert said. "You'd better come with us."

"What are the Germans going to do with a hatmaker? You can't make helmets out of straw. Go ahead, and don't worry about me. This is my third war. I always survive." He waved them on.

When Frank returned the Mullers' car to Sarreguemines in the afternoon of September 2, 1939, every civilian was gone.

The railroad tracks were littered with clothing, suitcases, and boxes. The door to the public library blew open and sheets of newspaper danced across the polished wood floor. A handful of reservists patrolled the empty streets—their families were gone. As darkness approached, no lights came on. Flies swarmed over unfinished meals while dogs and cats peered out from abandoned buildings.

Freight trains rolled west through the night hauling a cargo of 16,000 passengers who had known each other as neighbors, shopkeepers, schoolteachers, and friends. Now they were jammed together in boxcars without enough food and water. The only place to sit or sleep was the floor. There were no toilets. The train stopped twice to let people off who were too weak to complete the trip.

The exhausted refugees climbed out of the trains three days later in Cognac, a small town in a poor province. Local residents made room, as towns all over France absorbed a tidal wave of refugees. Hundreds of towns and villages in Alsace-Lorraine were evacuated and a quarter of a million people left their homes, land, and animals.

Their new landlord knocked on the front door early the next morning.

"Have you heard the news?" the priest said.

"No, we're just starting to unpack," Robert's mother said.

"France and Britain declared war against Germany."

He was a shriveled up old man with a bird's beak for a nose and he seemed to sniff the air for clues. His suspicions were confirmed when Bella trotted through the room.

"You didn't say anything about a dog," he said.

"Oh, Bella will be no problem," Robert volunteered.

"You didn't mention a dog," the priest said.

Five days later, Robert heard a rumble of distant thunder. Scattered clouds flickered in the evening sky and thunder hovered low to the ground.

His mother became very still. She whispered to Robert, "Listen carefully, son. Those are the cannons on the front."

The front. Robert wanted to know exactly where this human front was located and which way it was headed. As they stood silently at the window watching the flickering clouds and listening to the thunder, Robert pictured people's houses exploding, homes destroyed in less than a heartbeat, the ruins left to burn unattended by families who had built them, repaired them, filled them with their daily lives. He imagined soldiers pressing their faces against the ground in trenches, praying not to be tossed into the air by the ear-splitting explosions. He saw soldiers sliding shiny artillery shells into huge cannons and aiming them to take as many lives as possible. He saw his father in his new French uniform, hiding from the explosions as he counted every breath.

It was dawn before Robert fell asleep.

Robert felt anxious as he walked down the main street of Lutzelbourg later that day. Men in the streets were talking about France's surprise attack. Soldiers were pouring into the Saarland, they said, and the *Boches* were on the run. Newspapers reported that eight French divisions had taken control of the area between the Maginot Line and Hitler's Siegfried Line. The Germans hardly put up a fight before retreating. France had penetrated deep into German territory. The "Sarre Offensive" was a major French victory, they said.

With all the excitement, stores started raising prices. Winter sweaters disappeared from the shelves and coats could not be found. Refugees complained that they needed to go back home to get their winter coats and blankets.

The Germans didn't counter-attack. During the next three weeks, the French troops pulled back to their original positions. There were fewer than fifty casualties during the Sarre Offensive, mostly caused by land mines and booby traps in the German villages. People in town began to argue about General Maurice Gamelin, France's commander-in-chief. Allied soldiers, most of them French, outnumbered the Germans four-to-one on the Western front, so why did the French retreat? A verdict was reached on the streets of Lutzelbourg—the Sarre Offensive was a publicity stunt.[54]

The Mullers' apartment in Lutzelbourg was small and crowded. There was no place for Robert to study, nor was there room for him in the local school. Since the apartment was designed for summer vacations, it was cold and damp.

Robert and his mother started getting on each other's nerves. He began wandering through Lutzelbourg, taking time to appreciate the red sandstone buildings in the lush valley and explore the pine-covered hills. One day he paused to contemplate the jagged reflections in the clear water of the river when a sudden movement caught his eye. He looked up and saw a beautiful girl on the far side of the river. As he watched her, Robert felt a longing that was both exhilarating and terrifying.

He asked around. She was from Paris and she was staying in one of the patrician houses along the river. Robert had never seen such an attractive girl. Every day he waited by the river, hoping she might walk by. He rehearsed what he would say to her, but when she appeared, he forgot his lines.

Léonie's savings shrank. She had no income and the apartment rent was high. When the priest suggested that they get rid of their dog, Léonie and the children decided to leave. They hired a cab and moved to the attic of a farmhouse in the nearby hamlet of Trois-Maisons—three houses jammed together on a cold, flat plain exposed to wind and rain. The fields were bare where corn and wheat had been harvested, and Robert noticed deep scars in the land from previous wars.

He took a daily walk to the town of Phalsbourg, where ancient fortifications lay in decay as they sank slowly into the ground. Phalsbourg was the birthplace of authors Emile Erckmann and Alexandre Chatrian. Robert had read *Les Deux Frères* as a child. To pass the time, he started reading other works by the writing team of Erckmann-Chatrian.

The border between France and Germany remained quiet as winter approached. Hitler consolidated his gains in Austria and Czechoslovakia, while Poland stood up to Germany alone. France was required by treaty to attack Germany five days after Germany crossed Poland's border, but the French did nothing. On November 17, 1939, Poland collapsed. French newspapers reported morale was high on the Maginot Line.

Displaced residents argued with local officials, pleading for permission to go home and get their winter clothes. One morning, Robert walked into Phalsbourg just as a convoy of trucks from Sarreguemines pulled into town. He asked one of the drivers what they were hauling.

"Merchants are getting everything out of Sarreguemines so they can sell it in Paris and Lyon," the driver said.

The bitter north wind was cold when Robert marched back to Trois Maisons, but his mind was on fire. He sat up half the night writing a letter to Prime Minister Daladier:

> It is always the rich who get the favors. We are merely individual families who were suddenly evacuated from our homes. There is no fighting here. We want to go home to get our winter clothes but we cannot get permission. The merchants can go to their stores because they have the right connections, but little people don't count.

Robert decided it would be better not to show the letter to his mother. He walked to Phalsbourg and mailed it the next day. Even if Daladier never saw it, Robert felt better. His anger was gone.[55]

Robert's mother and her friend Marie coaxed a French army officer into issuing passes so they could visit Marie's husband at Rohrbach on the Maginot Line. When the taxi pulled up to the farmhouse, they decided to take Robert along. The car had a plush interior with vases attached to the back of the driver's seat filled with fresh cut flowers. With curtains drawn, they traveled through the combat zone without being stopped. It looked the same as always, except there were no people in the villages. When they reached Rohrbach, a sentry directed the cab to park by the family quarters. All they could see of the fortress was the entrance to a tunnel.

While they waited for Marie's husband, who was stationed underground, Robert drifted over to some off-duty soldiers who were lounging around a table near the entrance. Some of them were drinking wine with breakfast. A radio blared in the background, and Robert recognized the voice of Paul Ferdonnet, "the traitor of Stuttgart." He was going on about French officers and how they mistreated the soldiers. Everyone knew he was hired by Goebbels to provoke French soldiers, but at least he was entertaining. The soldiers were bored.

One of the men at the table described in graphic detail a disappointing visit to the local brothel. Another said that the problem was the bromides they put in the wine, which was freely rationed to off-duty soldiers. "Tell it to my wife," another shouted. They all laughed, but not joyful laughter.

The men spoke in the Lorraine dialect. Robert recognized one of the soldiers from Sarreguemines.

"Can I take a look inside?" Robert asked.

"Can't let you do that, son. Everything's a big secret in there." He pursed his lips with mock concern.

"What's the big deal?" Robert asked. "Everybody already knows about it. It was in all the newspapers. Anyway, my father is stationed on the Maginot Line, so it's not like I don't know anything. I just wondered what it looks like."

"Where's your father stationed?"

"We're not sure. He's probably at Simserhof."

"Well, Rohrbach may not be as big as Simserhof, but they're all the same inside. Everything is gray. The walls and the floors and the ceilings are all cement, and they don't waste money on paint or carpets. It's cold, that's for sure, and you wouldn't believe how boring it gets."

"How do people breathe underground?"

"Big fans push the air in from over there," he said, pointing to a grove of trees, "and the exhaust shoots out through the turrets. You don't want to be stationed in those turrets. It's so cold up there you can't even pick up the phone when they call because your fingers get so numb."

"How far underground does it go?"

"Now you're going to get me in trouble." He winked and took a gulp of wine. "Don't tell anybody I told you this, but it takes about thirty minutes to walk all the way to the barracks. That's why everything comes in by train. Once you reach the barracks, the tunnel goes off in two directions and it takes another half an hour to get to either end."

"So it's just a huge, long tunnel?" Robert said.

"Well, sure, if you're just talking about the fort. But then you have all your casemates up on the side of the hill, and the advance posts with the machine guns and the anti-tank guns. In front of that, railroad tracks are sticking out of the cement, and if that doesn't stop the tanks, the mines will."

"Some kids at school said that if a person dies in there, they put the body in acid and wash it down the drain."

"I've heard that one, but there's no truth to it. They have a mortuary down there—I've seen it—and there's a big stack of caskets, but I don't think we'll have to use them."

"What do you think is going to happen?" Robert said.

"I can tell you one thing, I'm not going to get myself killed over nothing, that's for sure." Now he was angry.

"What do you mean?" Robert asked.

"Look around, what do you see here? Everybody is from Alsace-Lorraine. You don't see any French regulars, do you? We're all territorials. Some of the officers are French, but they just hang around in the mess hall. Why should we be the only ones who get killed?"

Another soldier spoke up. "I used to be an officer for the Germans. When I reported to my French regiment last month, do you know what they told me? They handed me a stick and they said, 'Go over there and guard that bridge.' *Guard the bridge with a stick!*"

Other men groaned and spat on the dirt.

"I'm not getting my head shot off."

"The French don't want to fight. Daladier will hand over Finland next, you watch, and then it will be Sweden."

"What do you expect? Daladier is the son of a baker. He doesn't know crap about fighting the Germans."

Robert's mother called him over to the car.

"What's wrong?" she asked. "You don't look very well."

"Oh, it's nothing, just soldier talk," he said.

"Marie's husband looked up your father. He's at Welschhoff, just down the road."

The cab was almost to Welschhoff when they stopped at a checkpoint. A French officer reached through the open window, pulled back the curtain and frowned at the women. When he saw Robert, his eyes opened wide.

"*Mon Dieu!* What do you think you're doing?" he shouted. "Don't you know you're in the combat zone?"

"I didn't see any signs," Léonie said sweetly. "I wanted to say hello to my husband, and I'm told he's at Welschhoff."

"Do you have any idea..." he began. He looked at Robert again. The veins in his neck were standing out. "Is this your son?"

"Yes, this is Robert. He's not old enough for the army."

"I realize that. How old are you, boy?" the officer asked.

"Sixteen, sir."

"Sixteen! Madame, may I have a word with you?"

Léonie and the officer walked away from the car. Robert heard him shout the word *Arbeitsdienst.*

When Robert's mother returned, she said to the driver, "Follow him." A jeep escorted them out of the combat zone. Nobody said a word until they got back to Trois Maisons.

Two gendarmes knocked at the attic door.

"Do you have a Robert Muller here?" the older of the two asked.

"Yes, that would be my son," Léonie answered cautiously. "What is it you want?"

Robert thought, *My God, what have I done now?* He searched his mind for anything that might have gone wrong.

The gendarme removed a bundle of papers from a leather bag. On top of the stack was Robert's letter to Daladier. It was underlined in red with notes scribbled in the margins.

"Your son's letter was read by the Prime Minister," the man said. "There was an investigation. These are the reports."

Léonie looked at her son wildly, and then back to the stack of paper. Robert shrugged helplessly as he tried to calm down.

"We have been instructed to issue passes to all the refugees in this region to go back to their homes and recover their possessions. If you will come to our office tomorrow morning, I will put a truck and a driver at your disposal."

Each time the commander spoke his mouth twisted, as if he were in pain. Robert did not speak. When the gendarmes got up, the man in charge scowled and slammed the door.

Robert's mother stared at him. "Is there anything else

you haven't told me?" she finally said.

The following morning, Robert was waiting outside when the cab arrived to take them to the police station.

"You're not going," his mother said.

"But you'll need help, and after all—"

"I'll manage just fine. I can get the driver to help. I want you to stay here with your sister, and don't wander off while I'm gone."

Léonie got in the car.

"Be sure to drain the radiators," Robert said.

"What?"

"Drain the radiators so the pipes don't freeze."

Léonie returned in the evening in a truck loaded with winter clothes, linens, blankets and food. She handed Robert the portrait he had painted of his great-grandfather. There was a large box in the truck, which she asked him to carry upstairs. Inside he found the 1894 encyclopedia, his most prized possession.

A letter arrived from Lyon a few days later.

"It's from Mr. Petit," his mother said. "He says they have a very good school in Lyon. He has made arrangements for you to be admitted to the Lycée Ampère."

"This is no time for me to leave!" Robert said.

"You're wasting your time here. Do you want to lose the whole year? If you don't qualify for the baccalaureate, you can't go to university. Then what? Do you want to be drafted?"

"I can make up the time. This is more important than school."

"What's so important? Listening to old men make up stories about war? Reading your books? Do you think you are any help to me while you're hanging around here? The Germans won't do anything during the winter."

"All right, then why don't you come too?" Robert said.

"I'm not leaving, not while your father is here. He needs me here, but you don't have to stay."

"You don't even know where he is, and I promised—"

"Your father would agree with me. There will always be another war as long as people live and breathe, but our lives have to go on. Do you want what's best for me?

"I want the war to stop!"

"How are you going to do that? Do you want them to make you into a soldier so that you can shoot those boys across the river?"

"No, I—"

"Or how about Hitler? He'll give you a job. They'll put you in the *Arbeitsdienst* as fast as they can write your name."

"That would be insane."

"The *Boches* could walk in here tomorrow if they weren't still busy with Poland and Czechoslovakia."

"So what do you want me to do?"

"Get away from here. Go learn how to think."

"I am thinking! I'm reading Erckmann-Chatrian, and I have plenty of books that Mr. Hehn—"

"Hehn! You keep an eye on your Mr. Hehn, and you'll see. He'll be playing the German card before we see the end of this."

"Mr. Hehn happens to be the best teacher in the school, and what's the matter with reading Goethe and Schiller?"

"Hehn is a librarian, he's not a teacher, and he lives in the past. You're reading books now, and that's good. But books are supposed to lead you into the world, not take you from it. The Lycée Ampère is one of the best schools in France. It is time you challenged yourself."

"We can't afford this. You can't even afford this place."

"You will share a room with Jojo, and the cost of food is lower in Lyon. I can't afford to keep you here, not with these prices. You will take the train in the morning."

She handed him a note: *4 Rue Guynemer, 1ˢᵗ WW, Lyon.*

Chapter 5 – The Funny War

Gaul was a Roman province in the days of Jesus of Nazareth and Lyon was its capital. Surrounded on three sides by rivers, Lyon had been impenetrable. When Robert Muller arrived in Lyon at the end of autumn in 1939, it was a complex beehive of a city fitted tightly together on a narrow peninsula. On the map, the city looked like a slender neck adorned with an intricate necklace of 28 bridges. Over a million people lived around Lyon; it was second in size only to Paris. Two major rivers merged at the southern tip of the peninsula, and Robert guessed that a dozen Sarre Rivers could fit into either one.

Robert and Jojo walked together to school on Robert's first day. Jojo's family lived half a block from the Saône River on the west side of the city. The Lycée Ampère faced the Rhône on the east in the oldest part of town. They crossed a sprawling park by the royal palace as Jojo led them on a zigzag course through a jumble of streets.

"The Lycée Ampère is a lot harder than our school was in Sarreguemines," Jojo said.

"I hope I'm not too far behind," Robert said. "I've been out of school for six months now."

"They know you're from Lorraine, and we have plenty of refugees here. You'll do fine."

The school was set back from the Rhône half a block. It looked out on a high bridge that arched over the swirling current. The panoramic view from the front steps of the Lycée Ampère offered a rich contrast to the confined setting of Robert's high school in Sarreguemines. Robert felt free of the tensions on the border. He had slipped back into a time when things still made sense.

Robert found a seat near the back of his humanities class. The teacher was slouched at a huge desk reading a book, oblivious to his growing audience. Robert counted sixty students, twice as many as any class before, and there was a buzz in the air, as if something were about to happen.

Professor Cumin looked up and noticed the room was full. He pushed off from the desk and stood up. He was over six feet tall, and his eyes sparkled as if he had just discovered that all his best friends were in the room. He was a good-looking man with a very long face.

Cumin addressed the class in Latin for a few minutes, and then suddenly turned to a student. "Dupont! The principles of Descartes—quickly!"

Dupont stood up. "Never accept anything as the truth unless you know it to be true. Take each difficulty and divide it into as many parts as necessary. If there is a multiplicity of things, put it in good order, beginning with the simplest objects, and never leave anything out."

"Did everybody hear that? Always be careful not to leave anything out. That was good, Dupont," Cumin said with a huge smile. "You can forget everything I teach you, you can certainly forget me, but don't ever forget the principles of Descartes. They are a bible for your brain."

Cumin talked about the Roman influence on local dialects. Soon he was drawing a chart with arrows to map out the spread of the Latin language throughout Europe. For several days, Robert listened carefully to Cumin and took detailed notes. He tried to remain as inconspicuous as possible, but Cumin found him soon enough.

"Robert Muller, what is the main theme of *Le Cid*, the play by Corneille which I assigned last week?"

Robert was jolted out of his trance. As Cumin sat down, Robert got to his feet with the confidence of a student who had done his homework. He answered smartly, "May I suggest that it is the struggle between duty and one's own love or intention."

The whole class became dead still. Cumin's face drew longer, and he looked dazed, as if he had just been knocked on the head. He slumped forward on his desk. Then he raised his head slowly until he was tilted back so far that he was almost prone in the chair. Gradually his body slid down in the seat, inch by inch, until he disappeared under the desk.

Robert looked around the classroom in confusion. All the students seemed to be holding their breath. Jojo looked as if he were about to burst. Robert raised his hands in exasperation. "*What?*"

There was an explosion of laughter. Pandemonium broke out around him. Robert stood there helplessly, fighting the urge to run as the riot ran its course.

Gradually the room became quiet. Cumin pried himself out from under the desk, stood up with some effort, and pointed a long finger at Robert. The professor tried to speak, but he couldn't seem to get the words out and his arms dropped to his sides. He swallowed, steadied himself against the desk, and started rocking his arms in the air to imitate a small boat bobbing on the sea. Finally he caught his breath and blurted out, "Little boat!"

Robert remembered the words to a song memorized by every child in France, a song in which a little girl asks her mother if boats have legs. "Of course, little stupid one," her mother replies in the song. "How else could they walk on water?"

Robert's face felt like it was on fire.

"For heaven's sake, Muller," Cumin thundered, "don't ever repeat such a stupid thing in this classroom. I want your opinion, not something you got out of a textbook. Be yourself, Muller. Know yourself. Rely only upon yourself. Accept someone else's idea to be true only if you are totally convinced that it must be true. What did Descartes say, Muller?"

From behind his hot mask of embarrassment, Robert could see that Cumin was looking at him with kindness and humor.

"*Cogito ergo sum,*" Robert said.

"I think, therefore I am," Cumin repeated. "Why do you

suppose René Descartes, a prolific writer, is remembered for those six syllables?"

"It was the first idea Descartes concluded must be true."

"Very good, Monsieur Muller, and welcome aboard our little ship—and only fools may board her. I love this job! I wouldn't trade jobs with the Prime Minister of France! I just had a great idea," he said while writing on the blackboard. He turned back to face the class with a wild grin. "Let's not have any recess today."

To Robert's surprise, the class cheered.

On the way home, Robert complained to Jojo. "The way they stared at me, I felt like a complete fool in there!"

"Don't feel bad, Robert. It happens to everyone sooner or later. Your face sure turned red."

"You know something? I'm glad it happened. Maybe Cumin is right. If all I can do is repeat what I read in books, if I can't come up with my own ideas, why should anybody listen to me?"

"Why would anybody listen to us anyway?" Jojo said. "We haven't done anything but go to school and read."

"But this school really teaches us how to think! I feel like a dumb peasant here. The professors are incredible. Cumin reminds me of my father every time he finishes a new hat."

"You're doing well, Robert, and the worst part is over."

Letters arrived from Robert's mother every week. Winter on the border passed without any major incident, but there was no furlough for Robert's father. Their biggest challenge was keeping warm in the attic. Conditions for the refugees improved in March when Prime Minister Reynaud appointed Robert Schuman from Metz as Undersecretary of State for Refugees. Schuman had been a member of the French parliament since 1919, and with a staff he straightened out most of the problems. Robert's mother was trying to find a better apartment, but the refugee population was getting worse as people finagled their way back to Alsace Lorraine from the western provinces.

As Robert worked hard to make up the lost semester, Cumin's emphasis on Cartesian logic instilled a new discipline in Robert's thinking. He approached Cumin after class on his seventeenth birthday. "I would like to be able to write beautiful French prose, but in Alsace-Lorraine we speak a German dialect. Our French is not natural because we didn't speak it in the family; we had to learn it at school. Our French teachers told us that we would never be able to write like true Frenchmen."

Cumin looked at Robert with a warm smile. "Don't listen to all that rubbish. There is nothing easier than to learn a style. I'll teach you a trick we were taught at the École Normale Supérieure.

"You select a famous author whom you particularly like. Every day for six months, you copy ten lines from his work in a notebook. Copy the lines slowly, for no less than ten minutes, so you will learn them almost by heart. From time to time, go back and read the entire text you have copied. In six months, you can be writing exactly like Voltaire or Saint-Beuve."

He pulled an old collection of essays from his bookshelf and handed it to Robert. "Try this. Sainte-Beuve taught French literature at the École Normale Supérieure eighty years ago."

Robert sat at his desk and began to copy the long, complex sentences. It was an article by Charles Augustin Sainte-Beuve entitled "What is a Classic." [56]

A true classic is an author who has enriched the human mind, increased its treasure, and caused it to advance a step; who has discovered some moral and not equivocal truth, or revealed some eternal passion in that heart where all seemed known and discovered.

When Robert returned home that night, a letter was waiting for him from his mother. She had moved to an apartment in Metz so that they could all be together. There was a school nearby where Robert could finish the year. They still hadn't seen Robert's father.

Robert composed a farewell note to Professor Cumin, which concluded: *I will never forget you as long as I live. I feel like crying because I have to leave.*

While Robert packed the next day, Jojo delivered his message to Cumin and then met Robert at the train station.

"This is from Professor Cumin." Jojo handed him a letter and the book of essays by Sainte-Beuve.

"Thank you for all you've done, Jojo," Robert said. "I hope I'll see you when this whole mess is over."

"And I hope that happens real soon," Jojo said.

As the train rolled north towards Metz, Robert read the letter. It closed with a mix of French and Greek: *Oubliez-moi. Gnôthi seauthon.* Forget me. Know yourself.

Wide boulevards and Gothic architecture gave a touch of splendor to Metz, the capitol of Lorraine. Robert felt close to home, with Sarreguemines only an hour away. His uncle, Marcel Muller, had found them a small apartment. Marcel had a bakery on Rue des Allemands in Metz and business was good. Marcel greeted each woman with a pat on the derrière, leaving his trademark palm print of white flour. Women would greet each other on the streets of Metz and say, "I see you've been to the baker!"

The papers reported a speech by an American Senator who demanded that the United States stay out of the war. He ridiculed the standoff between Germany, France and England on the floor of the U.S. Senate and called it *The Phony War.* In France, it sounded like "The Funny War"—*La Drôle de Guerre*—and the label stuck. France was confident in the spring of 1940. With an army of 800,000 regular soldiers and another 5.5 million in the reserves, why should they worry? The Maginot Line was keeping the Germans at bay, and if fighting broke out, the two sides were evenly matched—136 German divisions compared to 135 Allied divisions in France, Britain, and the Netherlands.

Meanwhile, storm clouds were building up in the north. After Germany and the Soviet Union divided up Poland, the USSR attacked Finland while Germany drew up plans to conquer Norway and Denmark. Finland defended itself courageously throughout the winter, but the people were hopelessly outnumbered. Finland's defeat exposed the decrepit state of the French military. Prime Minister Daladier was forced out of office and replaced by Paul Reynaud.[57]

Robert enrolled in the Metz school—his third high school in nine months—and prepared for the baccalaureate exams, which would determine his eligibility for university. Robert had no time to think about anything but school. He usually stayed up late at night trying to catch up, going back over earlier assignments to fill in the gaps between schools and jumping over material he had already covered. His mother asked for daily reports of his progress, which merely added to the pressure.

On May 9, 1940, an unusually high number of German tourists visited Luxembourg by car and bicycle. Overnight they seized key border checkpoints and bridges, killing any customs guard who resisted. In the darkest hour before dawn on May 10, 1940, the serenity of Luxembourg was shattered by the roar of thousands of armored vehicles streaming westward towards France.[58] They encountered no resistance in Luxembourg's tiny villages as thousands of citizens followed their leader, Grand Duchess Charlotte, and fled in their cars to France.[59]

The attack was unleashed on a front 200 miles long[60] reaching from the North Sea to the Maginot Line. Every German maneuver was calculated to trick the Allies into thinking that the Germans were fighting a rematch of World War I. Army Group B flooded over the northern border of Germany and faked a main attack into Belgium and the Netherlands. The Allies raced north and turned east into the German trap, not aware that further south, three columns of tanks stretched back into Germany for 100 miles. After speeding across Luxembourg, the panzers fanned out on narrow roads through the Ardennes forest.[61]

London was bogged down in a cabinet crisis all day. In the evening, Winston Churchill emerged as Prime Minister in place of Neville Chamberlain. Churchill slept soundly that night, confident that the Allies and Germany were evenly matched.

Robert stayed up late to study. When he could no longer keep his eyes open, he crawled into bed and fell into an exhausted sleep. Two hours later, he was awakened by a terrific blast. He ran to the window and almost tripped over his mother and sister.

"What was that?" he asked.

"I don't know," she answered. "Maybe the gas reservoir blew up. It was too loud for a furnace."

She leaned out the window and looked up and down the street. Then she glanced at her watch.

"Do you think it might be Big Bertha?" Robert asked.

She closed her eyes, as if to erase the thought. Robert dreaded Big Bertha. The giant 420 mm howitzer was mounted to a platform on railroad tracks so that the force of the recoil would propel it into a tunnel and out of sight. It took twelve minutes to reload the one-ton shells and three minutes to roll the car back into position. They waited in the darkness, listening to barking dogs and the voices of neighbors as the minute hand on Léonie's watch crawled around a quarter of a turn. With a jolt, the sky lit up and another explosion demolished a building a few blocks away.

They tuned the radio to a German station and listened to Hitler's frenzied voice:

For 300 years it was the aim of the English and French rulers to prevent every real consolidation of Europe and, above all, to hold Germany in weakness and impotency. For this purpose alone, France has declared war on Germany 31 times in 200 years. Soldiers of the western front: the hour for you has now come. The fight you begin today will determine the fate of our nation for the next 1,000 years.[62]

Hitler's speech was followed by German reports of battles raging far to the north in Belgium, but nothing was said about the attacks to the south in the area of Luxembourg and Metz.

Robert heard the drone of airplanes in the distance. First the raspy sound of engines drifted in and out on the warm night breeze. Then it grew louder and spread across the sky until the noise shook the windows and rattled the dishes. The air erupted with the thunder of a thousand explosions.

"They're bombing the airport," Robert shouted.

La Drôle de Guerre, the Funny War, was over.

• • •

Seven divisions of tanks threaded through the winding trails and roads of the Ardennes forest, a region the Allies had assumed was impassable to tanks. A French cavalry unit north of Metz stumbled upon a huge column of tanks racing through Luxembourg and quietly retreated.[63] When they emerged on the other side, the panzers battled their way across the Meuse River at Sedan. Hundreds of thousands of men clashed in tanks, airplanes and armored cars along a 150-mile front in the Meuse River valley. [64]

Colonel Charles de Gaulle led France's 4th Tank Division into fierce fighting against one of Germany's most seasoned panzer corps. De Gaulle was ordered to stop the Germans from heading south to Paris, but Rommel had other plans.[65] The panzers took off straight for the English Channel so fast that Adolph Hitler tried to rein them in, thinking they must be racing into an Allied trap.[66] In reality, the Allies could not comprehend the speed of the panzer attack. They were caught completely by surprise.[67]

Robert listened to optimistic reports on Paris radio released by the French military. French columns held their ground, they said, as the Germans tried to force them out of Luxembourg. Germany called off the blitzkrieg in Belgium and the Netherlands after failing to take the Allies by surprise. German maneuvers indicated that they were reverting to 1914 tactics and would launch intensive assaults along a wide front. Paris radio boasted that France lost no planes when the Germans bombed the airfields.[68] Robert knew that couldn't be true.

The garrisons on the Maginot Line guarded France's German border, making sure that no invasion took place on the eastern frontier. Soldiers on the Maginot Line were the "forgotten army." They could hear German aircraft overhead, but they had no anti-aircraft guns, so all they could do was shoot machine guns at the planes, practice their drills, and listen to the radio.

Winston Churchill was awakened on May 15 by a telephone call from French Prime Minister Paul Reynaud. "We have been defeated!" Reynaud said. "We are beaten!"

Churchill refused to believe it. Holland capitulated to Germany later the same day, and only five days later, the panzers reached Abbeville on the English Channel at the mouth of the Somme River.

The people in Metz adapted to nightly bombardments. Robert's mother set the alarm in fifteen-minute intervals so that she would be awake for each explosion. Robert studied constantly, stopping to rest his eyes every time a shell was due to land. When the shells started falling in the daytime, some civilians built underground shelters. Robert's mother refused to live underground. She found a small apartment on the outskirts of Metz in the village of Ars-sur-Moselle, where Robert could still ride his bicycle to school. His sister objected, but Robert refused to quit. All that mattered, he said, was final exams. He had worked too hard to give up.

The explosions stopped as suddenly as they started. "Big Bertha must have gotten tired," some people said in Metz, but Big Bertha had been dismantled and moved by train to Schoenenbourg, a large installation on the Maginot Line near Haguenau, where the Germans tested Pétain's fortress.

Robert was riding his bicycle to school a few days later when he looked up and saw German planes converging on the Metz airport. Black puffs of smoke from French anti-aircraft guns splattered the sky. A plane fell screeching towards the ground, then another. One by one, the planes plunged out of the sky with piercing screams. People in the streets waved their arms and cheered wildly when they heard explosions on the ground. There was a surge of pride. Maybe the Germans were not invincible after all.

Robert watched the planes reappear in the distance. They climbed steeply into the sky. They were not hit after all. More planes howled and fell, released bombs, and pulled out of their dives. The Stuka dive-bombers continued the attack until every plane and hangar was destroyed.

It took the panzers just ten days to reach the English Channel, but France's leadership began to disintegrate in only half that much time. Six days after the attack started, Reynaud fired General Gamelin, his Commander-in-Chief, and Édouard Daladier, Minister of War. In an attempt to restore confidence, Reynaud called back France's distinguished 84-year-old ambassador in Madrid, Henri-

Philippe Pétain.

Reynaud hoped that Marshal Pétain's influence would help to restore confidence in his military leaders, but Pétain had already reached a different conclusion. After seven days of fighting, he could see the writing on the wall. "My country has been beaten," he said in Madrid before his departure. "They are calling me back to make peace and sign an armistice."[69] He returned to chaos.

Pétain believed that Hitler was destined to rule Europe.[70] France could negotiate a deal with Germany and start over, or it could wait a few days until Great Britain was defeated and then take whatever crumbs Hitler might toss them. With one exception, the military leaders sided with Pétain. Reynaud had only one more card to play when he asked for the opinion of Pétain's protégé—General Charles de Gaulle.

At forty-nine, de Gaulle had become France's youngest general on June 1, 1940. He was easily the least popular general among the elite officers. De Gaulle's reputation had never been tarnished by lack of confidence or inexperience. They hated him because he had needled them for twenty years to build tanks instead of forts. As a young cadet at the military academy at St.-Cyr in 1911, de Gaulle had been nicknamed *la Grande Asperge*—the Big Asparagus.[71] After he graduated the following year, he reported to an infantry regiment under the command of a colonel who, at the age of 56, was conspicuously old for a colonel—Henri-Philippe Pétain. Pétain's career had lacked distinction because he stubbornly insisted that military strategy should emphasize defense at a time when his superiors wanted to go after Germany and take back Alsace-Lorraine. De Gaulle adopted Pétain's lofty, aristocratic manner, while Pétain predicted a brilliant career for Charles de Gaulle.

Two years later when the First World War broke out, de Gaulle led his first attack across a bridge in Belgium and was injured when his leg was hit by machine gun fire. He spent seven months recuperating in a hospital. He was then promoted to captain and ordered to report back to General Henri-Philippe Pétain for the Battle of Verdun. While crawling along a trench, de Gaulle stumbled upon a group of Germans who stabbed him in the leg with a bayonet. A grenade exploded in de Gaulle's face and knocked him out.

The French gave de Gaulle up for dead and wrote him a glowing official citation. General Pétain put the finishing touches on his obituary:

> Captain de Gaulle, company commander, reputed for his great intellectual and moral worth...led his men in a fierce attack and savage hand-to-hand fighting, the only solution that met his sense of military honor. He fell in the fighting, a peerless officer in all respects.[72]

A German soldier saw that de Gaulle was still breathing. Rather than finish him off, the German dragged him off and he spent the rest of the war in a prison camp. Despite his wounds, de Gaulle tried to escape five times. The Germans sent him to a maximum-security prison, where he healed himself in solitary confinement for four months as he developed a bitter distaste for Germans. While in prison, he wrote to his father that his obituary much exaggerated the facts. [73] And for his own benefit, he wrote: *One must be a man of character...in action one must say nothing. The leader is the man who does not talk.* [74]

After the war, De Gaulle enrolled in École Supérieure de Guerre to complete officer training. While Marshal Pétain preached the virtues of defense to a war-weary nation and recommended construction of the Maginot Line, de Gaulle took the opposite point of view and criticized the French military establishment for its defensive posture. De Gaulle argued in favor of armored warfare and urged a build-up of tanks with such conviction that his instructors tried to flunk him out. Marshal Pétain made a special trip to the École Supérieure to interrogate de Gaulle's instructors. Pétain insisted that they raise his marks. De Gaulle's career was salvaged and he graduated with average grades, good enough to be an officer but not good enough for the General Staff.

The star students went to Paris. Charles de Gaulle was sent back to Germany to work in the Supplies Branch in the French-occupied Rhineland, where he dealt with issues relating to cold storage.[75] Eventually he was transferred to Paris, where he served 14 different French governments and developed a bitter taste for French parliamentary politics.

Charles de Gaulle, France's youngest general in June 1940, urged French leaders to accept Winston Churchill's offer of joint defense, joint economy, and joint citizenship for France and England.

When Paul Reynaud replaced Édouard Daladier as Prime Minister in 1940, he invited de Gaulle to the ceremony. On June 1, Prime Minister Reynaud promoted Charles de Gaulle and, made him France's youngest brigadier-general.[76]

On June 6, 1940, General de Gaulle advised Reynaud to stop fighting a losing battle and move his troops and his government to Africa, where France could join forces with Great Britain. When German troops paraded through Paris on June 14, the French government retreated to Bordeaux, a city bursting at the seams with terrified refugees who had abandoned Luxembourg, Belgium, the Netherlands, and northern France in tidal waves.[77] German planes cleared a path for the panzers through escape routes jammed with refugees by spraying the roads with machine gun fire.

De Gaulle dined at the Hotel Splendide in Bordeaux that day, where he recognized Marshal Pétain sitting at a nearby table. De Gaulle walked over to pay his respects without saying a word. Silently, Pétain shook his hand. It was the last time they would see each other.[78]

Reynaud sent de Gaulle to London arrange for the evacuation to Africa.[79] After a meeting with Winston Churchill, de Gaulle telephoned Reynaud with a stunning offer—joint defense, joint economy, and joint citizenship for France and England.[80] Such an arrangement had never been proposed in the history of the two countries. Reynaud was eager to accept.

De Gaulle flew to Bordeaux with Churchill's written offer. Pétain scoffed, "France should not enter into a union with a corpse." He believed that France would get better terms with Hitler by setting up an authoritarian regime along the lines of Germany, Italy, Spain, and Russia. "France must find its place in the new European order," Pétain argued.

When Reynaud's cabinet balked at Churchill's offer, Reynaud resigned without even bothering to ask for a show of hands. France's token president, Albert Lebrun, facing a constitutional crisis during a military meltdown, asked Marshal Pétain if he could form a new government. Pétain reached into his briefcase and pulled out a list of ministers for a new cabinet, men who had already agreed to an armistice with Hitler. [81]

De Gaulle went to his office and penciled in a few phony appointments for the afternoon. He then escorted General Spears, Winston Churchill's liaison officer, to the airfield. They shook hands and the English general boarded a small plane. De Gaulle turned to walk away as the plane ran up its engines, and then jumped in as the plane started to taxi. The French police watched helplessly as de Gaulle escaped to London. He had only £500 in his pocket, he couldn't speak English, and he had just broken every rule in the book.[82]

Robert rode his bicycle to school on the final day of the semester to take his baccalaureate exams. Students were waiting in front of the school when he arrived. Robert joined the others, his mind racing with anticipation. Dates and names and numbers percolated in his head like a kettle of soup. Robert's legs felt tired as he stood in the hot sun. He was thirsty—Metz's water facilities were destroyed—and his eyes ached from reading by candlelight now that the electricity almost never came on. He had slept only two hours.

The principal finally stepped onto the balcony. Robert felt a strange hollow emptiness in his stomach. The principal trembled as he held onto the railing with both hands.

"Dear boys, I beg you to go home. Your presence here is dangerous. German troops are now entering Metz. I know how hard you worked and how disappointed you must feel. I love you all. *Vive la France,* our beloved country."

He began to cry.

Robert stood numbly trying to make sense of what he had just heard. His hands were shaking. All the work...for this? How would he explain it to his mother?

A student shouted back to the principal, "Let us take our tests, sir!"

"No, it's impossible," the principal said.

"But it isn't fair! The Germans don't care what we do. They have other things on their minds. Please, sir, don't let them do this to us!"

The principal shook his head and went back inside without a word. Robert looked around at the faces of students whose names he didn't know. Some were angry, others frightened, but most of them looked like they were in a daze. Robert felt cold, then hot. The day seemed to have stopped, but his life was grinding ahead in slow motion. As the students drifted away, Robert stood still, trying to bring order to his hectic thoughts.

He rode his bicycle aimlessly through town for hours. People on the sidewalks looked up furtively as he passed. A blaring roar announced the arrival of the conquering army on the main boulevard. Motorcycles with sidecars paraded down the wide street. German soldiers laughed and waved at the pedestrians. Some of them waved back, but most of the people just stared or looked away. A motorcycle pulled up in front of a monument commemorating World War I, where a bronze French cock was perched on the pedestal clutching a German eagle in its claws. Two soldiers clambered up, pried it loose, and mounted it upside down so that the eagle appeared to be strangling the cock.[83]

A soldier waved to Robert with an excited smile. *He thinks he's liberating me!* Robert turned and walked away, reeling from the absurdity.

On the way home, he almost ran over a broken barrel. Tobacco had spilled across the street in front of a military warehouse. The door was broken off its hinges and people were arriving with shovels and wheelbarrows. Robert wandered into the building. Cases and barrels were stacked two stories high, but people were throwing them on the floor and smashing them open. There were no soldiers. A local militiaman shouted at the mob to stop, but more people kept coming. He fired several shots through the roof, but they didn't even look up. The looters dug into mountains of beans, lentils, and dried peas with shovels and bare hands, filling sacks and wheelbarrows.

Robert remembered his mother's words. *It is always the soldiers who get fed.* The enormous piles of food had been stockpiled for French soldiers while the civilians scraped by on war rations. Now the army was gone, leaving the civilians to meet the Germans face-to-face.

When Robert returned home, his mother was waiting.

"The principal wouldn't let us in. He said it wasn't safe for us to be there. The Germans—"

"You didn't take the tests?" she stammered. "Where have you been?"

"I rode around, saw some Germans. People broke into the army warehouse. There was tobacco all over the street."

"Where is it?" she demanded.

"Where is what?"

"The tobacco. Did you bring back any tobacco?" Robert had never seen her so upset. "Don't you think your father would appreciate a little tobacco?"

"What are you talking about?"

She handed him a knapsack. "You go back there and get some tobacco for your father so that he can relax when he comes home."

Robert was about to protest when Marcelle nodded towards the door.

"What?" Robert asked.

"Just go!" Marcelle hissed.

When Robert returned to the warehouse, people were pushing each other to get close to the piles of food. He filled a discarded bag with tobacco and crammed the knapsack full of peas, lentils, and beans. Robert filled his pockets, then took off his shirt and used it as a sling to carry more beans. He pedaled home with enough food for a month.

Fighting continued for three more days. After twelve days of continuous retreat, the exhausted French armies were cut into four ribbons with no continuous front. South of Metz, soldiers trying to flee from the Maginot Line were surrounded and pummeled by the German Air Force.

On June 17, Marshal Pétain broadcast a radio plea. "I have given myself to France to better her situation in this grave hour. It is with a heavy heart that I say we must cease to fight." [84]

Pétain appealed to Hitler to stop bombing French cities

and strafing helpless refugees. Hitler sent new instructions to his generals. France had to be cut off from Britain. The Pétain government must be given a "golden bridge" before the French escaped to North Africa with their ships and aircraft.

On the following day, June 18, 1940, the BBC in London broadcast a speech by France's youngest general. Reading from a prepared text of 360 words, Charles de Gaulle appealed to the French people to remember that France was not alone and the war was not over. "The flame of French resistance must not be extinguished and will not be extinguished," he said. His remarks were heard by only a handful of listeners in France, but French newspapers printed the speech.

German armored vehicles rolled through the French town of Locminé as a young man ran into the central square and shouted, "A general has just spoken on the radio and said that we must continue to fight. His name is de Gaulle." An old woman hanging on to the sleeve of a priest whispered, "He is my son."[85] Jeanne De Gaulle died four weeks later.[86]

De Gaulle was publicly repudiated by Pétain's Interior Minister and ordered to report to France for military duty. Instead, de Gaulle blasted the Pétain government on BBC, calling it, "a dissolving government enslaved by the enemy." He called upon the French people everywhere to fight.[87]

Conditions deteriorated in Pétain's makeshift capital as millions of refugees poured into Bordeaux. All roads leading south were jammed. Between six and ten million people tried to flee the Germans in cars, buses, bicycles, and on foot.[88] Most of them had no food, and soon their cars ran out of gas. People dropped by the side of the road, too exhausted and hungry to walk. Robert Schuman's refugee office was evacuated from Paris to a room in Bordeaux in the Faculty of Sciences. The staff of four was swamped with phone calls and pleas for assistance. They tried to cope with food shortages and epidemics, but they were overwhelmed.

German planes continued to strafe the roads to sweep them clear of refugees and open a path for their advancing army. They swooped in low over the streets of Bordeaux four times during the night of June 20, dropping bombs on

"Honor is saved," Marshal Henri Philippe Pétain proclaimed to the French people after he signed an Armistice agreement with Adolph Hitler.

crowded streets and blowing up buildings spilling over with refugees, priming Pétain to accept Hitler's terms.[89] Pétain protested the slaughter, but Hitler answered that several weeks had passed in 1917 between Germany's request for an armistice and the Allies' cease-fire.

As the location for France's surrender, Hitler selected the railway coach in which the Treaty of Versailles was signed in 1918. On June 21, 1940, Hitler handed Marshal Pétain an armistice agreement stating that the northern three fifths of France would be occupied by German troops and the French army would disband.

Pétain accepted. On June 25, Marshal Pétain broadcast, "Honor is saved! We must now turn our efforts to the future. A new order is beginning."[90]

On July 3, a French naval commander in Oran, Algeria was given an ultimatum from Winston Churchill to join forces with Britain so that his flotilla would not fall into German hands. When he failed to respond within six hours, Churchill ordered an attack. The British navy crippled three French battleships, two destroyers, and a seaplane carrier.[91]

The French Republic was abolished. Parliament was dismissed. Marshall Pétain, age 84, set out to govern southern France with dictatorial powers. A new constitution began, in regal terms:

> We, Philippe Pétain, Marshal of France, in accordance with the Constitutional Law of the 10th of July, hereby assume the functions of Head of the French State...

On August 2, Charles de Gaulle was court-martialed by the Pétain government *in absentia* as a deserter and he was condemned to death.[92] De Gaulle replied on BBC to his former mentor and benefactor: "The savior of Verdun has become a traitor...it is the shipwreck of old age."[93]

Chapter 6 – Occupation

How peaceful the town seemed when they drove into Sarreguemines. Everyone had been away for ten months, and yet the streets were clean, as if they had been freshly swept. Flowers were blooming in the central plaza and someone had tended the beds. There were no collapsed roofs or scorched walls, and all the bridges were standing. But here and there, Robert saw a broken window or a piece of furniture in the street.

"Prussians," Léonie snarled.

The car pulled up in front of their house. "Wait here," Léonie instructed the driver. "You too, Marcelle."

Robert ran up the stairs. The door was unlocked and the key had been removed from the keyhole.

"Hallo!" he yelled in German, then "Bonjour!" in French.

His voice echoed with a hollow sound. The sofa was gone from the living room and there was some discoloration where the painting over the mantle had been removed. The kitchen table was missing.

Robert and Léonie searched from room to room.

"We should make a list of everything that was stolen," Robert said. "We will file a demand with the Germans and insist that every item must be returned."

"Go downtown and check the shop," his mother said.

Robert found the door to the hat shop locked but the hat-making machines were gone. He made a mental list on his way home of the things he could do to make money if his father didn't get back soon. When Robert reached the front door, he heard boisterous laughter inside.

"You're home!" Robert shouted.

"Oh my, can you believe how much you've grown!" his father laughed. "But you don't look very happy to see me. Is anything wrong?"

"They said on the radio that the Germans captured two million French soldiers. I thought you were locked up."

"French soldiers, yes, but we're all Germans now. The *Boches* let most of us go home from Alsace-Lorraine. Crazy, huh? So why the long face?"

"I went down to the shop. Everything is gone, Papa. I'm sorry."

"My God!" Léonie said.

Robert's father rolled his eyes, as if he had suddenly remembered something. "Nothing was stolen—it's all just hiding from the Germans."

"What are you talking about?" Léonie shouted.

"Please, don't get so excited." Then he waited until she was ready to explode. "Don't worry, I borrowed a truck and we moved everything to Metz."

"Where would a soldier like you get a truck?" Léonie asked playfully with her hands on her hips.

"We had plenty of trucks in the army, but we weren't using them very much. Boring drills all day, freezing cold every night, and for what? So we could sit around and watch the Germans fly over our heads every day?

"The truck!" Léonie interrupted.

"Anyway, the army wasn't really using all those trucks, so my friend and I borrowed one and we took the machines to Metz."

"They let you do that?" she asked.

"Well, officially we went there to pick up some supplies."

"How are we going to get them back?" Robert asked. "I haven't seen any trucks since we came home. There aren't many cars either."

"We're alive, son, that's the only thing that matters. We'll get them back, and then we'll be making hats faster than you can count."

A limousine pulled up in front of the Muller's house a few days later. Léonie saw it through the window just before they heard a knock at the door. Robert started to get up, but his mother motioned for him to sit down.

"You will please send out Herr Robert Muller," the German soldier said. "The Vice-Gauleiter will wish to speak to him."

"I'll see if he's here," Léonie said dryly and shut the door. She called upstairs to her husband. "Robert, you'd better come down. A German officer is here!"

Robert's father hurried downstairs. "Did he say what he wants?"

"There is someone in the car."

Robert's father opened the door. A man stepped out of the limousine wearing a crisp German uniform.

"Erwin Raiffenrat, my God," Robert's father muttered as he went down the front steps.

"Hello, Robert," Raiffenrat said in a voice that was a little too loud. "I am now a powerful man in Lorraine. The Führer has appointed me to be his Vice-Gauleiter for the entire province of Lorraine. I will be living in a castle near Metz."

"That must be quite an honor," Robert's father said, shifting his feet uncomfortably. He shoved his hands deep into his pockets.

"I haven't forgotten how much I owe your family," Raiffenrat continued. "If there is anything I can do for you, please do not hesitate to ask. I will do everything I can."

"One thing the Germans could do is help me get back my hat-making machines," Robert's father mumbled. "You see, everything was evacuated to Metz."

Raiffenrat snapped his fingers and pointed to his orderly, who stiffened and nodded. It would be done. Robert was aware of his father's extreme discomfort. He watched the black limousine glide away from the curb as his father came up the steps, shaking his head and scraping his shoes against the cement. He looked at his wife and children, and then stared at the ceiling in exasperation as he bit his lip.

"I don't ever want to hear that man's name spoken in this house again!" he said. He left and headed for the pub.

Vichy had been a popular resort before the war. Half a day

south of Paris, the town was famous for its mineral baths and bottled water. "Good for the liver," people said. Vichy was filled with hotels, restaurants, nightclubs, and bars. Business had been good before the war, but when the Germans marched into Paris at the start of the summer season in 1940, Vichy's tourist economy spiraled into the ground. Rooms sat empty, restaurants were boarded up, and everyone was out of a job.

When Marshal Pétain needed a place to set up his new government, Vichy rose to the top of his list. Despite the dubious propriety of running a government out of an assortment of resort hotels, Vichy had its share of amenities. There were plenty of empty hotel rooms for offices and apartments, an army of unemployed bartenders and chefs who could set a table fit for a King, and a limitless supply of that famous Vichy water.

The Vichy government walked a fine line, trying to keep order in France while collaborating with Hitler. The Germans agreed that they would refrain from stationing uniformed soldiers in the Vichy capitol. They also promised to give a 24-hour notice before entering to inspect government offices.

Maintaining an appearance of sovereignty was calculated to hamper de Gaulle's efforts to mobilize the French people who, for the most part, seemed willing to go along with the new regime. Hitler decreed that the demoralized, politically decadent French should be taught that the German soldier was courteous, cultivated and forthright, always exhibiting their best conduct. This was the beginning of a new Europe.

Residents trickled back to Sarreguemines during the summer, but the first trainload of refugees did not return until August 29. German civilians moved into town to take over the administration. Marshal Pétain urged Robert Schuman to remain in Vichy, but he soon grew weary of collaboration politics and returned to Metz in August. A month of Nazi rule in Metz was enough for him. When Schuman applied for a permit to travel as a *Volksdeutscher Lothringer*—a Lorrainer of German stock—he became the first French parliamentarian to be arrested.

Robert's high school scheduled a day for graduating students to make up their final exams. Robert prepared again for his baccalaureate. A German official walked into class when everyone was seated and the tests were about to begin.

"You will be required to attend one more year of classes before you graduate," he announced. "The books you have been reading are full of lies."

"Wouldn't it be better if we studied German history at a good German university?" one of the students said.

"How could you possibly qualify for any university with your heads full of propaganda? You are very fortunate to have this opportunity."

There were sighs and groans.

"Mr. Kroener will be your teacher."

As soon as the Nazi left, Robert hastily wrote a request for an exemption and handed it to the teacher.

"Ah, we can begin right here!" Kroener announced to the class. He printed Robert's name on the blackboard in big block letters, underlining the *u*.

"There! We will begin with the correct spelling of your names. In Robert's case, the correct spelling is *Müller*."

The students were handed a list of new rules for the recovered territory of Alsace-Lorraine. Speaking French in public or wearing French berets was prohibited, and the penalty for each offense was fifty pfennig.

On the way home from school, Robert complained to a friend about losing another year in school. They passed a German policeman.

"What's that I hear?" the policeman said. "Speaking French, are you? That will be fifty pfennig, young man."

Robert fished around in his pocket for the money. He handed a hundred pfennig note to the policeman.

"Here you go, and keep the change," he said in German. Then in French, "*Au revoir!*"

Robert and his mother laughed about it at dinner, but his father shook his head. "You're taking after your mama," he said. "One rebel in this family is enough!"

"Which reminds me," Léonie said, "everybody is asking for berets. Our customers would not have been caught dead wearing a beret a year ago."

"Oh no, I'm not starting a beret factory," Robert's father said. "I have enough problems trying to make hats."

"You don't have to make berets. We can get all we want in Paris."

"Are you crazy?" Robert's father laughed with his arms folded, the way he laughed when he felt cornered. "We don't even have any credit in Paris. It's two completely different currencies now."

"We still have thousands of francs. I can take the train tomorrow!"

"And what if you're caught?" Robert's father asked.

"I'll hide the money in a book. When I get to the customs station in Metz, I'll leave it on the seat. If it's discovered, I can always say the book doesn't belong to me."

Robert's father couldn't sleep after Léonie left for Paris. A telegram finally came announcing her arrival time.

At the station, Robert's father paced up and down the platform until Robert warned him that he was attracting attention.

"Where is she?" he kept asking.

"It's not time yet," Robert said.

When the train arrived and the doors opened, Léonie was standing proudly in one of the compartments with two huge cartons. Robert's father scolded her all the way to the car, while he and Robert struggled with the heavy boxes. "You take too many risks," he said.

"How did you get these boxes through German customs?" Robert asked.

"It was simple," she said. "I asked two soldiers at the checkpoint in Novéant to be gentlemen and help me. They carried the packages very gallantly through customs, and the customs officer didn't dare to stop them."

Robert's grandfather came to visit them a few days later.

"The living area was hit by two bombs," Laurent said. "It's a total mess in there. At least the factory is okay. I set up a bed in the storage room until I can repair the damage. Nobody is going to buy Panama hats while there is a war."

"You can work here," Robert's father said.

"Are you selling hats again already?"

"Not really. People are still too afraid to spend money."

"You'll do all right after things settle down, but I'll stay where I am. I have to put everything back together and it will give me something to do. What about Robert? Is there any danger that he'll be drafted?"

"Marshal Pétain claims that Alsace-Lorrainers cannot be forced to join the German army," Robert said.

"Pétain is an old fool," Laurent said. "He has no power over Hitler."

"They're making us Germans again," Robert's father said. "It won't be long before they teach us to walk like ducks."

"What do you think, Robert?" Laurent asked.

"I don't like the people who have taken over," he said.

"Robert will be all right so long as he stays in school," Léonie said.

"They're teaching us to be future Führers," Robert said. "They have two goals—to convince us that German culture is superior, and to change us into disciplined Germans who never challenge authority. Today our teacher talked about the *bipolarity of the German being*."

"What does that mean?" Robert's father asked.

"First of all, they tell us that we're Germans by blood, whether we like it or not!" Robert said. "So that is supposed to give us the innate capacity to switch from one extreme to the other without feeling any conflict. They're very proud of this, which they compare to the unimaginative, decadent permissiveness of the French."

"So a good Nazi can go off and commit atrocities all day long, then come home at night and be the perfect father and husband," Léonie said.

"I will not go along with those people, Grandpère," Robert said. "I will never join their army."

"Good, but I hear rumors the Germans will deport the whole family to Poland if their son is caught trying to escape," Laurent said.

"Under no circumstances will I allow my son to wear a German uniform!" Robert's father said in German, which he always used when he was upset. "The French fight among themselves and they never seem to get organized, but at least they let people live in peace! We were always free to do what we want."

"The Germans are too controlling," Laurent agreed.

"I won't go away if that means they'll come here and arrest you," Robert said.

"It's just a rumor, probably started by the Germans," Laurent said. "Nobody has been deported, as far as I know."

Vacancy rates were high and money was scarce in a town that had been shuttered for almost a year. Some relief came with the arrival of German officials sent to take over administrative positions. Léonie rented the downstairs apartment to a civil servant from Germany named Karl Beitz. Beitz brought with him a fine set of furniture and paintings, which he said he obtained from a Jewish lawyer in Czechoslovakia. Beitz had separate living quarters on the left side of the first floor. The Mullers kept their voices down whenever he was home.

A draft board was set up in the building next to Robert's school. As part of Hitler's effort to integrate the Lorrainers into the Third Reich, a campaign was launched to enlist boys in the German army when they reached the age of 18. Every boy who turned sixteen was pressured to sign up for the *Arbeitsdienst*, a paramilitary German youth corps that prepared boys for military service. Robert noticed that not all the boys who had shouted Nazi slogans in the streets were eager to sign up, but they were bullied into joining. They marched in formation on the soccer field carrying spades and shovels in place of guns. One cold morning during the winter, they were ordered to strip naked and swim in the icy river. Three boys died of pneumonia.

Robert stopped sleeping through the night when British bombers started passing over Sarreguemines on their way to Germany. The local officials handed out instructions spelling out mandatory precautions. Every attic was to have pails of sand for dousing incendiary bombs. All windows had to be sealed so that no crack of light would be visible. Robert and his father reinforced the basement ceiling with extra beams and installed a heavy door at the entrance.

Robert's father asked him to join him for a walk one evening after dinner. "You've probably heard me say that I sometimes have a beer with my old friend Guehl," he began.

"Guehl the baker?" Robert asked.

"Right, Guehl the baker. He told me the other day that he has two brothers living in Thionville. One of them is also a baker and the other owns a coal barge. He takes it back and forth between Lorraine and France. I want you to pack a few things and take the train to Thionville in the morning. We have to get you out of here before they start drafting soldiers. You can stay with the baker until his brother is ready to take you across."

"What about you?" Robert asked.

"There hasn't been any trouble here, so you don't have to worry about me. Who knows where all this is leading."

When Robert packed that night, he felt like he was going on a short vacation. Only his father saw him off at the station. The train to Thionville stopped at two checkpoints, where German soldiers inspected identification papers and travel permits. Robert's passport granted him unrestricted travel in Lorraine as a *Volksdeutscher Lothringer*, but it was intimidating to be subjected to German inspections. [94]

After a few days at the home of the baker, Robert was taken down to the coal barge. The baker's brother showed him a little wooden shack hidden under the coal.

"Get in," he said.

Without a word, the brothers shoveled coal against the door until the shack was completely covered. Robert heard the brothers' muffled voices as they talked to someone on the deck. He took shallow breaths to keep the black dust out of his lungs, but fear began to take over. He finally relaxed, taking long, slow breaths. After fifteen minutes—it seemed like an hour—they shoveled away the coal and he stepped into the sunlight.

"You'll do fine, son," the captain said kindly.

Robert returned to the baker's house and waited. The long days alone in the house were almost as much of a strain as hiding under the coal. On the morning of his escape, a telegram arrived from his father. "Return at once." That's all it said. Robert thanked the baker and took the next train to Sarreguemines.

• • •

"I've been talking to a German from the Rhineland," Robert's father said. "His name is Peters, and I think he's trustworthy. He's a better Catholic than I am, that's for sure, and he hates the Nazis. We had a few beers and some brandy, and then we talked about crossing the border."

"Do you think that's a good idea?" Robert asked.

"I know, I know, we have to be careful, but you have to trust somebody. You can't figure everything out by yourself. Peters said it would be foolish for you to leave right now. They've received orders to prepare to deport the families of any young men who refuse to join the *Arbeitsdienst*."

"That settles it, I have to join," Robert said.

"Maybe so, but listen. Peters is a member of the Draft Committee. He thinks he can get you a student deferment if you sign up for the *Arbeitsdienst*. He said it's not really such a big deal, compared to the army. All you have to do is pass the medical exam and you will be deferred!"

"Are you sure you can trust him?" Robert asked.

"He strikes me as a good man, very religious and warm-hearted. I don't think he would lie to me. In any case, if it doesn't work out and you are drafted, we can always get you across the border."

Robert despised appearing before the *Arbeitsdienst* Draft Committee. The boys were herded into a room and told to take off their clothes. A young man sitting next to Robert refused to undress.

"Why do you refuse?" a Sergeant asked him.

"Because you do not have the legal right to enlist me."

"And why is that?"

"Because I am French!" the boy said.

"Oh, so you're French? Well, that explains it. So tell me, how is it that you happen to telling me this in German?"

"I was trying to be polite," the boy said, hesitating.

Two Nazis yanked him to his feet and dragged him out of the room. They were smiling when they returned. Robert overheard one of them say in a low voice, "A few days in solitary and that boy will discover in the depths of his heart that he is a good German."

The soldiers laughed. Robert felt ashamed when his name was called.

"Robert Müller!"

He stepped forward to face the committee. Peters handed a slip of paper to the chairman, who spoke without looking up. "Robert Müller, you are deferred for one year to attend classes at the University of Heidelberg."

Robert's shoulders relaxed for the first time in weeks as he walked through the gardens in the park on his way home, but he was haunted by the face of the young man who refused to comply.

When he neared his home, Robert noticed a young, blond German woman sitting in the window across the street. She had rented a downstairs apartment in the neighbor's house, where she lived alone with her infant son. She was holding the child and humming softly, but she had a sad tone in her voice as she stared off into the distance. Her husband, a German soldier, had moved them there when he was stationed in Russia. She had no friends, and her pale face looked lonely and frightened.

Robert opened the front door of his house and saw an ugly portrait of Hitler hanging inside the door.

"What's this?" he asked his father.

"New rule—hang Hitler in the hall or go to jail. But look, I finally found a good use for that idiot." He lifted the frame to show that it was hiding a bundle of fuses and switches.

Students trickled in from the occupied countries to attend the University of Heidelberg, making Heidelberg one of Germany's most cosmopolitan cities.

After Robert rented a room in a boardinghouse, he walked across an intricate bridge into the center of the old town. The narrow streets led to an ancient church with a tall clock tower. He climbed the steep steps to the top of the tower and looked out across a jumble of ancient tiled roofs. *The Nazis could never build a town as beautiful as this*, he thought. Despite an amphitheater on top of a wooded hill across the river, where Nazi rallies were held, Heidelberg had the appearance of a sheltered medieval city.

Robert's landlady introduced him to Slavko Bosnja-kovich, who rented the room next to Robert on the third floor. "Even though he's 27 years old," she said, "Slavko tells me he was a colonel in the Yugoslav army."

"Well, I said that in order to rent a room in this fine house, not to make myself sound important," he responded.

"A colonel is good enough for me," the Landlady said. "Now that you're acquainted, I'll leave you alone."

"So what classes are you taking?" Robert asked.

"I will be studying law," Slavko said. "And you?"[95]

"I'm interested in economics."

"Most of the good professors are gone," Slavko said. "The Nazis fired half the professors, researchers, and deans in Germany. Hitler accused them of being Jews and 'white Jews.'"

"Hitler also said that nuclear physics is *Jewish physics* and Einstein's theory of relativity is *a Jewish bluff*. Are they going to feed us that Nazi line here?"

"Maybe this is not such a good time to study science in Germany," Slavko said. "As for law, that's another matter. There are enough atrocities to employ an army of lawyers."

"Economics is a new field, so it's as much an art as it is science," Robert said. "Have you heard anything about Walter Thoms?"

"Thoms—he's the worst Nazi in the school!"

"He's the head of the Economics Department."

"Don't worry about it. He can't dictate what they teach," Slavko said. "If the Nazis tried to rewrite all the textbooks, the students would just laugh at them. Here in Heidelberg, things are not so bad because it's an international city. At the University of Berlin, the Nazis replaced the rector with a storm trooper who was a *veterinarian*. He added 25 courses in racial science, and another 86 courses in veterinary science.[96] Forget about the Superior Race. The Third Reich is going to bestow upon the world a Superior Dog!"

Slavko was a slender, soft-spoken aristocrat with a gentle manner and a fine appreciation for irony. They became friends as time passed and traded ideas about how to stay out of the German army.

"How did a Serb wind up in Heidelberg?" Robert asked.

"Prince Paul was a gentleman, in my opinion, and he was the regent of our nation. After the Germans marched into Rumania and Bulgaria, Prince Paul gave permission to his government to make an accord with Hitler, since we were surrounded and we were no match for the Luftwaffe and the panzers. The Royal Guard revolted, thinking the British would come to our aid. They threw out the Prince and took over the government. Then the army splintered into factions of Serbs, Croats, and Albanians. Hitler went crazy. The Luftwaffe started bombing Belgrade. Ten days later, I was in a prison camp, along with 300,000 of my fellow patriots.[97]

"How did you get out?" Robert asked.

"I have a friend who has a friend who made me promise that if I ever get into university I will study law so that I can help the others."

"What is it like now in Yugoslavia?" Robert asked.

"There is no Yugoslavia. Hitler took his knife and cut off little pieces for Hungary, Italy, and Bulgaria. In the part he kept for himself, he set up two puppet states: Serbia and Croatia."

"Isn't that more or less what the Serbs wanted when they set off the First World War—a separate state for the Serbs?"

"I beg your pardon, Robert. A few schoolboys murdered an Archduke. You can't blame the whole war on us."

It was apparently a sore point.

"All right," Robert said with a smile, "I'll concede it wasn't entirely the Serbs' fault. They just lit the fuse."

"But we do keep going around the same circles, and, to answer your question, my friend, it is still a big mess."

Slavko had not forgotten how to have a good time. On the night after the United States declared war on Germany, Slavko dragged Robert to Seppel's Tavern in the center of town. He introduced Robert to Louis, a student from Metz, who was already drunk. Others joined them as the hours passed. The walls were covered with paper, photos, and poems. After a few beers, Slavko climbed up on a chair and started reading the notices.

"Well, Robert! Look what we have here." Slavko lifted up a yellow slip of paper and examined it. "It says here that a certain Robert Muller, or should I pronounce it *Müller*, was arrested—"

The others at the table started listening.

"—and he was subsequently fined for pushing a naked man through the streets of Heidelberg in a wheelbarrow!"

Robert shook his head to ward off the roar of approval.

"No, look—it gets better. A second ticket was issued to the suspect, Robert Muller, for urinating—*urinating* on the arresting officer's leg!"

"You peed on the cop's leg, Robert?" Louis marveled.

"Let me see that," Robert mumbled as he climbed up on a chair next to Slavko. "Hey, there's no date on this ticket!"

"Robert," Slavko admonished, "next time you're arrested, you must call me. I will introduce this wall as evidence that you are the innocent victim of an imposter."

Robert held up his hands. "I honestly cannot remember peeing on any German officer's leg since I arrived in this fair city."

With that, Robert was unofficially promoted in Slavko's gang from humble student to rowdy animal.

"Slavko is in the hospital!" the landlady said when Robert returned from Christmas vacation. "I found him on the floor a few days ago. He was unconscious and he had blood coming out of his mouth."

"What did the doctors say?"

"Your friend has tuberculosis. They fear the worst, Robert. I'm sorry to give you such bad news."

Robert left his suitcase on the landing and rushed to the hospital. He had been away only three weeks, but he regretted that he had left his friend alone for the holidays. Robert found him propped up against a pile of white pillows. His face was moist and yellow, like beeswax, and his long, thin hands were transparent.

"I wish you had come with me to Lorraine," Robert said. "My family is living a very secluded life now, but even so, I could have insisted—"

"I wasn't in any shape to travel, Robert." Slavko smiled weakly but his eyes were still bright. He drew each breath with care. "Don't worry about me, I'll be fine. This will help me stay out of the army. But I need to ask a favor of you."

"Does it involve a wheelbarrow?"

Slavko smiled and took a few shallow breaths. "Not this time. I want you to go to the library and bring me every book you can find by Dr. Émile Coué." [98]

At the university, Robert found a copy of Émile Coué's *Self-Mastery Through Conscious Autosuggestion*. He claimed that people could use their imaginations to build their self-confidence and restore their bodies to perfect health. Robert skimmed through the little book while he rode the bus to the hospital:

> We human beings have a certain resemblance to sheep, and involuntarily, we are irresistibly impelled to follow other people's examples, *imagining* that we cannot do otherwise. Thus, we who are so proud of our will, who believe that we are free to act as we like, are in reality nothing but puppets of which our imagination holds all the strings. We only cease to be puppets when we have learned to guide our imagination.
>
> Whereas we constantly give ourselves unconscious autosuggestions, all we have to do is to give ourselves conscious ones. Autosuggestion is the influence of the imagination upon the moral and physical being of mankind. It is the training of the imagination, which is necessary.
>
> When the will and the imagination are antagonistic, it is always the imagination that wins. When they are in agreement, one is multiplied by the other.
>
> The imagination can be directed. Autosuggestion is an instrument that we possess at birth. To make good suggestions it is necessary to do it without effort. The latter implies the use of the will, which must be entirely put aside. One must have recourse exclusively to the imagination.[99]

Robert jotted down the autosuggestion taught by Coué to every audience and prescribed to every one of his patients:

> Every morning before rising, and every night upon getting into bed, shut your eyes and repeat this little phrase twenty times in a monotone voice: "Every day, in every way, I am getting better and better."

"Do you practice Coué's method?" Robert asked Slavko when he reached the hospital.

"I have trouble sticking to it, but I think it will help me get out of here."

"It sounds too easy. There is no depth to his philosophy."

"How can you know that if you don't try it?" Slavko said. "In any event, what do you have to lose?"

"You're right, it's not a big effort," Robert conceded.

Robert repeated Coué's phrase every morning and night. "Every day, in every way, I am getting better and better." He was soon adding his own phrases. "I feel wonderful. I feel happier than yesterday. I have never felt this good before. It's marvelous to be so alive and feel so healthy."

Slavko recovered and was released from the hospital a few weeks later. By then, Robert was convinced that Coué's method was having a positive effect. The intensity of his happiness, his enthusiasm for life, even his views about the world had improved as a result of the suggestions he fed to his unconscious.

"You showed me a simple tool to make my life richer!" he told Slavko.

"I merely asked you to bring me the book, but someday Émile Coué may save your life. He saved mine."

The Royal Air Force sent 1,130 bombers to Cologne on the night of May 30, 1942, and destroyed 600 acres of the city. It was the 105th air raid for the residents of Cologne, but the area destroyed in one night was greater than all the damage throughout Germany caused by thousands British air raids since the beginning of the war.

Leaflets were dropped on the city by the RAF announcing the start of the *Thousand Bomber raids*: [100]

This proof of the growing strength of the British bomber force is also the herald of what Germany will receive, city by city, from now on."

Robert was ordered to work at the Haffner safe factory in Sarreguemines during the summer of 1942. The factory had been converted into a munitions plant, and Robert was assigned to assist a lathe operator. The assembly line work was tedious, but Robert was grateful he could go home at night and sleep in his own bed. His co-workers were mostly women and girls from Poland, slaves who had been taken from their families. They worked sixteen hours a day performing the most menial, repetitive, dangerous tasks. At night they were locked up in a crude barracks.

After two weeks on the factory floor, Robert was ordered to go upstairs and report to the office. He could see by the charts and graphs in the anteroom that the Germans were keeping track of everything the workers did. Robert was not surprised that he had been called for a reprimand. He was not quick on his feet and he hated making ammunition for the Nazis.

The dour expression on the receptionist's face in the office did nothing to ease Robert's discomfort. She was heavy and hard of hearing, judging by the way she yelled at callers and demanded that they repeat everything twice.

The plant director, Herbert Reuther, came out of his office and greeted Robert with a smile. "I see that you're attending the University in Heidelberg."

"Yes, sir."

"Is that a good school?"

"It's one of the best schools in Germany." Robert said.

"Yes, I've heard it's good. What are you studying?"

"Mostly economics, sir, and some courses in literature."

"Your favorite author?"

"I suppose that would be Goethe, or perhaps Schiller."

"Goethe! You see? I knew this boy was smart."

The receptionist looked up without comprehending.

"I knew you were smart the minute I saw you. I can tell a lot about a man by the way he looks at me. You know, Müller, I appreciate a good mind and I could use an extra hand in here. I need someone who's good with numbers."

"What sort of work would you be looking for?"

"Nothing fancy, certainly nothing that would tax a mind like yours—just basic office work and accounting."

"I could probably help with that."

"Look around here Müller, what do you see?"

"Nothing much, really. Just some charts and graphs. It looks like things are well organized."

"Exactly! You don't see all those stacks of old reports and

records, do you? When I first got here, this room was piled up so high with junk you couldn't even see the walls. I think you'll like working here, Müller. We use our heads around here."

Reuther assigned Robert a desk in the corner of the reception room. He added up columns of figures, figured out the time it would take to do tasks and the cost per unit. The work was as tedious as assisting the lathe operator, but it was less tiring. Reuther took every opportunity to point out the efficiency and effectiveness of the German approach to business, never once stopping to consider the purpose of the product or take into account the cost in human lives. Labor costs were measured in calories and life expectancy. Robert's heart sank every time he walked past the assembly line and saw the faces of the workers. Hitler preached that the Poles were sub-human, which made their bondage all the more tragic.

The Mullers were awakened almost every night by the wail of air raid sirens. As the horns blared, they fled into the basement and listened to the house rattle, first in tune with the growling percussion of British bombers, then to the staccato of anti-aircraft batteries. When the planes returned a few minutes later, they hummed on a higher note. If a bomber was hit and parachutes opened, German soldiers on motorcycles raced into the fields to catch the downed airmen, followed by dozens of policemen with German shepherds.[101]

Robert was staring up at the sky in front of the house one night when a huge black mass lunged out of the sky with a terrifying sound. Three, maybe four bombers roared across the sky so close to the house he thought they would hit the roof. Dozens of sparkling fires started burning in the street.

Robert ran into the house.

"What happened?" his father yelled.

"Firebombs!" Robert shouted as he raced upstairs. The attic was already filled with smoke and the biting odor of phosphorus pentoxide.[102] He counted three fires on the floor, and then his throat started to burn. Explosions rocked the house.

Robert shoveled sand on two of the fires, breathing

through a sock. His father ran in with a bucket of water.

"No, not water! Use the sand!" Robert yelled. "There!" He pointed to a fire behind the bed. They shoveled silently until the fires were out.

"Look at that," his father said, pointing to three holes in the ceiling where bombs had ripped through the roof.

"We shouldn't breathe the phosphor," Robert said. His father's eyes were watering so heavily that Robert took his arm. When they were safely downstairs, Robert ran outside. Several houses were on fire, and people were starting to panic. There were not enough hoses to put out all the fires.

Robert banged on the prison door and demanded a fire hose. The guard refused. "This is government property."

When a crowd formed around Robert, the guard gave in and brought them a long fire hose. They hooked it up to a hydrant down the street. Robert's former house was burning out of control—the entire roof was in flames—but the house next door was only starting to burn. They poured water on the flames until firemen arrived to finish the job. Then they moved to the next burning house. It took all night to bring the fires under control.

Robert was exhausted when he climbed the steps to his house in the morning. His father greeted him at the door.

"You saved the wrong house," his father said.

"What?"

"You should have saved our former house. There were hundreds of premium hat cones hidden in the basement. We were trading them for food and money. Oh well, I suppose it doesn't matter. We'll get by somehow."

"Robert, look at you!" his mother cried out.

He looked at himself in the mirror. His face was smeared with black soot and dirt, and his chin was bleeding. His pajamas were burned and ripped in more places than he could count.

Herbert Reuther took Robert under his wing. He seemed to think it was his duty to steer at least one errant Lorrainer back into the fold, and Robert was always handy when Reuther felt the need to beat his Prussian drum. It was in the middle of one of those pep talks—Reuther was going on about the virtue of orderly channels of distribution—when a foreman barged in.

"We've got several women on the sick list, Mr. Reuther. They think it has something to do with the toilets in their barracks. They said they're all stopped up. I haven't had time to check them yet."

"Very well," Reuther said without hesitating. "Maybe the commissary food does not agree with our guests. Now that's a pity. Tell them they can go without food for the next two days—that should make them feel better—and since they have so much free time on their hands, they can fix the toilets themselves—with their hands."

When the foreman was gone, Reuther looked startled to see that Robert was still in the room. "Müller, where was I? Oh, never mind, I'll tell you what. Why don't you come over to my house after dinner tonight and we can chat."

Reuther lived near Robert's home in a beautiful villa. The house had belonged to a candy-maker named Philippe before the war. Robert and his friends used to call it "Candy Philippe's house." As he approached the front door that night, Robert thought about the women in the barracks. Reuther's wife directed him through an ornamental garden to a beautiful orchard in the back. Music blared from a radio next to Reuther, who was sitting with his back to Robert sprawled across a lounge chair. He was listening to a chorus singing the triumphant finale to Beethoven's *Ninth Symphony*, broadcast live from a concert hall in Berlin. Robert listened to the finale while he stood in the shadows, haunted by images of the women lying on their mattresses, weak from dysentery and starvation, missing their loved ones and burning with hatred for the Nazis who had stolen their lives.

Reuther sat in rapt silence after the performance ended, his shoulders rising and falling with long, deep breaths. He shuddered, and Robert wondered if he regretted his cruelty to the women. Finally he rose and turned to face Robert, tears streaming down his face. He wiped them on his sleeve.

"Müller, whenever I listen to Beethoven, it makes me so happy, I always end up crying!"

Robert stared icily at the man. He had attained the state

of mind extolled by German high school teachers: *die polarität des deutschen wesens*—the polarity of the German being. Reuther's soul was divided between incompatible extremes, and yet he seemed to be blissfully free of internal conflict.

No, Robert decided. Reuther was not a man. He was a monster.

Chapter 7 – Birds in Flight

I saw Peters last night," Robert's father said at breakfast. "The Germans are abolishing student deferments. He said they're afraid of the Americans, and now they're fighting the Russians for their lives."

"Can he help me get any other kind of deferment?"

"He said there's nothing he can do. He doesn't have any influence over the military, just the *Arbeitsdienst*."

"Maybe I can get across on the coal barge," Robert said.

"He doesn't think you should cross the border yet. He says it's still going to be a long time until Hitler is defeated. If you go too soon, we will all be deported. He said we should try to get you a health deferment."

"But I'm in pretty good shape," Robert said. "The only thing that isn't very good is my eyesight."

"We might be able to get you some thicker glasses. I'll talk to Welters this morning."

Welters had a medical supplies outlet near the hat shop. He had supplied Robert's glasses for years. He told Robert's father that he still had blank prescription forms signed by an ophthalmologist who hadn't come back after the evacuation. He would see what he could do.

Robert felt dizzy when he reported for his medical review at the Kommandantur three weeks later. His new glasses were so thick, he felt like he was swimming under water when he tried to walk.

"Take off your glasses and read the letters on the wall," a German sergeant ordered.

"I can't read anything," Robert said.

The sergeant marked a piece of paper and said, "Now put on your glasses."

Robert stared at the chart with his glasses on, walked a few steps forward and squinted as he read the biggest letter.

"Good," the sergeant said. Robert handed him the new prescription. "Ah, I see what the trouble is. Your glasses are not strong enough." He concentrated hard on some mental calculations and added a few numbers to his report. "How can you possibly study with such bad eyes?"

"It is hard, sir, but I try."

"I'm sorry, lad, but I can't pronounce you fit for active service. You would probably shoot your buddies instead of the enemy. The best service I can render the German army is to send you back to the university."

Robert went straight to the hat shop, where his parents were working.

"How did it go?" his father asked.

"He gave me a deferment. He said my glasses are not thick enough."

Robert's father put on the thick glasses and squinted. "So this is how the world looks when you're a *Boche!*"

"Peters must be behind this," Robert's mother said. "There's no other explanation."

"No, he told me he couldn't do a thing...but I'll ask him."

Robert stopped in the park on the way home. He sat on a bench to relax and let his imagination wander. He thought of a remark by Émile Coué: "When you make conscious autosuggestions, do it naturally, simply, with conviction, and above all *without any effort.*" Robert allowed himself to imagine what life would be like after the war. He pictured men in different uniforms laying down their guns and shaking hands. He saw mountains in the distance, and then he heard a child squeal and a woman's laughter.

Robert opened his eyes. The young German woman who lived across the street was tickling her little boy as they wrestled on a blanket on the grass. It was the first time he had seen her smile. The woman stopped playing with the boy and looked up at the sky. When she picked him up and he became quiet, Robert heard a low rumble in the distance. It couldn't be British bombers, he thought. They flew at night. The sirens started wailing. The woman grabbed her blanket and hurried up the path carrying her child.

Robert started up the path behind her, watching the sky for planes. The rumble grew louder and his stomach started vibrating. He stopped in a clearing and scanned the blue sky until he saw the slow motion of white streaks, four fine, white threads spreading out into one wide stripe behind the silver specks. He picked out perhaps a dozen planes in a diamond formation, and then he saw other diamonds formations, seven in all, inching across the sky.

Flying Fortresses! Robert had heard the Americans were building B-17 "Flying Fortresses," but he never thought he would see them in daylight. A squadron of Messerschmitts shot up in the air and buzzed around the American bombers like angry bees as they flew out of sight to the east.

When Robert's father came home from the tavern, they talked about the Americans. They seemed larger than life flying those huge planes across France in broad daylight. The "Flying Fortress" looked like a giant porcupine, Robert said, thinking a "Flying Fortress" was the formation, rather than the individual plane. Everyone had gone outside to watch the American bombers, ignoring the sirens.

"Those Americans are not afraid of Hitler," Robert's father said. "They'll blow up every factory in Germany."

"What about the Haffner factory?" Robert's mother said.

"I don't think they would bomb anything here," his father said, "but it's a good thing you're going back to school."

"Did you talk to Peters today?" Léonie asked.

"Sure, I bought him a beer. He said Hitler was going to lose for sure, but it will still take quite awhile, even with the Americans. Things are going badly for Hitler in Russia."

"Did he say anything about my physical?" Robert asked.

"He swears he had nothing to do with it. He said that it was pure Nazi stupidity, that they are so blinded by their feelings of superiority that they can't see straight. Their arrogance is clouding their judgment."

On his return trip to the university, Robert's train slowed to a crawl in Saarbrücken. The tracks were uneven and the train creaked as it crawled past collapsed buildings. People went about their business, while others picked through the ruins and cleared rubble in the streets. There were gaping holes and fallen buildings in almost every block. The train station was shut down, so passengers switched trains in the yard. The next train started east into Germany late at night, but it stopped halfway to Heidelberg on the outskirts of Ludwigshafen, an industrial city across the Rhine from Mannheim.

"You have to walk from here," the conductor said.

The train tracks in front of the locomotive were twisted like pretzels in the moonlight. A path had been cleared on one side of the track, where passengers filed past each other in the darkness walking in opposite directions. Robert started down the cinder trail and tried to walk quickly past the collapsed buildings on both sides of the tracks, but he soon slowed to the weary pace of the others. People walking towards him were covered with gray soot. Ahead, he noticed several columns of white smoke. The number of collapsed structures increased as he walked, until finally he passed the final shell of a building and saw that almost nothing was left standing ahead. There were only fragments of walls and chimneys jutting out of flat waves of unrecognizable debris. Smoke was rising from pyres of burning bodies.

As dawn approached, he saw groups of people crying in the ruins. Heading into the glare of the sunrise, Robert walked for miles through flattened blocks, square upon square of smoking dust where houses had been pulverized. Unimaginable fires had left no trace of tens of thousands of people. Ludwigshafen was reduced a powdery tomb.

"How did this happen!" he asked a man passing the other way when they both stopped to rest. The man's gray face was sagging with grief.

"The firestorm—you ask how did this happen? First they

covered the city with incendiary bombs, spreading fire all over the city, and the British kept coming in waves and dropping the phosphor bombs, the ones that burn your eyes and nose until you can't breathe, and they explode if you spray water on them. Some of them were time bombs and they'd go off while people were trying to put out the fires. After a few hours, the whole city was on fire. It burned all day until it turned into one huge flame, and you could feel the wind, like a hurricane, pulling air into the fire, and people were getting sucked into the fire, pulled right off their feet. If you were down in the shelters it didn't matter. Either you couldn't breath because the air was gone or you burned to death. What's the difference?"

"That's what they call a firestorm," Robert said.

"No, that was just to get it hot. Then they came back the next night and dropped explosives down the center of the furnace. When those bombs went off, everything turned to dust. You couldn't stop it."

The man's eyes seemed to be pleading with Robert.

"Is there really a God in heaven?" Robert said.

The man shook his head and walked away.

Slavko tried to cheer Robert up with his latest theory—how the Serbs won the war.

"First of all, the war's not over," Robert interrupted.

"No, of course not, but we both know Hitler can't win," Slavko said.

"All right, I'll go along with that." Robert was in no mood for Slavko's humor, but he didn't want to be alone.

"And what's beating him—Russia," Slavko explained, like a patient teacher. "Almost every German soldier and tank and plane is now in Russia, which means Hitler doesn't have enough men to stop England and the United States."

"So you're saying the stubborn Russians are winning the war, not the troublesome Serbs," Robert said.

"You don't see my point. If the Serbs hadn't defied Hitler, which made him so crazy he went after Yugoslavia and Greece, he would have attacked Russia at least a month sooner and he would have won! He went for the cape instead of the matador.'"

"So what's your point—the Serbs drove Hitler crazy and changed the course of World War II?"

"Exactly!"

"What about the Croats and the Slovaks?"

"They're mad at us too! We're very good at getting people riled up. So what is that you're reading?"

Robert showed Slavko his philosophy book. "I saw some bad things on the way here, and then I read this passage by Immanuel Kant. *It will be proved, I know not when or where, that the human soul stands, even in this life, in indissoluble connection with all immaterial natures in the spirit world, that it reciprocally acts upon these and receives impressions and help from them.*"

"But what about Thomas Carlyle," Slavko said, turning the pages. "*Everywhere the human soul stands between a hemisphere of light and another of darkness; on the confines of the two everlasting empires, necessity and free will.*"

"Slavko, do you think there are spirits in the universe who can visit us and they might help us to end the war?"

"We will win because Hitler will make mistakes," Slavko said. "Is that because Hitler can't listen to Kant's invisible spirits, or because he has fallen into a hemisphere of darkness? Maybe they are the same thing. I believe that Kant inspired Émile Coué. Kant's Copernican Revolution brought forward the idea that the human mind is the originator of experience, rather than a passive recipient of perception."

"But even if the mind can generate perceptions, does this have anything to do with the real world?" Robert said. "I don't feel that I have any power to change the reality of a city that was reduced to ashes in a few hours."

Slavko saw the sorrow in Robert's eyes. "Robert, your train passes through Mannheim, doesn't it?"

"And also Ludwigshafen—the residential area was gone!"

"Ludwigshafen has the largest chemical manufacturing center in the world. It's three miles long, right across the river from Mannheim. They have refineries there and they make rubber. How can they stop Hitler if they don't stop his trucks and his planes?"

"If we have to fight, how do we make the world any

better?"

"You can't change it with will power, but maybe if you let your imagination wander, it will show you a better way."

Fifty-four thousand American and 23,000 British troops landed between Morocco and Algiers on November 8, 1942. Marshal Pétain stayed his course, appeasing Hitler by ordering his commanders in Africa to resist the Allied "aggression." On the other hand, he hinted to his officers in North Africa that he was acting against his wishes and was sympathetic to the Allies. This only added to the confusion.

French admirals and generals in Africa argued with each other for three days over the legality of joining the Allies. The French commanders took turns locking each other up, switching internal allegiances, and issuing and rescinding orders so many times that General Mark Clark, Deputy Commander-in-Chief for Operation Torch, started pounding tables with his fists and slamming doors.

After three days of sporadic fighting between French and American troops, Hitler lost patience with Pétain, who vacillated every time the Germans offered him military support. German armored convoys and planes swooped into southern France on November 11, 1942—Armistice Day. The German invasion sent shock waves through French commanders in Africa. General Clark threatened to arrest the French leaders and lock them up on a ship. They came to their senses and joined the Allies on November 13, bringing France back into the war. [103]

After Hitler invaded Vichy France, thousands of French men fled into the hills to join the *Maquis*, the guerilla units of the French Resistance. Pétain's government retaliated by organizing its own militia, the *Milice*, to function as an auxiliary of the German Army. The *Milice* recruited 25,000 Vichy Frenchmen and trained them to infiltrate *Maquis* units. The *Maquis* and the *Milice* started waging a civil war in Southern France with such fury that even the Gestapo was impressed by their brutality.

. . .

In March 1943, legal blindness no longer qualified as an excuse to avoid serving in the German army. Hitler needed every man he could get.

Peters warned that Robert would be called up with the next group of draftees. "Do not do anything foolish," he told Robert's father. "Buy time. Do anything you can to survive this insane war. Can you trust your family doctor?"

"Dr. Frederich is a very good friend," Robert's father said. "Our families came from the same town."

"Maybe he can perform an operation, but it has to look real. I can find out the date when the next draft notices will be issued. If your son is in the hospital when the order arrives in the mail, that may save him for another month or two."

Dr. Frederich scheduled several appointments for Robert. He showed Robert the exact location of his appendix and told him to press hard on that spot every day. He arranged for X-rays to be taken by a friend who was a radiologist, who then certified that there was a strong suspicion of an infected appendix.

Robert returned to the university. Dr. Coué had taught his patients how to cure illnesses. Robert went to the library and looked through notes of Coué's sessions that had been transcribed by one of his disciples. Robert wanted to learn how to get sick.

> Every one of our thoughts, good or bad, becomes concrete, materializes, and becomes a reality...Man is what he thinks. The fear of failure is almost certain to cause failure, in the same way as the idea of success brings success.[104]

It didn't matter what the thought was. Autosuggestion worked either way, for good or for bad. Robert guided his imagination to think that his appendix was infected. He pictured it getting more swollen and inflamed each day. He pressed on it for hours while he practiced autosuggestion, persuading himself that he had severe appendicitis. The spot became so sensitive it was almost too painful to touch.

Slavko dropped into Robert's room. "I've been reading some Goethe, and it started me thinking about some of the choices I've made. Tell me what you think about this:

> Until one is committed there is hesitancy, the chance
> to draw back, always ineffectiveness.
> Concerning all acts of initiative and creation, there
> is one elementary truth, the ignorance of which kills
> countless ideas and splendid plans:
> That the moment one definitely commits oneself,
> then Providence moves too. All sorts of things occur to
> help one that would never otherwise have occurred.
> A whole stream of events issues from the decision,
> raising in one's favor all manner of unforeseen
> incidents and meetings and material assistance,
> which no one could have dreamt would come his way.
> Whatever you can do, or dream you can, begin it.
> Boldness has genius, power, and magic in it.

"This is a good time to be bold," Robert said. "Audacity is the first step in any worthwhile adventure."

"I'm going home, Robert. There is a war to be won, and I don't think lawyers are going to win it."

"There will be plenty of time for lawyers. We will need a whole new system when the fighting is over."

When Robert got up the next morning, a copy of Émile Coué's little book was resting against his door. He wondered if he would ever see his friend Slavko again.

A telegram arrived from Robert's father a few days later asking him to come home. He took the next train. The following morning, Dr. Frederich checked him into the hospital across the street from Robert's home in Sarreguemines. A draft notice was delivered to Robert's home the next day.

Nazi nurses in brown uniforms had replaced all the Catholic nuns at the hospital, and the *braune Schwester* assigned to Robert was as beautiful as she was suspicious.

Schwester Erika would have been quite a lovable woman, Robert decided, if she were not trying so hard to be strong, heartless and efficient. She was contorting herself to be a good German soldier, loyal to her Reich. It was her duty to expose Robert Muller as a fake. Her Führer needed soldiers, all the soldiers he could get.

It was Robert's first operation. Brown Nurse Erika didn't stop asking questions as she shaved Robert's belly. "Where does it hurt? What kind of pain is it? How long has it been hurting? Does it hurt here...here...here...here?"

Robert jumped and screamed every time she pressed the precise spot.

She was a good looking, strong, healthy German girl who, under different circumstances—but the questions kept coming as she wheeled him into the operating room. She placed a mask over his nose and mouth. The ether started dripping.

"Does it hurt here—start counting from one to a hundred—here...here?"

A faucet near the bed was dripping, and as Robert watched her beautiful, grinning face, the drops got louder—*keep counting*—and louder. He closed his eyes and saw beautiful colorful circles expanding into ever-wider circles—the drips now echoed like a gigantic gong hit by slaves—colossal circles, colors, and sounds reverberating in the universe, infinite, eternal color, a stunning world he had never imagined.

"How about here?" she cooed, and the lights went out.

Nurse Erika was holding Robert's hand when he awoke the next day. She was asking him about his studies, about his politics. How about Dr. Frederich—was he Robert's regular doctor? How long had Robert known him? Did he ever talk about the war or mention the Germans or say anything about the draft?

Robert had expected this interrogation and had prepared himself. His self-imposed brainwashing was paying off.

Dr. Frederich entered the room with a big grin. "I have seldom seen such an enormous, diseased appendix, and it was about to rupture. You would have been in great danger if it had not been removed."

Robert's family and friends visited him during a cheerful

week of recovery. The *braune Schwester* came by several times a day, and stayed to discuss philosophy, literature, and politics. He had passed the interrogation with flying colors, and now she wanted to talk about more important things. After experiencing the anesthesia, Robert was eager to talk.

"Where does life end and death begin?" he asked her. "Which little drop of ether makes all the difference between life and death, or is there is no discontinuity between life and death and matter is simply changing?"

"I don't know," she answered, "but many people have told me about reactions like yours to the anesthesia."

"The religions have all their Gods," Robert said, "but we are all part of the universe. All these Gods tell us that there is a reality that goes beyond our life on this Earth."

"What I *feel* is bigger than what I can see or touch," she said. Erika let him see her softer side when she talked about deeper subjects. She never mentioned, though, that a Gestapo officer had stood at Dr. Frederich's side during the operation to be certain the appendicitis was real.

A group of teenage girls brought books and flowers to Robert—he was one of the only boys their age in town, so they stayed as long as they could. Finally the nurse became furious and told them that visiting hours were over.

"You have a good mind, Robert," she exploded. "You must not waste time on those silly geese. Your ambition will take you far beyond this little town."

Erika visited Robert more frequently as the week passed, and stayed long into the evenings after she was off duty. He wrote:

I began to like her very much. Behind her stern appearance and military gait, there was a marvelous intelligence and a warm woman, beating with all the loving impulses of life. The military, the toughness had been added only superficially by education. No regime can really change the fundamental nature, warmth and uniqueness of a human being.[105]

Robert brought Erika a bouquet of flowers a few days after he was released, and she invited him up to her room in the hospital for dinner. They talked late into the night about what held the world together, and when it was time for him to leave, they looked into each other's eyes for a long time without saying a word, but the whole time their eyes were talking. They knew they lived in different worlds.

Robert and Louis, a student from Metz, were the only ones left in Slavko's gang. Seppel's tavern continued to be their meeting place, but most of the seats were empty. Students who still attended the University of Heidelberg at the end of the spring semester in 1943 were an odd assortment that could not be trusted. Conversations about the war were evasive, and any emotion other than grim determination caused alarm and aroused suspicion.

"My mother used to smuggle schnapps across the border into Belgium in my baby bottle," Robert said to Louis.

"My father used to say that he had two suitcases," Louis said, "one for business and the other for pleasure, and the one for pleasure had a false bottom."

It had started out as a tentative conversation, a possible door opener that either of them could end by changing the subject. They had seen each other at Seppel's with Slavko and the others for over a year, but Robert still didn't know Louis's first name. He always went by the family name, Louis, which Robert guessed was a prosperous Metz family. But the name Louis was so common he would almost be untraceable.

Everyone in Germany was up to something, but *you have to trust someone*, and the conversation seemed to be going in the right direction.

"Smuggling is a way of life on the border," Robert said.

"Border people don't do it for profit," Louis added. "It's just a way of testing the system and defying the borders."

"My mother went to Paris and brought back a whole shipment of French berets after the armistice," Robert said.

"No kidding. I wouldn't mind going there myself," Louis said. "I hear the girls in Paris are terrific."

"The women around here are too serious," Robert agreed.

"They have forgotten how to have a good time, Robert.

Wouldn't it be fun to hear a woman laughing?"

"The only way we can get there is in our dreams."

"Who knows, we might be able to find a way," Louis said. The door was open.

"How do you know that we can trust this man?" Robert's father asked. Robert had finally told him that he had been meeting with Louis throughout the summer.

"I just feel I can trust him," Robert said.

"All right, so what do you know about him. His name is Louis, right? What's his last name?"

"That is his last name."

"Okay, then what's his first name?"

"I don't know."

"Oh, for God's sake, and you're putting your life in this man's hands? Help me out," he said to Léonie.

"You've always said we can't do it alone," she said to her husband. "Are you sure the barge is no longer an option?"

"The barge is gone, the owner is gone, and his brother Guehl the baker is gone. God help us!"

"What about Peters?"

"He can't help us. He said if you can walk, the army will take you, and the notices will be coming out any day. I'm surprised they haven't drafted *me* yet."

"Louis said it's a pretty normal thing now," Robert said. "There are quite a few *passeurs* taking people across the border, and his father knows where to find one in Metz."

"After the draft notice comes, we're sunk. You must get out now," Robert's father said. "That's the only thing that matters. If you stay here, you're finished."

"Now remember, Louis and I are only going to Paris for a week, that's all you know. We'll have round trip tickets from the nearest town across the border to Paris, and we have both registered for the fall semester."

"You should carry the school papers with you," Léonie said. "And you'll need a receipt from your landlady for October."

"It's all here," Robert said.

"What about the bank?" she asked. "A student wouldn't

leave money in the bank if he was about to escape."

"That's why I left enough money in there, and I have my bank book with me. We thought about it carefully."

"I don't like it," Robert's father said.

"It sounds like it will work," Léonie said.

"It makes me nervous," he muttered. "But you can probably stay with my cousin Marcel above the bakery."

"Crossing the border shouldn't be a big problem," Robert said, "but when the draft notices come out, you'll need to tell them a story."

"Don't worry about us," Robert's father said.

"We're not taking any chances. Louis and I are going to Vienna for a mountain climbing expedition in the Austrian Alps. We'll send you letters from Vienna before we return to Metz. When the draft notice comes, tell the Germans we disappeared in the mountains and you think we must have been killed."

"So if you get away, you went to Austria," Léonie said, "and if you're caught, you were on your way to Paris for a week."

Robert and Louis couldn't sleep on the crowded train. They arrived in Vienna at dawn. After a bowl of goulash, they found a hotel room and slept for a few hours, then wrote letters to their parents. In the first letter they described their search for mountain climbing equipment, and said they would be leaving for the Alps in a few days. They deposited those letters in a mailbox. The second letters were entrusted to a French maid at the hotel. They were to be mailed a few days later.

Louis's father met them at the Metz station. "I have bad news, boys. The *passeur* was arrested."

"Do you know anybody else?" Louis asked.

"I haven't found anyone yet, but I'll keep looking. You can stay at the house, if you like, Robert."

"We can't do that, Mr. Louis. We're supposed to be in Austria. We can hide at my uncle Marcel's bakery at 82 Rue des Allemands for a few days. If you find anyone, let him know the arrangements."

While they hid in a room above the bakery, Robert and Louis went over their alibi. Ten days later, Robert's uncle found a *passeur* named Bernard from Montigny-les-Metz. Half the money had to be paid in advance to his intermediary, a girl named Yvonne. The rest would be due after the crossing.

Robert's mother came to Metz to wish him off.

"You shouldn't have come," he said.

"I wouldn't miss this for anything," she said. Léonie stuffed a big chunk of smoked ham and fresh underwear into his small suitcase.

Robert and Louis left Metz for St. Privat, a village to the north, where Yvonne met them at the station with two other people, a woman and wiry man about Robert's age. They became acquainted at a restaurant while waiting for the *passeur*. Robert and Louis joked about the French girls they would meet in Paris, while the man smoked cigarettes and the women made polite conversation about the problems with rationing. Bernard arrived late in the evening, a nervous, redheaded squirrel of a man. Leaving Yvonne behind, they walked to the woods, where three others were waiting—an adult couple and a weary young man.

They walked for hours through the trees along an old railroad track. The ties were too close together for one normal step and a little too far apart to skip every other one. The man who smoked in the restaurant had trouble keeping up with the group. The other man walked with a limp. They finally left the track and followed a path towards a field, pausing when a German patrol passed behind them. Robert offered to carry the suitcase of the smoker who kept falling behind, since his own bag was not heavy.

"We just crossed the border," Bernard said. "Welcome to France. We will wait here until the other patrol goes by up ahead."

As they stood in silence, Robert felt the pulsating, warm fragrant body of the Earth beneath his feet. The full moon cast a luminous shadow in the branches overhead. Robert felt the joy of approaching freedom. It was 15 August 1943.

They walked another hour. Bernard gathered them in a wheat field on the outskirts of a village. "You are safe now. In the morning you can take a train from here into France.

If you want, you can sleep in that barn over there near the farmhouse. The peasants are used to it. I'll return to Metz now and inform your relatives. Good luck to you."[106]

The couple and the woman went to sleep in the barn. The smoker said he would spend the night at his uncle's place in a neighboring village. Robert and Louis and the weary young man stacked a few bales of freshly cut wheat together and laid down between them to sleep out of sight in the field.

Robert removed his suit and carefully folded it, then put on extra undershirts and briefs to stay warm.

He slept for about an hour and then awoke to the sound of crickets, more crickets than he had ever heard in his life. He was finally free, lying in an open field with stars overhead and a new life that would begin with the dawn. There were so many crickets chirping, he could hardly believe that he was feeling so much fear. Fear gripped him, a deep terror like he had never felt before, as if demons were being released from beneath the earth. The fear consumed him and crowded out any sense of reason. A cold chill made him shiver and his lungs worked hard because his ribs felt tight, as if a steel cage was squeezing the life out of him. His heart was beating fiercely.

Then a voice called out inside his head. *Run! Get up and run away from here as fast as you can!*

He pictured himself running away, running across the field and into the forest and running until he was far away.

Run the voice commanded. *Don't think. Run as fast as you can.*

But his body wouldn't move. It felt tight and cold as he lay there, trembling.

"This is nonsense," he said. "I'm free. Thank God it's over and I can finally relax. The Germans will never find us."

He took a deep breath, and then another, and felt his muscles relax a little. "It's over," he whispered. "I'm letting go now. I am in France, I am free...happy to be free..."

Run, the voice said, but it was softer now. *Run away...*

His body was relaxing. His breathing was easier and the steel cage was releasing. The terror was subsiding. His forehead stopped squeezing. The voice had been pleading, but now it was leaving, and the pasture was filled with the haunting call of an owl and the pounding sensation in his temples subsided.

Robert heard two owls calling back and forth. An ocean of calm engulfed him in a warm feeling of...perfection! It was all unfolding, revealing itself, knowing itself in the shadows, in the starlight, in the shrill song of crickets singing.

The crickets stopped.

Robert lay calmly, breathing slowly in the silence. His chest was rising and falling evenly and he felt peaceful. He had seen a fleeting glimpse of perfection. His mind was calm, quiet, alert.

He heard a light crackling sound, followed by footsteps. A raspy voice shattered the silence.

"*Heraus, sie Schweinehunde! Hände hoch!* Get up, you pig's dogs! Hands up!"

Half a dozen men surrounded them, Gestapo wearing dark leather jackets. Two German shepherds lunged at them, yanking against their chains. Robert could barely see the barrels of their guns in the glare of their flashlights. Black boots kicked his companions. They groaned and awkwardly stumbled to their feet.

"Flying away from the army like birds, eh?"

"You have no right to say that," Robert snapped back. "We're on our way to Paris for a vacation, that's all."

"Nice story." The Nazi laughed. "We'll see."

He stared at Robert closely, then Louis, then the other man. The Nazi hesitated. The triumph melted from his face.

"I know you," he said to the weary young man, who pressed his shoulders back and stood at attention. "You failed to return to your regiment after your leave." He glanced at his men and let out a sigh. "I have the sad honor to inform you that you were awarded the Iron Cross for your courage under fire on the Russian front."

Chapter 8 – Escape

J ust a squalid apartment building!" Robert thought. "Is this the best they can do?" Robert waited and stared at the armored steel door. The Nazis guarding him waited for the driver to unlock Louis's shackles inside the military truck that had transported them from the St. Privat jail. Robert felt his aching feet on the gravel. His body sagged from lack of sleep and his legs were sore from the hike the night before.

He hunted for clues to his surroundings, something that might save his life. It was a Gestapo steel door. It was bolted to the back of an old building that was almost identical to the others in the neighborhood, except that no laundry hung from the windows, and the curtains were all the same color, a depressing slate gray. Apparently the Gestapo had taken over an apartment building.

Louis stepped awkwardly out of the truck.

"This is the Metz Gestapo headquarters?" Robert asked.

Louis nodded soberly. Metz was his hometown, and this was the last place he wanted to see. They should have been in Paris by now. Louis looked pale and unsteady. In the harsh sunlight, Robert noticed that he was trembling.

Guards in black uniforms forced them down a flight of steps into a concrete catacomb. The air was stuffy and hard to breathe. They passed several corroded metal doors. Robert was ordered to stop, while Louis continued around a corner.

A guard fumbled through his keys and opened the door. Robert's nostrils flared when the smell hit him. He sealed his lips as they shoved him into the cell and closed the door against his back. Sweaty faces in semi-darkness looked fearful and weary. The low ceiling seemed to press down on their heads. In the gloom, desperate eyes glanced at him.

Robert's optimism began to fade. He counted heads—at least 30 men were stuffed into a narrow storage room. Robert's legs were wobbly, but there was no place to sit. His chest ached. He was breathing in shallow gasps. The only ventilation was a small window by the ceiling. A nauseating odor rose from a pail in a corner. Robert eyed it warily, hoping he would get out before he needed to use it.

The men were crowded together around the window. Robert stayed by the door, where a small peephole admitted a trickle of air. He counted time in breaths as the humid morning melted into an oppressively hot afternoon. No one talked or moved, to save precious oxygen. It was impossible to sit on the floor or lay on the two wooden beds. The air near the floor was too stale to breathe and fear of suffocation battled with fatigue. A few men dozed, leaning against the others. Robert's mind refused to let go.

There was nothing to do but retreat into private thoughts and rummage for hope. Robert remembered Dr. Coué: *Be the happiest man in the world, wherever you are.*

Robert whispered, "Every day in every way I am feeling better and better." It was comforting to repeat those words.

He thought, "I never could have imagined a depressing place like this. What an incredible opportunity to observe how my feelings and thoughts are shaped by circumstances out of my control. My God, my life has turned out to be such an adventure!"

He started feeling better. Their alibi was good. Both Louis and Robert had enough money in the bank to give the impression that they would be returning to school. They both had rent receipts. They had registration slips for the fall semester. Neither of them had any record of trouble with the Gestapo.

Robert went over their story again—two university students trying to slip across the border for a last-minute fling in Paris before going back to school. He rehearsed the particulars of their story until he found a hole. How did they find Bernard, the *passeur* who guided them across the border? What would Louis say? He knew better than to give them the name of Robert's uncle, but their stories might not match. Robert made up several explanations—some of them absurd. He settled on the simplest one, and then all he could do was wait.

Each time the guards called out a name, fear rippled through the cell. After the prisoner was taken away, the tension subsided. There was a brief shuffling of feet, and then there was a little more room.

Robert's mind wandered. He thought about the voice he heard in the field. Something had spoken to him while the others were asleep. Someone was yelling at him to get up and run away, but how could that be? Was it some kind of disembodied voice? No, it was more like a guardian. It must have been an intuitive voice, he decided. It could see the Germans coming for him, but his rational mind wouldn't listen. That logical, balanced, finely-tuned instrument trained in the French Lycée to excel in moderation, balance and equilibrium, a mind cautioned to be wary of extremes, that cultivated French mind of his had ignored the voice because it was certain they were too far across the border to get caught.

Next time, I will listen!

The number of prisoners dropped with each round of interrogations. Robert counted the minutes between footsteps of the guards patrolling the corridor. In the interval, he spoke to a man in the next cell. "Tell Louis, I wish we were back at the train station with those pretty students who told us about Bernard."

Louis's reply came back a few minutes later. "*D'accord.*"

Robert stopped worrying about their alibi and gave up wondering how soon they would get out. He concentrated all of his attention on the intricate landscape of the metal door as it spooled a precious thread of oxygen into his nose. Between all the tiny pockmarks and pimples—craters and mountains—he found a hidden network of winding valleys through which he might find a way to escape with his mind.

"How can I get to my luggage?" he asked a man who was

standing nearby.

The other man confided that one of the guards was poor, and sometimes he would grant a favor in exchange for something of value. Robert pleaded with the guard to take him to his suitcase for fresh underwear. Then he winked. The guard reluctantly escorted him to the storeroom.

Prisoners' belongings were organized into two heaps. Robert found his suitcase and set it on the floor. He gave the guard a bar of soap and two shirts, keeping for himself a sweater, a change of clothes, and the smoked ham from his mother. Robert removed his underpants, and when the guard looked away he wedged a pencil between his buttocks and smuggled it into the cell.

He sharpened the pencil by sanding it on the door, and then he began to string tiny letters together to form words which laced around irregularities on the corroded door to build sentences which became roads on which he could escape to the Jura Mountains where, just before the war, he had discovered the poetry of Goethe.

Robert began in the top left corner of the door:

> She was a ravishing woman, and I fell madly in love with her the very moment we met in the first days of spring. We held hands on a majestic, snow-covered mountain, where cold, pure water flowed into the stream and tickled our feet.
>
> "From heaven love doth rain," I whispered.
>
> "Love gives love the strength to grow," she said.

And so Robert escaped from the suffocating heat.

Each time footsteps approached outside, Robert stopped writing and stepped back from the door. He paid close attention to the reaction of each new prisoner and organized the various behaviors in his mind. Each man's response to the oppressive conditions indicated many secrets about his character. Years later, Robert wrote:

> Imprisonment is a great test in the art of living. One can see the walls, the ugliness, the darkness, the misery, the despair, the loss of freedom, but one can also concentrate on one's mind and heart, on the

image of a beloved person, a flower, a souvenir, the moment of recovered freedom, or one's future plans for life. Sometimes I think that to be really happy in this world and to appreciate life, a person must have been imprisoned.[107]

Robert recognized a prisoner who was led past the door and placed in the next cell. It was Bernard, the *passeur*. Robert waited until the guards were gone.

He hissed through the peephole, "Bernard, Bernard!"

"Who's that?" Bernard whispered.

"It's Robert."

"Robert? What the hell are you doing in here?"

Bernard sounded tense and disoriented. He said he returned to Metz after leaving everyone in the field. He visited the families to share the news of the escape and collect the balance of his fees. His last stop was the apartment of the young man whose suitcase Robert had carried. The man's uncle asked a few questions and went to get the money. That's when the Gestapo stormed in.

Robert decided to say nothing about his arrest. The less Bernard knew, the better for both of them.

Robert felt waves of fear when Bernard was taken away. A few minutes later, the prisoners were escorted up the stairs. Every day, they were given a few minutes in the courtyard to exercise, wash their faces at a pump, and hang their blankets on ropes to dry. Every man indulged in a primitive human pleasure—inhaling sweet, intoxicating air. They took turns carrying the heavy bucket up the stairs to an outhouse in the courtyard. The man with the bucket was always given plenty of room. Robert stood off to the side by himself and looked around for any possible way to escape. An agile person might be able to scale the wall on the far side of the enclosure, but the guards watched every move.

Bernard returned to his cell a few hours later. Robert heard a shrill note of panic in his voice. In the courtyard the next day, Bernard cautiously surveyed the perimeter. He walked slowly past Robert. "I want you to make a big distraction tomorrow." Robert nodded and turned away. That was not a Nazi talking. His face was swollen and bruised.

Robert stood next to the pail when the guards arrived the following day. He carried the heavy bucket slowly up the stairs, letting the others pass him. He couldn't avoid breathing the putrid fumes. He stopped in the sunlight and gazed from side to side as he sucked in a deep breath. Some men were already walking in circles while others waited in line at the water pump.

Robert plodded unsteadily across the courtyard, stopped to wipe his brow, and then continued forward a few steps. Bernard was adjusting his blanket on a rope near the wall. Robert rocked a little, stumbled slightly, and set the pail down. He placed one hand on his stomach and looked up, blinking, into the sun. Nobody moved. Even the handle on the pump stopped squeaking.

Robert tilted his head back and took a deep breath, sweat pouring down his face. He stumbled, lurched forward and slammed his foot against the pail. The pail flipped, bounced off the ground and launched into a grotesque arc, fanning its contents across the dirt and leaving a stain like a giant buzzard's claw.

As Robert regained his footing, an irresistible compulsion drove every man in the courtyard, prisoner and guard alike, to stare.

There was a sudden explosion of pent-up fury. Germans barked commands as they rushed forward. Prisoners scrambled to get out of the way. Only Robert heard the faint explosion of glass as Bernard disappeared over the wall and fell through a skylight. In the distance, a woman screamed.

Robert completed his romantic novel as the pencil wore down to a nub. The population of the prison rose and fell with each successive purge. In exhaustion, Robert laid on the floor. He pried a chip of wood from the bottom of a bed and wrote the final words with his pencil: "August 21, 1943. Gestapo, Metz, thirst, heat, lying on the floor, no air."

"Robert Müller!"

Robert's heart beat wildly as the guards led him up two flights of stairs. He was ordered to sit at a polished dining room table with his hands folded. Robert saw a reflection of his whiskered face in the glass door of a china cabinet. He tilted his head to get a better look at the beard.

An inspector sat down with a grunt and mechanically read a list of questions. Robert's answers seemed to be of no interest to him, although he was irritated by any answer that was longer than a sentence.

It was over in a few minutes. Robert was called back twice to answer the same questions during the following week. It was always the same bored interrogator. The depth of his weariness was amazing. *Perhaps the final outcome of Nazi aggression is terminal depression,* Robert thought. *At least I still cling to the hope that someday I will walk out of this prison with my humanity intact.*

Robert and Louis were transferred without explanation to Le Grand Seminaire, a former Catholic seminary. Robert began to suspect that Louis's father had bribed a German official so that he would accept their story. Their monastic cell seemed luxurious after the prison, but their only entertainment was the incessant search for uncommonly large gray lice.

A guard banged on their cell a week later.

"You're free to go."

There was no admonition, nothing about going back to school or staying out of trouble—no emotion whatsoever.

"See you in Heidelberg," they said outside the monastery, loud enough to be overheard. They knew they might never see each other again.

Louis headed to his parents' house in Metz while Robert walked down the wide avenue to the train station. It looked like a church from a distance. The Metz train station was a sprawling edifice built during the German occupation. Robert entered the building under five giant arches filled with stained glass windows. Enormous statues supported a vaulted tile ceiling; intricate bas-reliefs adorned the walls.

The train to Sarreguemines was scheduled to depart at half past eight. Robert bought a ticket and wandered through the lobby. If the station was a shrine to the Industrial Age, its abbey was the finest restaurant Robert had ever seen. He sat at the bar, ordered a bottle of amber-colored Alsatian beer, and slowly untwisted the cage on the ceramic cork. Then he experienced the most satisfying pleasure of his life. He wrote:

> To caress, to hold, and to gulp down with heavenly
> delight an enormous glass of ice-cold freshly drawn
> Alsatian beer, seeping through its egg-white collar of
> bittersweet foam, this is the apex of life. This is
> liberty.[108]

As the tension in his shoulders subsided, Robert wondered
why the beer tasted so good. Drinking beer was an ancient
rite of the Germanic tribes. Beer was their symbol of liberty.
Robert was raised to be a Frenchman by German-speaking
parents whose own parents had spoken French at home
while they were taught in school to think like Germans. It
hadn't crossed Robert's mind to order a bottle of French
wine for his celebration. Did that make him a German?

It was possible that the tribal rhythms beating inside his
cells dated back eleven hundred years to Charlemagne. The
Frankish emperor, who stood six-foot-four and wielded a
sword too heavy for most men to carry, forged France and
Germany into one land—Francia. Charlemagne (Charles I)
conquered, subdued, and governed Saxons, Aquitains,
Lombards, Spaniards, Bretons, Beneventans, Bavarians,
Slavs, Huns, and Danes for 47 years. Charlemagne's only
surviving son, Louis the Pious (Louis I), aspired to please
the Pope, who in turn preferred rulers who could keep their
subjects in line. Louis the Pious raised a set of quarrelling
sons who took after their grandfather. When they were not
busy fighting each other, his sons were ganging up on him.

In the last years of his life, Louis the Pious gave France
to Charles the Bald, Germany to Louis the German, and
Italy to his eldest son, Lothar. Louis the German cultivated
German literature as he consolidated his realm, giving
Germany a distinct cultural and political identity for the
first time.

After their father died, Louis the German and Charles
the Bald met in Strasbourg in 842 to partition Francia into
France and Germany, but Lothar wouldn't settle for Italy.
The deal fell apart and negotiations resumed. Resolved in
the year 844 by 120 commissioners, the Peace of Verdun
awarded France to Charles the Bald, Germany to Louis the

German, and gave a slice down the middle to Lothar. Charlemagne's realm disintegrated during the next generation under Louis the Young, Charles the Fat, and Louis the Stammerer, followed by Charles the Simple, Louis the Child, and Louis the Coward. Lothar's narrow kingdom in the middle acted as a buffer between France and Germany. Lacking natural boundaries or cultural identity, it became known as Lothar's kingdom, or Lotharingia, and would eventually be called *Lorraine*.[109]

Here we are, Robert thought, *heirs to the ancient empire of Charlemagne, and we are still fighting the same battles.*

Robert ordered another beer. He wondered if France and Germany would ever stop killing each other over Lorraine. He raised his glass to Charlemagne, the only man who had ever given Europe a taste of unity.

With his German cells flushed with a deliciously French feeling of liberty, Robert ventured out into the streets of Lorraine's capital to visit his uncle Marcel and tell him about the Gestapo prison and the escape of the *passeur*.

Strolling in the warm afternoon sunshine along Rue Serpenoise, Robert recognized a passing face—the man whose suitcase he had carried across the border. Robert followed him for several blocks as he quickened his pace and walked faster and faster until they both were running. He turned a corner and ducked into an apartment building.

Robert waited at the entrance for several minutes. When the man came out, Robert grabbed him by the shirt.

"What's going on here?" Robert shouted. "You're trying to avoid me, aren't you? I just got out of prison! Why aren't you in France?"

The man looked at him wildly. As soon as he recognized Robert, he relaxed.

"Perhaps I could explain," he said with a friendly smile. "You really scared me for a minute."

Robert released his grip.

"I don't feel like talking here. Let's find a place to sit."

"All right, why don't we go have a beer," Robert said. "And I want to know why you're still here."

They found a pub in the next block. The man told his story with disarming ease.

"My parents were sent to Metz from Germany in the 30's.

They raised me to be a Frenchman so that someday I could get a job as an undercover German agent."

The man talked about working for the Gestapo the same way Robert might talk about making hats.

"I pretended I was trying to escape when I went to the *passeur* for help," he said. "I stayed at the back of our group in the woods so that I could signal to the patrols with my flashlight, but the idiots never saw me. After I left you, I had to walk most of the way back to Metz to report your location. Our main objective was to arrest the *passeur*, and we got him a couple days later."

The man did not talk like a Nazi. He had an easy-going manner, probably the result of his French education.

"Why do you suppose they let us out?" Robert asked.

"I knew you weren't trying to escape—you had no reason to lie to me—so I put everything in my report. I'm glad they let you out. Is your friend okay?"

"Oh, sure. He's taking it easy until school starts. But we never got to see Paris, because of you."

"I wouldn't mind a little time in Paris," the man confided. "The women here are much too serious, don't you think?"

Robert felt a chill when he heard this. "I don't know, I suppose so. We just wanted to see the famous city." Robert extended his hand. "No hard feelings."

Robert paid for the beer.

"What a crazy world," he thought as he walked to the station. The train pulled out after dark, less visible to bombers. Robert wrote about confinement:

Man on this planet is always a prisoner of something. He is a prisoner of his time, his beliefs, his class, his possessions, his education, and his God. He is a prisoner of the atmosphere—a few minutes without oxygen will kill him. [110]

As the train rolled east and south to Sarreguemines, Robert drifted into a tumultuous sleep.

"You must go see Erwin Raiffenrat," his father insisted. "He still owes me a big favor."

The name of Erwin Raiffenrat had not been spoken in the Muller household for three years, ever since he had pulled up in a limousine and announced that he was the Vice-Gauleiter for Lorraine. Now Robert's father couldn't seem to say enough good things about him.

"Friendships are more important than borders," he said. "There always comes a time when you have to ask for help from your neighbors. Erwin's family was not so bad."

Robert's mother was wary, but she kept silent. If Robert could get to France, her relatives there would help him. Her family was in danger. If Robert were arrested again, the whole family would be deported to Poland and Robert would be sent in a prison regiment to the Russian front.

"Erwin Raiffenrat and I grew up in the same town," his father said. "We were always in the same class. His family never forgot how much my father helped them. He said he is living in a castle near Metz. You have to go see Erwin."

His mother perked up. "You can stay with my sister Marguerite."

Robert hesitated, but his father pressed him. "Go see Erwin tomorrow. There's nothing to worry about. All he can do is refuse."

The castle was close to Ancy-sur-Moselle, the village where Marguerite had lived with her husband, Alphonse, until he fled to France at the start of the war. Marguerite sat down with Robert and they shared a basket of fresh strawberries and yellow mirabelle plums from her garden. Then Robert told her the purpose of his visit.

"Raiffenrat is the worst Nazi in the world!" she said. "I wouldn't trust that *Boche* for a second. You are a fool if you see him, and so is your father. He will have you arrested, and that will be the end of you. I'm begging you, do not go."

Robert promised his aunt he would be extremely careful. She loaned him a bicycle for the short ride to the castle. The narrow road closely followed the border between Lorraine and France. Long strings of houses without windows bordered the street. In old times, counts and princes had levied a tax based on the number of windows and doors facing the street. As a result, people had built their kitchens and bedrooms in the back and piled manure heaps along the road. Robert was surprised how often the German police stopped him, but every time he told them he was going to see Raiffenrat, they clicked their heels and shouted, "Heil Hitler!"

The waiting room in the castle was adorned with antique tapestries, but they were hidden by blood-colored banners with Hitler's twisted cross. A loud party was underway in the next room. Robert peeked through a heavy curtain and watched the German army officers and Nazi officials with growing discomfort. Their bravado was crude and menacing as they congratulated each other with champagne toasts.

Raiffenrat finally staggered over to see Robert, who meekly reported that he was the son of Robert Muller, the hatmaker. "I'm spending my vacation with my aunt and she told me that you live nearby. My father wanted me to come by and say hello."

Raiffenrat indulged in Robert with a few questions about Robert's family and his studies. When he offered a glass of champagne, Robert shook his head and said his aunt would be worried if he did not get back quickly.

The return ride seemed longer. Robert felt depressed. Another option had evaporated, and now he realized how tightly the border was guarded. It was worse than he had imagined, yet birds darted freely back and forth across the border in the trees.

"There has to be a way to get across that line without being noticed," he thought. "I'm getting better at this business of outsmarting the Nazis."

His weariness lifted at Marguerite's cottage.

"I can't tell you how happy I am," she said after hearing his story. "Thank God you have better instincts than your father. I made some inquiries. I have friends who work for the railroad. They will take you across the border next Wednesday night on the train from Metz to Paris!"

"That's incredible!"

"They need a few days to make the arrangements."

She opened a bottle of mirabelle brandy, made from the plums in her garden. It tasted bold and sweet, like nectar.

"No more *passeurs*!" Robert said.

· · ·

Robert's family greeted him with grim faces. His father handed him a blue sheet of paper. Robert was ordered to report to the German Army at 6:00 a.m. on the following Monday—four days away. He read the notice carefully and sat in the living room in silence. He reminded himself that optimism could accomplish miracles, even in the worst circumstances.

"Do you still have that bottle of French champagne, Papa?"

"Yes, but why do you ask me that? Certainly you don't intend to celebrate your induction into the Nazi army?"

"Of course not. First I'll get rid of this notice and then we will celebrate."

"You are crazy," his father said, shaking his head. But he went down to the cellar to look for the champagne.

Robert walked down the steep hill and marched into the office of the Kommandantur. It was swarming with draftees. He demanded to see the official who had issued such a ridiculous notice.

"You people come here to Alsace-Lorraine," he said to the German official, his voice heating up. "You tell us how smartly you are going to run this country. That's all we ever hear about in school. What are we supposed to think of people who are so poorly organized that they send me this notice right before my final exams? I've killed myself to prepare for those tests. Is this what you mean by orderly administration? It's nothing but bad management. If you continue like this, you will alienate the entire population of this region!"

The officer stiffened. "It's not our fault if you don't keep us informed. How are we supposed to know everything? Sit down and wait your turn, like everyone else."

Robert shook his head with disgust.

"Next!" the German exploded.

Robert stood by the wall in the waiting room with his arms folded, glaring at the Germans behind the counter. Finally he was ushered into the office of the Kommandant, an enormous man in his late 50's.

Robert started to explain that he was studying law and economics in Heidelberg when the man interrupted him.

"I was a lawyer before the war and guess what! I studied

economics at Heidelberg! Who's the chairman of the Economics Department these days?"

"Professor Thoms," Robert replied.

"Walter Thoms? I had him. Very bright! Of course, he was just a professor in those days."

"He has certainly made a good impression on Adolph Hitler," Robert said.

"Oh, I didn't know. But of course, it makes sense."

Robert and the Kommandant talked casually about mutual professors. After a few minutes, Robert mentioned his situation. The Kommandant listened carefully, and then pondered his options before he spoke.

"I will consider withdrawing the draft notice as soon as I receive a letter from the University confirming the date of your exams."

"All right, but this is Thursday afternoon," Robert said. "It will never get here by Monday. What if they send it by telegram?"

"All right, as long as they confirm it with a letter."

Robert ran back up the hill. He gathered up every official document he had saved from the university and took off down the hill on his bicycle.

"Where are you going at this hour?" his father called out.

"Heidelberg!"

The northbound train was already chugging into the tunnel when he reached the overpass. Robert pedaled through downtown. When he passed St. Nicholas church, he shouted, "Life is a miracle!"

He raced past the old house in the Goldstrasse and pedaled as fast as he could on the shoulder of the road to Saarbrücken—an hour away. Trucks with no headlights almost knocked him into the bushes. He ran to the platform and caught the last train to Heidelberg.

On Friday morning, Robert went to the University office. He asked the clerk questions about classes and professors until she finally went into the back room to get a catalog. He reached over the counter and took a sheet of letterhead.

Returning to his hotel room, Robert composed a letter from Walter Thoms requesting that a telegram be sent to his student Robert Müller in Sarreguemines. Robert transferred the official seal from one of his documents to the letter, using a freshly cut potato. Another seal was transferred to a telegram form stating that final exams for Robert's master's degree would be given in mid-October.

The post office accepted the telegram without question.

Robert rode the train to Saarbrücken, pedaled his bicycle back to Sarreguemines, pushed it up the steep hill, and waited in the house for his telegram. "Why do you suppose it is taking so long," he asked his mother.

"In wartime, nothing is certain," she said. As the hours dragged on, she left him alone.

The telegram was delivered at ten minutes to five. Robert rushed into the Kommandant's office just before they locked the front door.

Robert's father was waiting on the front steps when he returned home.

"Champagne!" Robert shouted, waving a pink certificate.

His father read the certificate slowly. Robert's induction was postponed until the end of October. Shaking his head, his father took the bottle of Champagne from the mantle and released the cork, spilling champagne on the floor.

For the first time in a long time, his father laughed and laughed until tears were streaming down his cheeks.

October 4, 1943 was Robert's last day in Sarreguemines. The sky rumbled with the sound of heavy bombers flying towards Germany from England. Robert silently cheered the American pilots. He looked out the window and spotted a plane through the clouds, the bright glint of a distant bomber trailed by a flurry of glitter fanning out like a cloud. The heavy roar of the planes was drowned out by anti-aircraft fire from German installations all over town.

A few minutes later, thousands of leaflets fluttered to the ground with strips of aluminum foil dropped by the B-17s to scramble German radar. It reminded him of Christmas tree tinsel. The pamphlets announced that the Allies had landed in Sicily. It would only be a matter of time before they drove the Germans out of France.

As Robert went back to packing his belongings, he worried that the Kommandant might notice he was missing.

He would certainly find out at the end of October, when Robert failed to respond to his next draft notice. Hitler was desperate for manpower. When a draftee disappeared, his father was promptly arrested. If that happened, Robert would return and face the consequences, but it was something he could not discuss with his parents. They would never agree to that.

He heard the roar of the American bombers returning to Sarreguemines, but their engines were making the same heavy sound as before. A huge explosion knocked Robert to the floor. He scrambled for cover in the doorway. There were shouts downstairs, but the anti-aircraft guns drowned out everything but the sounds of bombs exploding. It seemed to go on forever, a riot of explosions and creaking timbers and shattering glass. After the explosions stopped, the wail of sirens gradually died down.

Thirty Boeing B-17 Flying Fortresses had dropped almost 100 incendiary bombs and 200 explosives. Most of the bombs landed on bridges and railroad tracks, but here were hundreds of casualties. The fish merchant ran by their house shouting the names of his wife and children. He found them crushed beneath a collapsed bridge, where they had run for cover. A bomb destroyed the house across the street and killed all the inhabitants, including the young German woman and her child.

"No one will feel safe any more," Léonie said. "When they hear sirens from now on, everybody will run into the fields."

Robert went upstairs to his room and closed the door. He looked across the river, turning the sorrow in his heart over and over while his mind kept repeating over and over—*war*.

Robert crouched in an oily trench next to a railroad track. Aunt Marguerite and Yvonne Antoine were hiding next to him. Yvonne's brothers worked together on the midnight shift as engineer and brakeman. It was half past one. The women giggled and whispered, then froze at the slightest sound. Robert was silent. He was dressed in oily clothes and his face was smeared with candle soot. They heard whistles coming from Novéant, a busy station where every train stopped for military and customs inspections. German soldiers shouted orders in the distance.

They waited for more than an hour. A locomotive slowed to a stop at the signal tower next to their hiding place. A man waved a kerosene lantern in a circular motion. Robert kissed the women goodbye and scampered up the gravel incline. Steam wheezed and hissed as Robert climbed the steep metal steps to the cab. He was thrilled to be on the monstrous machine.

With a slight nod, the engineer guided the locomotive back into the station. Coal burned in the firebox, flickering molten orange and white. Germans in uniform swarmed over a string of freight cars as the locomotive rolled into position. They tested doors, shouted, and scribbled on clipboards. The locomotive backed into the line of boxcars with an emphatic shove, sending a sharp jolt rippling down the length of the train that caused the soldiers to jump.

The engineer flashed an impish smile. The locomotive groaned as it pulled out of the station. After they picked up speed, Robert leaned his head out and felt the wind. He watched the black shapes of farms slide by in a lazy procession between the pale spokes of country roads. As the moon set, patches of stars appeared in the clouds.

The engineer tugged on a chord and the whistle sang his trademark tune. The engineer's brother raised a bottle of schnapps as the train raced across the border. Robert took out his harmonica and played to the rhythm of the train.

Uncle Alphonse had parked two blocks from the freight yard. He drove slowly, looking up and down each cross street at the intersections. It seemed to Robert they were driving in circles until they reached the edge of town and headed north.

"Are you afraid that somebody might be looking for me?" Robert finally asked, breaking the silence.

"You? No, no, they don't have any idea you're here. But the Germans are everywhere. They inspect all the trains; they stop cars on the road. You never know when they'll show up."

"I thought it might be a little easier here in France."

"Oh sure, it's better. They don't force the French to sign up for the army and wear German uniforms. That'll be the day! They don't expect children to speak German in school. Hitler is a big idiot but he's not a fool. They aren't stupid enough to think that they can control France, but they may try to split it up. It never works though. People don't forget."

Alphonse worked his way northeast on narrow country roads for two hours while Robert dozed. They finally stopped in Chauny, a town halfway from Paris to Belgium. Alphonse led Robert to a small shed behind a building—two rooms without a kitchen.

"Will I be safe here?" Robert asked.

"Here? No!" He laughed. "You can't even walk down the street without being stopped, and if they come up to the door—pfft! We will both disappear. Anyway, why would you want to stay here?"

"Well, I have to live someplace."

"There's nothing to do here. It's been over three years since the Nazis took over. They watch everything we do."

"What about Paris?" Robert asked. "I could go to Paris."

"No, you don't want Paris, but Vichy! There are plenty of jobs there, and the Germans are more restrained. They know better than to march around in the streets of Vichy, as long as they want to pretend that Vichy is the capital of a foreign country."

"What can I do there?" Robert asked.

"Fight the Germans! After the Americans landed in Africa and Hitler sent his troops into Vichy, thousands of people joined the Resistance. You speak German like a German and your French sounds like the French, and you've been to university. Fight with your mind, Robert! Guns are no way to win a war."

"My mother told me you were wounded in Verdun."

Alphonse thought about it for a minute.

"Not exactly. Over 300,000 men were killed in Verdun. To say I was *wounded* would not be right. I was shot in the hand all right—by another German soldier. He was a draftee from Alsace-Lorraine, just like me."

Tears welled up in his eyes and he paused a moment.

"We were hiding in a crater. After nine months of bombs

and machine guns, Verdun looked like the moon—that's what everybody said, but it was a lot worse. You don't have mud on the moon up to your chest, and it's not crawling with rats. The rats would crawl into the crater to see if you're dead. Do you know what they called it? *The mincing machine!* How would you like to wake up every morning and find yourself in the *mincing* machine?"

"No thanks," Robert said.

"Winter was coming back, the second winter in the Battle of Verdun. We all knew we were going to die. There wasn't any way a man could live through that. So I told him, this guy in the crater, I said, 'Shoot me! Go on, shoot me right here!'"

Alphonse pointed to a crimson starburst on his right hand.

"The guy just shakes his head, like I'm out of my mind, and then without even saying a word to me, he pulls the trigger. Now I'm lying there in this hot mud—it feels hot now—and I'm rolling around trying not to scream—God, it hurt! And I see this guy, he looks all blurry, and he's pointing *at his leg*!

"Now I'm supposed to shoot him in the leg with my left hand. I take two shots and I'm not even close, my hand is shaking so bad! You can't shoot a man in the leg with your left hand. I got him on the third shot, right below the knee. That was twenty-seven years ago...it was supposed to be the left hand...don't ever tell him to shoot you in the right hand. I wasn't thinking."

Alphonse stared at the scar on his hand, his lips moving.

"You did the right thing," Robert said.

"Maybe, maybe not. Maybe I was a big coward, Robert, but I didn't want to die in that mud and get eaten by rats. They said that General Henri-Philippe Pétain won the Battle of Verdun. They called him the Savior of Western Civilization, and then they built the Maginot Line—why? Because Pétain said they should!"

"And it was useless," Robert said.

"Now look at Pétain—he's a foolish old man who thinks he's a king, but he takes his orders from Hitler."

"But people still speak highly of him," Robert said. "They say he saved France from total disaster by talking to Hitler."

"He's a traitor!" Alphonse shouted. Then he smiled. "But you should go there anyway, Robert. Get a good job with Pétain's government. That's where you can do the most good."

"What can I do in Vichy? All I've ever done is make hats."

"You'll find a job. They're very sympathetic to refugees from Alsace-Lorraine. Your uncle Maurice will put you in contact with the Resistance in Vichy. If it doesn't work out, you can always go into the hills and join the *Maquis*."

"Why do they call it the *Maquis*?"

"It's a word for *wild, bushy land* in Corsica, and they're the guerrilla units in the Resistance. They get some help from de Gaulle, but they're mostly on their own. Oh, by the way, this is for you."

He handed Robert an engraved certificate. It was a birth certificate for a man named Louis Parizot.

"My sister sent it," Alphonse said. "She works in the City Clerk's office in St. Etienne."

Robert read the inscription. Louis Parizot was one day older than he was. He felt an eerie sensation reading somebody else's birth certificate and telling himself, *That's me.*

"This man, Louis Parizot, is he still alive?" Robert asked.

"She couldn't find any death certificate in the records." Alphonse said. "Ah, but who knows in this crazy war?"

Chapter 9 – The End to War

K eep calm," Robert said to himself. "It might just be an oversight." But he wasn't certain. There was no way he could tell and no one he could ask.

Robert Muller was known as *Louis Parizot* in Vichy. He worked for the French Ministry of Information on the second floor of the luxurious Hotel de Grignan. He was assigned to the French Communications Center, where radio transmissions from around the world were monitored and recorded for the Vichy government. He was an office worker with a monotonous job working for the increasingly repressive Vichy regime, but Robert secretly reported to a technical center for the French Resistance hidden in a wooded area outside of town. His life was anything but boring.

Through correspondence from his mother, Robert—he always signed his letters *Georgette*—learned that the jolly Kommandant in Sarreguemines had covered up his escape. If the Kommandant had reported the mix-up to Nazi officials, it would have cost him his job, and Robert's father would have been arrested.

Robert had just returned to his room after learning that André Royer, a friend at the University of Strasbourg, had been arrested. The room did not feel right, so he had examined all his possessions. A pair of socks in the top dresser drawer was facing the wrong way. It could have been an oversight on his part. He wasn't sure.

The next morning, Robert reported to work as usual. At ten o'clock, his secretary, Madeleine Grange, received a phone call from a guard at the entrance to the building. "Three gentlemen are here to see Louis Parizot on behalf of André Royer."

Robert's heart started racing. He instructed Madeleine to telephone Pierre's office down the hall as soon as the men arrived. Pierre was in the Resistance. When she called, she should ask for Louis Parizot.

Madeleine phoned Pierre a few minutes later.

"I am looking for Mr. Parizot. Three gentlemen from the *police* are here to see him." Her voice was unsteady.

"He's not here," Pierre answered.

Robert and Pierre heard a man with a heavy German accent yelling, "If you don't tell me where he is, I will have you shot!"

Robert fled to the attic of the hotel, where Pierre joined him a few minutes later.

"There are five or six men from the Gestapo in the building," Pierre said quickly. "They are searching all the offices, and they are not in any hurry. They seem to think they will find you, as long as they're patient and thorough."

"Germans are the most methodical people in the world," Robert said.

"The entrance is blocked. They have a prison van parked at the curb. I wish I knew what to tell you."

"If I climb out on the roof, they'll shoot me like a pigeon!" Robert said. "Maybe you could roll me up in one of those old carpets over there?"

"We can do that if you wish, but they will look there if they don't find you anywhere else."

"You're right," Robert said.

"I can't think of anything." Pierre lit a cigarette and smoked it nervously. His distress was not helping.

"That's all right," Robert said. "Go back to your office and act like nothing has happened. I'll figure something out. Leave me one of your cigarettes and the lighter."

Alone in the attic, his mind raced. *What can I do? What can I possibly do? If they see me on the roof—*

He tried to steer his mind away from the roof.

They were systematically searching offices—exactly—so that was...that was good! They were very relaxed because they knew Robert was in the building—fine! The entrance was blocked; that was fine too.

Why can't I see a logical way out? Because it doesn't exist, that's why! Everyone in the building has to do what they say and the Germans are taking their sweet time. I'm going to be arrested!

Robert took several deep breaths.

I must overcome my fear and think rationally, he decided. This was the moment of moments to be creative. What an opportunity, what a tremendous adventure—a 20-year-old student trapped by Nazis in a fancy hotel. *Won't it be great if I slip through their fingers?*

Robert tried to come up with something new.

How do Germans think?

He let his mind wander for a few minutes, feeling a growing sense of adventure.

"What is the one thing a Frenchman would do that a German would never expect?" he whispered.

Robert casually started down the stairs from the attic. His hair was slicked back with water, and parted down the middle. He was smoking a cigarette. On the fourth floor, he picked up a file folder on a desk in the hall and tucked it under his arm. On the third floor, he saw two Nazis with their backs to him, talking to someone. Then another office worker stepped into the hall and waited. They were ordering everybody out of their offices.

Robert continued walking towards the majestic staircase leading to the mezzanine. He took off his thick glasses and put them in his pocket. Everything dissolved into a seamless blur.

From the top of the wide marble staircase, Robert heard a loud murmur of voices. *My God, they've put everyone in the hall. What if one of the collaborators sees me!*

He took a puff on the cigarette.

Oh well, if they recognize me, they'll arrest me. So what? They were going to arrest me anyway! At least this way I have a chance!

Robert started down the staircase, carrying the file in one hand, the cigarette in the other. A crowd had assembled near the bottom of the stairs. He couldn't make out the faces. He took another step towards the bobbing images. There was a sudden hush. He took another step. Silence! His throat tightened; he took another step. They started talking again.

When he reached the bottom, Robert noticed a blurry cluster of shiny bald heads. He walked straight up to them.

A German was shaking Madeleine violently. Another was holding a photograph of Robert.

"What is going on here?" Robert demanded.

"These gentlemen are looking for Mr. Parizot," she said.

"Parizot? But I just saw him! He's on the fourth floor!"

"*Schnell hinauf!*" shouted one of the Germans. "Upstairs quickly!"

They charged up the staircase.

Robert shrugged. He waited on the mezzanine while the others returned to their desks. There was not a single nod of recognition from his co-workers. Taking his time, Robert wandered down to the hotel lobby. German soldiers were standing outside the front door. He asked the concierge to take him to the cellar. The man shook his head. Robert leaned closer and growled, "Right now!"

The man led him to a door inside the entrance to the kitchen and scurried back to his desk. At the bottom of the stairs, Robert found a row of bicycles. He picked one that still had air in the tires. A door led to an alley, where a fence enclosed the back of the hotel. He rode the bicycle down a driveway on the side of the hotel to the street and casually pedaled away from the prison van.

The Germans did not stop searching for Louis Parizot until they had looked under every desk, checked every closet, pried open the vents and unrolled the dusty carpets in the attic.

Robert was introduced to his "fiancée" three weeks later on a quiet street corner in St. Etienne. She was younger than he was, perhaps seventeen, and he noticed that she didn't smile when they were introduced, or when they shook hands. The girl listened intently to his voice when he mumbled hello. Her somber eyes studied every feature of his face as if it were a map.

"You have a strong chin," she said and walked away.

Robert shrugged. The man next to him was an officer in the *Maquis*, a fellow fugitive from Lorraine. Robert's uncle, Maurice Tonnellier, had introduced them after Robert showed up on his doorstep.

"Go back to your uncle and stay inside until I come," the man said.

While Robert waited at his uncle's apartment, he wrote a coded letter to his parents and signed it Georgette, as usual. It described a carefree adventure through the Loire Valley and ended with a promise to return home before the end of winter. The messages Robert sent to his family were filled with fictitious names and false clues. He never told them he was in the Resistance. Maurice promised to send the letter, but he seemed uncomfortable for reasons Robert could not fathom.

The officer arrived at Maurice's apartment before dawn. "You're going to visit your fiancée today," he said. There was a pick-up truck waiting for him on the street. He rode in the truck until afternoon, when the driver let him out at a railroad station in St. Bonnet le Chateau.

Robert was surprised to see members of the Resistance openly milling about at the station. They spoke with each other and mingled with others in civilian clothes. He stood alone and waited, feeling self-conscious. He was the only one who looked like a German. Finally, the girl appeared.

"Come with me," she said. He wished she would smile.

She led him over to a small group of men, and then walked away. That was how strangers were introduced in the Resistance, through an intermediary. Robert stood before a wiry, intense, short man who examined him from head to foot like a specimen. He had a strangely inquisitive face and seemed to be irritable. Robert felt transparent.

Robert thought he seemed like a scoundrel, but at least he was smart.

As Robert answered his questions, he became acutely aware that he was the only person in the group with blonde hair, and he still spoke with a German accent. The man gestured to Robert to go with another man in the group. As they walked away, he heard him say, "Keep a close eye on that one for a few days."

"Who was that?" Robert asked.

"You don't know who that is?" the man said, laughing. "That's Jean Marey. Always do exactly what he says."

After sunset, three Peugeots drove into the hills filled with men. Some wore uniforms and others were dressed as civilians. It was almost midnight when the cars suddenly stopped. Men with machine guns surrounded them.

"What's your mission?" a man shouted to the lead car.

Robert couldn't hear the reply, but after several minutes they were allowed to pass. Twice again they were stopped by gunmen during the night. About 5:00 a.m. they reached La Chapelle, a village high in the hills above the Loire River. The cars stopped at a farmhouse for a quick breakfast of wine, cheese, cold cutlets and cigarettes. Then a man led Robert up a steep path through the woods to a combat training camp.

For the first time in his life, Robert slept on the ground. His was told his name was Marco. They issued him a partial *Maquis* uniform—khaki pants, a khaki shirt, a belt, an armband, a Colt revolver, and a Sten submachine gun. No jacket or helmet. He kept his own boots. They showed him how to shoot and how to throw a grenade. They taught him how to kill a man in his sleep and how to die without confessing to the *Milice*.

No group was more hated by the Resistance than the *Milice*. The *Maquis* used a form of torture for interrogation introduced by the Gestapo in southern France. It was called *la baignoire*—the bathtub. With hands tied, a prisoner's head was held under water until he almost suffocated. The dunking was repeated until the prisoner confessed. The *Milice* retaliated with "the seesaw." After torture, a pair of prisoners would be hung by their necks from both ends of a suspended beam, their toes dangling a few inches from the ground. When one managed to touch the ground to relieve the pressure on his throat, the other started to strangle. To the amusement of their captors, it could take as long as half an hour for both victims to die.[111]

After completing combat training, Robert was assigned to Lieutenant Albert Oriol's unit. They were called *le G.M.O. 18*

Juin, the *Operational Mobile Group 18th of June*—a tribute to the first radio broadcast from London by General de Gaulle. Their hideout was La Chapelle.

On Robert's first outing, his unit stumbled upon a group of German soldiers. When the Germans saw the *Maquis,* they started shouting. The *Maquisards* raised their guns.

Robert waved his arms. "Stop!"

"What do you mean?" Oriol yelled. "Are you crazy?"

"Don't fire!"

The Germans waved their arms frantically as the *Maquisards* gripped their rifles tightly and waited for Oriol's order.

"Shut up, Marco!" Oriol said. "What are you doing?"

"These guys speak the worst German I've ever heard."

"Tell them to throw down their guns!" Oriol commanded.

Robert gave the order and they dropped their guns. Oriol and his men moved in cautiously, circling the soldiers while looking around to see if anyone was hiding in the bushes. There were eighteen men in German uniforms. They backed up against each other with their hands up.

"Check their weapons," Oriol said nervously.

"Hey, these guns are nothing but junk," a corporal said.

Their guns were old and broken, and they were not loaded. While the prisoners were searched, Robert pieced together their story, straining to understand their broken German.

"We'd better go see Marey," Oriol said.

Commandant Jean Marey had been an officer in the French army before Marshal Pétain dissolved it. De Gaulle put Marey in charge of several mobile Resistance units with a total of about a hundred men.

Robert translated for the leader of the captives.

"This is Colonel Gregory Trifonof," Robert said. "They are Russian soldiers. They were captured on the Eastern front and sent here so that they would not be tempted to escape. They were locked up at the military building in St-Etienne, but after the Allies landed in Italy, the Nazis put them in German uniforms and marched them around town so that it would look like the Germans are still in charge."

"What do they want?" Marey asked.

"He said his men are good soldiers. They fought hard in

"Marco" was Robert Muller's name in a combat unit of the French Resistance.

Stalingrad before they were captured."

After dinner, Marey summarily promoted Robert to the rank of Sergeant and placed him in charge of the Russian unit. Robert could barely fire a gun, but he was the only man in the camp who spoke German. Robert and the Russians were each issued a mound of hay for a bed and a potato sack for their belongings. They were quartered in a barn.

The following evening, Robert and his comrades gathered around the village fountain in La Chapelle. As Trifonof coached Robert, they sang Russian folk songs. A group of villagers gathered around them. They had never seen a Russian and were enchanted by the soulful melodies. Nuri Akshurin soon had everyone laughing at his antics while Robert acted as interpreter. Each time Robert asked him to repeat a word—his German was atrocious—Nuri shrugged and said, "But that should be clear to a hedgehog!"

When the Resistance could not get enough food from local farmers, they raided German warehouses or robbed French banks and businesses suspected of collaborating with the Germans. One unit got away with $400 million from a Banque de France armored car near Clermont-Ferrand. That record was broken by a *Maquis* train robbery in the town of Neuvic that netted nearly a billion dollars in gold.[112]

Because of Robert's training in economics, his unit spent many days counting money in a little school that was Marey's headquarters. Robert taught the Russians to speak French and they taught him Russian. When a radio signal was received from London, Robert's unit drove three trucks into a large field late in the night, parked them in a triangle and waited. When they heard the drone of a transport plane, they turned on the headlights. Sheet metal containers floated into view on parachutes. The heavy boxes were filled with arms and equipment.

On June 7, 1944, they found a note in one of the boxes. The Allies had landed in Normandy. One week later, they heard a radio broadcast describing a hero's welcome for Charles de Gaulle in the city of Bayeux in Normandy. It was de Gaulle's first encounter with the French people since he had become known the world over as the voice of France.[113]

. . .

An informer working for the *Milice* was captured near La Chapelle and brought to the schoolhouse for interrogation. Robert and his men were ordered to leave the building when the prisoner was brought in. He was a stocky man with a ruddy complexion—a typical middle-aged Frenchman.

After three days of torture, the Russian unit was ordered to escort the prisoner to a clearing in the forest. Robert barely recognized the prisoner when he stepped into the sunlight. His face was red, blue and green, his eyes and lips were swollen, and his shirt and pants were shredded and wet. He walked proudly past his neighbors in the village with his hands tied behind his back. He held his body erect. Halfway up the dirt road to the clearing, out of sight of the villagers, the man started to tremble. He cried and threw himself on the ground, pleading to be spared. Robert tried to comfort him, but he looked around wildly without hearing the words. The Russians tried to get him back on his feet, but he squirmed and kicked. They grabbed his feet and dragged him up the hill. The man clawed at the dirt with his fingers until his fingernails were gone. Then he tried to bite the ground, scraping the rocky earth with his teeth. He coughed violently as his lungs filled with dirt. Robert stepped gingerly over a broken tooth glimmering in the dirt.

At the clearing, they lifted the man to his feet. He walked a few steps, until he saw a freshly dug grave. His legs buckled. He rolled on the ground, sobbing like a child, and tucked his head between his legs. His pants were soaking wet. Suddenly he jumped to his feet and threw his arms up, shouting, "*Vive le Maquis! Sauvez-moi!*" At that instant, the guns fired and he fell in a heap.

Robert felt dizzy. He looked around at his comrades. The men seemed bored and indifferent, except for Nuri. He was scowling at Robert.

"You not good soldier, Marco," Nuri growled. "Too much good feelings."

Robert sat up late that night trying to comprehend what had happened. The man's physical and mental anguish had revealed a desolate component of human nature, one that

Robert had never imagined. He could understand that a man could be driven to such deep remorse and despair, but to die so wretched and alone, so utterly lost in desperation and terror—that was no way to leave the Earth.[114]

On August 15, 1944, an armada of 1,500 ships landed on the French Riviera between Toulon and Cannes. The French First Army marched up the Rhône Valley while the U.S. Seventh Army followed a parallel course along the foot of the Alps. As the Germans retreated up the Rhône Valley, the *Maquis* was ordered to slow down their retreat and prevent them from regrouping in Germany.

Commandant Marey assembled four *Maquis* groups near the village of Estivareilles to attack a column of German soldiers retreating from the city of Le Puy. Marey ordered his men to spread out on the edge of a forest overlooking the escape route. They obtained shovels from the local farmers and dug foxholes for hours. As the Germans marched up the valley, Marey's men opened fire. Hidden from view, they ran back and forth and shot from so many positions, it seemed as if they were a battalion. The Germans scattered. That night, the *Group 18ᵗʰ of June* slipped into Estivareilles before the Germans arrived and blew up the only bridge crossing the Loire River. After the Germans started building a temporary wooden bridge, Marey extended an offer to negotiate. The Germans finally agreed to surrender.

At dawn, Robert met a German soldier in the middle of the wooden bridge. The German handed over his weapons, including a heavy, ornate revolver.

"That looks like a special gun," Robert said. "Where did you get it?"

"I won it in a shooting contest in my home town in northern Germany."

"I'll take good care of it," Robert said.

Over 700 German soldiers were taken prisoner, captured by fewer than a hundred *Maquisards*. The Germans were furious when they realized their captors were so few in number. Among the Germans, a dozen French collaborators were identified who were trying to escape to Germany. The German prisoners were fenced off, but the French collaborators were tried as criminals. After a military tribunal in La Chapelle, six were sentenced to die. The other six were sent back to Le Puy for trial. Robert was ordered to assemble his unit to escort the prisoners to their execution.

The six prisoners walked with dignity through the village and started up the dirt road through the woods. A sweet-looking woman about twenty years old walked with them. Her name was Guichard Blanche, from Le Puy. She had fled from her beautiful city with the retreating Germans so that she could be with her husband, a young Frenchman who had been head of the *Milice* in Le Puy.

Her delicate features startled Robert. She had been spared the humiliating ritual of shaving the heads of women collaborators. Unlike the five condemned men, she had not been tortured or beaten. She walked silently in bare feet with her eyes fixed on the ground. Robert stopped to let her pass and watched her lips moving. He strained to hear her voice as he followed her up the hill. Her words brought back distant memories. He followed her haltingly, torn by ambivalent feelings. She was praying! The Latin words of the Ave Maria came back to him. "Hail Mary, full of grace," she said in Latin, "the Lord is with thee, serene Virgin..."

When they arrived at the freshly dug graves, the five men stood with pride and gazed at the horizon, but Guichard Blanche knelt in the moist soil, looking directly at the guns aimed towards them. She prayed loudly in a crystal-clear voice. "Hail, glorious one in all angelic virtues, whose Assumption was our glorification."

The condemned men suddenly shouted in unison, "*Vive la France!*"

An explosion of gunfire silenced their voices and stopped her prayer in mid-sentence. Her body was lifted into the air by the blow and landed in the grave.

Tears rolling down Robert's cheeks as he completed her prayer. "Oh, Mother of God, remember me."

That night, Robert couldn't sleep.[115] The devotion Robert had forsaken as a young child—drummed out of him by ridicule in the French schools—had been stirred by the spectacle of Guichard Blanche's prayer. Her deep faith had saved her dignity, even while fear and anger consumed the men standing with her who proudly defied death. She had managed to hold onto a vision that transcended mortal fear.

It was a better way to die, he decided.

As a German unit fled up the Rhône Valley, Robert's unit drove north to establish a new position in the town of Givors, ten miles south of Lyon. There was a hushed feeling of elation in the truck, a sense of impending liberation. Marshal Pétain had retreated to Germany. General de Gaulle was walking down the Champs Élysées in Paris through an enormous crowd.

De Gaulle described the experience in his memoirs:

> Huge crowds are massed on each side of the avenue. Perhaps two million people...As far as I can see, waves of humanity surge before me in the sun beneath the Tricolor.
>
> I go on, full of emotion yet undisturbed...through the storm of voices echoing my name...It is one of those miracles of the national feeling which mark our history down the centuries...We are one thought, one feeling, one voice together...And I in the midst of it all, I feel not a person but an instrument of Destiny. [116]

Robert's unit met up with a party of 30 *Maquis* recruits hiding in a ditch. They were waiting nervously for three trucks reported to be heading north filled with German soldiers.

Colonel Trifonof selected a position on a knoll with a clear view of the road. They set up a Russian 76-mm cannon, which they had captured from the Germans. Trifonof decided to operate the cannon himself.

Three trucks raced towards them. The eager recruits in the ditch opened fire too soon and the Germans stopped ahead of the trap. Trifonof fired the cannon and missed. He fired again and hit the lead truck. German soldiers clambered out of the wreckage and spread out across the fields, caught in a crossfire. They fired back wildly as they tried to run away. In minutes, all three trucks were burning and the bodies of Germans were scattered on the ground.

The _Maquisards_, flushed with adrenaline from their first battle, ran into the field and grabbed wallets, watches, gold rings, and anything of value. Robert wandered across the field in a daze, sickened by all the blood and the looting. Nuri tossed Robert a wallet and asked him to inspect it. Inside he found pictures of four children with a woman. Robert unfolded a letter from the woman to her husband. He sat next to the man's body. There was news about each of the children, a report that the village had been damaged and a brief account of how their neighbors were coping with the famine. The letter concluded with a prayer that God would end the war and bring him home safely.

Through tears, Robert looked at the man lying on the ground. His green uniform was soaked with blood around the stomach. The man did not have the face of a ferocious Aryan warrior. He looked like an ordinary father who had been in a hurry to get home to his family.

Robert became pale and started shaking. Nuri shook his head. "Marco, this is war. You could be dead instead of him. It is time you be real soldier."

Light drizzle was falling. Nuri picked up a can of lard, which German soldiers carried for quick energy. He opened it with a knife. Using his fingers, he gulped down the white fat with a satisfied grin, his eyes fixed on Robert. The air was rancid with the smell of blood. Black smoke billowed from the burning trucks and blew across the field, searing their lungs. Robert felt faint under Nuri's gaze.

The Russian put his foot on the dead man's belly, still licking the fat from his fingers, and stepped hard. Blood squirted out the holes in the uniform. Robert turned away and vomited.

Laughing, Nuri shouted, "Marco is not soldier!" He walked away in the drizzle.

Again their unit moved north. Robert sat wearily with the Russians as they rested in a meadow near Givors, waiting for orders. The weather turned warm and the sun came out. Finding a four-leaf clover, Robert turned his imagination loose to find an image of peace. The sound of bees and the fragrance of flowering clover lulled him to the edge of sleep.

A motorcycle pulled up and a courier shouted, "Sergeant Marco!"

"I'm Marco," Robert shouted.

"We stopped a Red Cross truck on the road to Lyon. The men inside were Germans, so we shot them. Marey wants you to read what's in the wallets."

Robert sat down wearily on the grass. He found more pictures of children and wives, more letters filled with hope that the war would end. There was only one difference. These men were officers. Robert was about to toss the wallets on the ground when he had an uneasy feeling. He opened each of the billfolds again. One had an inside lining. He carefully slit it open. Slipping his fingers between the cloth lining and the leather, he removed a thin piece of paper.

Robert's heart raced as he examined the Gothic handwriting.

"Take me to Commandant Marey."

The motorcycle rumbled to a stop and they were ordered to take cover. *Maquisards* were crouching behind trees and boulders with their rifles drawn. Marey gestured to Robert to drop to the ground. Keeping low, Robert maneuvered to Marey's side.

"We trapped about 20 Germans in that barn," Marey said. "They look like *Arbeitsdienst*—youth corps."

"So they're just kids," Robert said.

"Well, these kids are carrying guns. Speak to them in German. See if you can get them to surrender."

Marey handed a megaphone to Robert.

"Hello!" Robert said in German. "My name is Marco. Your officers lied to you about the *Maquis*. We are young men, just like you. We are trying to end the Nazi occupation of our country, that's all. If you surrender, we will keep you here for a few days. Then you can go home to your families. You have my promise. Why start fighting now and get killed for nothing? The war is almost over."

Slowly the boys emerged from their hiding place, blinking in the bright sunlight. As they were led away,

Robert was touched by how bewildered they looked.

Robert removed the slip of paper from the wallet and handed it to Marey.

"The Germans in the Red Cross truck were officers," Robert said. "This is their plan for Lyon."

Marey's eyes widened. He looked at the scrap of paper with wild anticipation, trying to make sense of the writing.

"The Germans are not going to defend Lyon," Robert said. "They are already retreating north to Belfort. They will leave behind a few platoons and two anti-aircraft guns in Lyon to fire at tanks. This paper lists all the bridges and the number of Germans stationed at each location. Can you believe it? There'll be nothing but snipers there when the Allies arrive, but they're going to blow up all the bridges."

"Does it say when?" Marey asked.

"Tonight!"

"We have to stop them," Marey said, turning to leave.

"Wait," Robert said. "The Americans will probably veer west and join the French to capture Lyon. If they keep going straight north, they might beat the Germans to the Belfort Gap."

Marey called for his radio.

"One more thing," Robert continued.

Marey glared at him.

"It says that the next information will be delivered on Thursday in Belfort in front of the main church. Let me go there. I look like a German and I speak perfect German."

"Forget it, too dangerous," Marey said. "Three German officers are dead. They'll know something is wrong. It would be suicide."

As dusk approached, Robert wandered into Givors. The French First Army had arrived and people were celebrating wildly. The modern arms and tanks of the French regulars made the Resistance equipment look preposterous.

A *Maquisard* stopped him. "Marey got into a big fight with General Brossolet at City Hall. They say it's real bad."

A few minutes later, Robert found Marey brooding in his makeshift office. "What's the matter?" Robert asked.

"The French general refuses to go to Lyon. He says he has orders to spend the night in Givors," Marey muttered.

Robert had never seen Marey so agitated. His eyes rolled as he stood up and sat down, then got up again and paced the room.

"I told the General that I don't give a damn about his orders," Marey shouted. "All he has to do is keep going a little further and he can save every bridge in Lyon. They're blowing them up right now!"

Marey pounded the table and kicked the chair.

"He kept telling me, 'I have my orders.' I told him, 'You can get new orders.' I told him that we'd do it ourselves, that I would take my men to Lyon. We can get there in 20 minutes. It will take years to rebuild those bridges. He told me to stay out of Lyon. 'The French Army is in charge,' he said. That's when I let the bastard have it."

"You hit a general?" Robert asked.

"I slapped him." Marey slumped in his chair.

It was over for Marey. Robert felt sorry for him. He had made so many smart decisions in the chaos of battle, but now his nerves were shot. Marey was finished.

Robert spoke quietly. "I would like your permission to take Colonel Trifonof and drive towards Lyon in the truck with the loudspeaker."

Marey shrugged. "Do whatever you want. I don't care. What difference does it make?"

It was dark when Robert and Trifonof headed north out of Givors. People were celebrating in the streets. Thundering explosions rolled across the sky from Lyon. In village after village, Robert appealed for German soldiers to surrender over the loudspeaker, but they were already gone. Villagers found one German soldier hiding in a barn. Muller and Trifonof put him between them in the front seat of the truck and continued north.

At dawn, a great column of armored cars overtook them as the French First Army streamed towards Lyon from Givors. Trifonof tucked their battered truck between two French tanks and joined the column as they entered the outskirts of Lyon. Thousands of people flooded around them on all sides, embracing the soldiers and showering them with flowers. Robert and Trifonof were swept along in the celebration. Young women reached inside the truck, grabbing and kissing them hysterically. Even the German prisoner was overwhelmed with emotion and cried like a child.

A barrage of gunshots ripped into the buildings over the crowd. Robert traced the sharp explosions to a hospital in the old section of Lyon across the river. People screamed and dove for cover as German snipers or Vichy militiamen fired from the highest attics with long-range rifles. People scattered in every direction and ran inside buildings and hid in the alleys. Soon the crowd was gone and only the armored column remained. A small contingent of American troops approached the city from the other side of the Rhône.

Robert and Trifonof turned their prisoner over to the local militia. Twenty-seven bridges had been destroyed during the night.[117] Only the Wilson Bridge was still standing, saved by Resistance fighters. Robert parked by the Wilson Bridge and they waited for their comrades, smoking cigarettes and talking in German.

Robert felt a gun press against the back of his head.

"Haut les mains!" several young voices shouted.

Local underground fighters had watched them speaking in German for several minutes. They were marched to a police station, where Robert explained that he was from Alsace-Lorraine and he only *looked* like a German. By the time the police let them go, it was nighttime. The French First Army streamed across the Wilson Bridge into Lyon.

Their *Maquis* unit was nowhere in sight, so Robert and Trifonof returned to Givors. Robert saw Marey sitting alone in his dark office. He felt a chill in the camp. Nuri motioned for Robert to join him outside.

"We were ordered to stay in Givors. Marey lost his roof. He ordered us to march the prisoners up the road and line them up against the cemetery wall. A priest got between us. We had to drag him out of the way. That's when we shot those boys."

Robert could not believe it. "All of them are gone?"

"All dead."

Robert started breathing in quick gasps. Pressure squeezed his head. Anger exploded into a raging fury as he crashed through Marey's door.

"What is this insane story they're telling me?"

Marey looked at him wearily.

"I talked to those boys," Robert shouted. "I promised we wouldn't hurt them. They were just children. They look like me—we speak the same language. They all have mothers, just like me...like you. They have their own dreams. What madness has gotten into you? Who gives you the power to take the lives of those boys?"

Marey closed his eyes.

"Answer me!" Robert cried. "Can you?"

"We were getting reports that the Nazis were evacuating prisoners from Fort Monluc in Lyon, but we didn't know where that butcher, Klaus Barbie, was taking them."

Marey spoke in a low, hoarse voice. Robert could barely hear him.

"Some peasants came to see me. They saw a big wooden building on fire just before we arrived here, and they asked me to take a look. There were dozens of bodies in there. Some of them, their feet and hands were tied with barbed wire. Others had nails in their jaws. The Nazis threw cans of gasoline on those people and burned them alive. Do you know anything about Monluc?"

"No one ever comes out alive."

"Unless they turn into collaborators. Klaus Barbie is a monster. When I returned, I assembled your young Nazis and told them what their compatriots had done."

"They were boys! They weren't like Barbie," Robert said.

"Don't worry about those *boys*. They were arrogant to the end—they almost looked happy they would be sacrificed for their insane Führer and the fatherland. The master race..."

He spat on the ground.

Robert walked blindly out of the camp and up a hill, past the tall cemetery wall into a field. In the impassive gray light of the full moon, a hundred stone crosses peered over the cemetery wall at him like frozen sentries. He stomped and kicked his boots against the ground.

The whole world had become a madhouse—all the blood he had seen, soaking into the dirt, fathers who were tortured, daughters humiliated to their last breath, sons who would never be found—not even a stick to mark their graves. Yesterday those boys were alive, trusting Robert and throwing their guns down. Their hopes and dreams were alive; their hearts were beating, their mothers were waiting and their fathers, who wanted to be proud—all their hopes gone for all eternity.

A terrifying guilt seized Robert. He wanted to take back what he had said to the boys, to tell them something different, tell them...tell Marey...

"My God, what have I done?" he shouted and collapsed in the tall grass. The ground absorbed his tears. His chest heaved. It ached so much he wanted to scream. It was the end. He was too tired to fight any more. No more...no more.

An immense determination seized him. Robert glared at the moon. He searched furiously through the stars for any sort of answer to the questions that were forming, questions that raged against the sky and raced through the stars and burned a hole in the black void.

Then he noticed the emptiness was shimmering. The black void was filled with light.

Gripping his rifle, Robert pulled himself up to his feet. His legs were wobbly.

"I swear to God," he sobbed, and then he shouted, "I swear to God...I will spend the rest of my life...working for peace...in this wretched world."

His legs couldn't hold his weight. The grass folded under his body and he closed his eyes and slept for two or three hours, until the moon had disappeared and the first light of dawn stirred him awake.

Gazing toward the pale blue horizon, Robert watched the hills come into view. The valley was quiet. The war had moved on.

Robert felt like a new man.

A few days later, General Charles de Gaulle paid a visit to the region. Huge crowds welcomed him in Lyon.

For the benefit of Russia, England, and the United States, he said, "The hope of France lies in her greatness; that is to say, the right of occupying her place among the greatest, a right she has had for more than 2,000 years.

She has not forfeited this right."[118]

Leaders of seven Resistance groups in Paris had announced to a stadium crowd the previous day that they would continue their activity even though liberation had been achieved. De Gaulle's message for them was stern—the days of guerrilla fighting were over and the Resistance would not play a political role in the future of France.[119] He would not tolerate insurrection. When told that a Resistance leader admitted to conducting trials and executions, de Gaulle dispatched an investigator from Paris.

On his tour of the Lyon region, de Gaulle inspected Resistance groups, sometimes allowing them to stand rigidly at attention in the hot sun while he chatted, seeming to be unaware of their discomfort—which was not his usual treatment of men in uniform. During one inspection, de Gaulle walked past a line of youthful colonels with their officer's bars sewn neatly on their sleeves. At the end of the line, he came to a solitary private. De Gaulle stopped and looked him up and down. [120]

"What's the matter with you?" he said. "Can't you sew?"

A new France was emerging from war. The Resistance was finished.

It was time for Robert to go home.

Chapter 10 – Victory

L ookin' for a ride, kid? Hey, d'ya know any back roads outta here?"

The American soldier looked around to see if anyone was watching. Robert had picked up some English, but this was not a dialect he had ever heard. *Roads*—the soldier said something about roads.

"Pardon?" Robert said.

"Back roads! Saar-gwa-mean!" he said slowly.

"Sarreguemines! Yes, I go to Sarreguemines!"

"Back roads!" the American repeated. "No roadblocks."

"No roadblocks. Good, I show you no roadblocks. I know this area like my pocket," Robert said in his best English.

"Your pocket, huh? Okay, hop in kid. I'm in a big hurry."

Robert shoved his duffel bag behind the passenger seat of the American jeep and climbed in. The bag was full of bread and sausages for his family. Back when he was a teenager riding through the countryside on a girl's bike, he had found more than one way to get back and forth between Sarralbe and Sarreguemines without being seen. He pointed to a muddy road that disappeared behind a barn. The jeep took off so fast he almost fell out.

Robert was weary and the air was cold in the open jeep, but it was New Year's Eve, 1944, and his luck had finally changed. He had been stuck in Sarralbe for weeks trying to get through the roadblocks set up by the Americans. His grandfather was still rebuilding the living quarters at the factory, so Robert had stayed with his uncle, René Muller. They slept every night in a bunker built by the Germans next to the Solvay nitrate factory. Robert hadn't slept well in a week. German warplanes flew over Sarralbe all day long and Big Bertha lobbed shells into the town at night. It was hard enough to sleep in a crowded bunker without being blasted awake every 15 minutes by a ton of explosives screaming through the air and blowing up four or five houses. It was Metz all over again five years later, and there was no getting used to that scream.

"Are you with General Patton?" Robert asked the soldier.

"Patton's in Bastogne now. Helluva mess up there."

"I was born in Malmédy. Is there heavy fighting there?"

"Put it this way kid, there won't be a tree left standing in Bastogne when Patton's finished. General Alexander Patch is in charge around here. I'm with the Seventh Army, thank the Lord! General Patton is Commander of the Third."

"Why is it so hard to get through?" Robert asked.

"Got to keep the roads open. There are about 30,000 refugees in Lorraine—Russians, Poles, Slavs—slave labor from the mills and mines.[121] None of them speak the language, and there's a big risk of typhus, so that's why there's a stand fast order."

The jeep swerved around an unexploded shell and almost sank in a mud hole. Robert grabbed the windshield as the jeep stopped. "Keep an eye out, kid. We're in enemy territory."

"I heard the Americans were already across the river," Robert said. "

"We thought we had it nailed down for a few days but the Krauts keep coming back. Why do you want to go there?"

"My parents live in Sarreguemines with my sister."

"Aw geez, that's tough. A lot of people are hiding in the cellars. If you don't find them, you might try the caves. Say, do you know how to shoot?"

"I was in the Resistance."

"Pick up that gun, will you, and keep an eye out."

"Watch out!" Robert shouted.

They crashed through a wooden gate and skidded into a field of trampled wheat. Hundreds of tank tracks pointed the way to Sarreguemines.

American and British planes had bombed Sarreguemines for months, because of its importance as a rail center at the confluence of two rivers along the border.[122] Robert saw buildings everywhere with gaping holes and collapsed roofs. The railroad yard was nothing but black craters and twisted steel. When the jeep finally reached the top of the hill, Robert almost cried for joy. Their house was standing. It hadn't been seriously damaged.

As the jeep drove off, Robert stood in the gloomy winter light watching for some sign of movement inside. The windows were lifeless and the steps had not been swept. All the houses looked abandoned. Even the fortified entrance to the prison across the street was standing open.

Robert heard a burst of machine gun fire down the hill. He found the front door was locked, but the spare key was still hidden under the step. Inside the hall, he listened for a moment until his eyes adjusted to the darkness—not a sound. Then he recognized a portrait of Charles de Gaulle hanging a few inches in front of his nose in the dim light, where Hitler used to hang. Robert lifted it off the hook and turned it around. On the back was the ugly poster of Hitler. He laughed so hard he dropped the frame on the floor.

Voices whispered in the basement.

"Is anybody there?" he shouted.

"Robert?" his father said.

"Papa!"

The door opened. They embraced and wept. Robert's father yanked him inside and barricaded the door. At the bottom of the steps, Robert was smothered with hugs and kisses. Marcelle stood nearby, trembling.

"What's wrong?" Robert asked.

She tried to speak, but she kept sobbing. He took her hands. Finally she said, "It's been awful. I didn't think we would ever see you."

"Look at me, I'm fine. I never even got shot. Just this hole in my shirt."

They took turns poking their fingers through the hole.

The Mullers' house was only slightly damaged after four weeks of fierce fighting when Robert returned to Sarreguemines on December 31, 1944.

"Thank God we're all together again!" Léonie said.

"I heard that people are hiding in the caves," Robert said.

"It must be hard for the people down there," Robert's father said, "but with all the bombing and the shooting, it would have been a big mess if everybody had stayed in their houses."

"You're okay, Papa!"

"Sure, I'm fine."

"When Papa was across the street, Mama took him dinner every night," Marcelle said.

Léonie's eyes rolled.

"In prison?" Robert said. "You were arrested? Mama, you didn't tell me he was arrested."

"So what?" his mother said. "If I had told you, you would have come home."

"Exactly!"

"And gotten us all in trouble," his father said. "But it wasn't so bad. Your mother talked to the guard—"

"The assistant warden was a friend of mine," she said.

"—and they let her bring me a hot meal every day, and when I stood on the bench, I could wave to Marcelle across the street."

"You still should have told me," Robert said.

"And I suppose you just forgot to mention in your letters that you had joined the Resistance?" Léonie said.

"I didn't want you to worry. How did Papa get out?"

"The Americans were on their way here," Robert's mother said. "The Germans panicked and took off across the river, and before they could get organized, some people called the prisons and told the wardens to let the prisoners out. They said it was on Hitler's orders."

"And they let everybody go?"

"We walked right out the front door," Robert's father said. "But the Americans stopped in Nancy."

"I heard that they ran out of gas," Robert said.

"Either that or it was the mud. We've had nothing but rain since the summer. When Hitler found out the Germans ran away and they let the prisoners out, he went crazy and ordered Gauleiter Bürckel to take his own life."

"He refused, of course," Robert said. "Hitler is finished."

"You want to know something? Bürckel killed himself."

"That's crazy," Robert said.

Robert's father opened the last bottle of wine and Léonie cooked an elaborate dinner in the laundry room.

"I'm surprised there aren't any Americans staying here," Robert said, half joking.

"Oh, they came, all right, about three weeks ago," Léonie said. "A whole group of officers asked if I would let the general use our house as his headquarters. I said, 'Of course not! I'm here alone with my daughter and it would not be proper.' They saluted me and left! It was about time I met a real gentleman in this bloody war."

"Did they mention the general's name?" Robert asked.

"They said it was Patton."

"What! You turned down General Patton? Do you know who he is?"

"I don't really care who General Patton is. I'm tired of all these generals. We had a French general here, and he was going to win the war. Then a group of German soldiers moved in. They all think they have to sleep in this house."

"But Patton is famous. You could have put a plaque on the house that said *General Patton slept here*."

"I'll tell you what. When this war is over, you can put up a plaque that says General Patton did *not* sleep here."

While his mother made dinner, Robert looked around.

"What's this?" he asked, pointing to a German bazooka against the wall.

"Oh, it's nothing," Léonie said. "A soldier left it."

"No German soldier in his right mind would forget this. He would have to account for it."

"When the Germans retreated," Léonie explained, "they left behind a few soldiers to shoot at American tanks. When I saw a soldier hiding behind our garden wall, I was furious. After all this, why should our house be destroyed at the last minute? I went outside to make him leave, but it was so cold out that I invited him in for a cup of hot coffee. Then I offered him some schnapps."

"*My* schnapps!" Robert's father complained, playfully.

"So I asked him to tell me about his mother. I said, 'What is the point of risking your life now? Your officers are all safe across the river. Do they really think you can stop the Americans with that gun?' Then I told him about you, and how hard it was to be a mother in the war. I said, 'What am I going to do when I discover your dead body in my garden? Am I supposed to go to Germany and find your mother and tell her what a great hero you were so that we can both cry together? She'll want to know why I didn't stop you.' "

"What did he do?" Robert said, laughing.

"He kissed me on the cheek. Then he thanked me on behalf of his mother and he asked for some more schnapps, and then he went home. I don't think he even knew how to shoot that gun."

"He was just a boy," Robert's father said.

"You probably saved his life," Robert said.

"Then the Americans showed up with one tank," Robert's father said. "Just one tank! They must have gotten lost or mixed up or something. But the tank got here on December 6—St. Nicholas Day. Since he's our patron saint, everyone thought it was a good omen."

"So the whole town surrounded the tank and cheered and yelled," Marcelle said. "We didn't want them to leave."

"Those two colonels looked pretty worried until the other Americans showed up," Robert's father said.

"Is anyone hungry?" Léonie asked. "I've made you a nice dinner."

They celebrated in the soft lamplight with smiles and quiet toasts. Robert watched his father's face relax. He lifted a glass and said with a sweeping gesture, "After the war, everybody will need new hats. You and I will be quite busy. Maybe we can find a bigger shop."

"I'm not sure, Papa."

"Sure about what?"

"I've been thinking about taking up a new profession."

Robert's father looked at him expectantly, waiting for the punch line. "There is no better profession in the world than making hats, I can tell you that." He looked at Léonie and shrugged. "Okay, maybe a doctor is *almost* as good. So if you want to be a doctor..."

"I want to work for peace, Papa," Robert said quietly.

"Work for whom?" his father asked.

"I want to be a peacemaker."

"I have never heard of such a profession. Who is going to pay for a thing like that? Do you see any future in it?"

"There has to be a way, Papa. We can't keep getting into bigger wars and killing more people."

"There has always been war, and somehow we always make it through." He got up impatiently and paced in a circle. "But we don't need to figure this out now. We can talk about it later."

"We're all tired," Léonie said. "Let's try to get some sleep. Our son has come home from the war."

Robert studied their precious faces in the orange light. He saw changes—creases around the eyes, more roundness to their posture, and everyone was thin.

Fatigue finally caught up with Robert and he curled up on a bed in a corner of the cellar. In what seemed like less than a minute, Robert awoke to machine gun fire. The ground trembled with an explosion. He sat up. His mother was sitting by a candle watching him.

"Did I make too much noise?" Robert asked.

"It's okay, son," she said softly, as if he were a little boy. "It has been like this every night for the past few days. It's going to be all right now. The worst is over...just a few more days. You can go back to sleep."

The Germans took over the city during the night, but they were driven back in the morning. The Mullers celebrated New Year's Day in the cellar listening to heavy aircraft overhead. Hitler deployed 800 planes that day to bomb airfields in France, Belgium, and Holland.[123] The next day, Germans tried to blow up the only remaining bridge over the Sarre, but Resistance fighters drove them back. There was nothing for Robert's family to do but wait in the basement while the war passed over their heads. There was no news and it was never safe to go out.

"This talk about peace," Robert's father said, "will you do it on the weekends when you're not working, or at night?"

"I don't know how to go about it. I may become a lawyer."

"What? Do you want to be a poor lawyer all your life?"

"If I were a lawyer, then I could go into politics."

"You're a hatmaker's son!"

" Daladier was the son of a baker."

"Yes, and look what happened to him. They threw him out! You have to build up a business first. Then people will respect you and you can branch out, if you like."

"I am already a hatmaker."

"Yes, of course you are," his father laughed, "but I still have a few things I could teach you—if you weren't always in your books!"

"Keep your voices down," Léonie said.

"Why keep my voice down? He's talking nonsense."

"There could be Germans outside. Do you want them to come down here?"

"They have better things to do than to crawl around in people's basements," Robert's father mumbled.

They remained trapped in the basement while their food supply dwindled. The shooting finally stopped on January 20 when Americans troops entered Sarreguemines for the last time. Thousands of people walked out of the Caves of Welferding into the hazy sunlight on a gray winter morning. They talked about surviving underground, how babies were born, people died and were given a decent burial, surgeries were performed, collective kitchens prepared the food, and some merchants even built wooden platforms to keep their families off the ground.[124]

A few days after the Mullers moved upstairs, Ervin Raiffenrat's brother-in-law came to the door. Robert stood next to his father in the doorway.

"Ervin is in town," the man said, "and he needs a place to stay for a couple of days. He told me that perhaps you could help."

"Erwin is in town?" Robert's father said.

"He is fleeing from the Americans. My house obviously wouldn't be safe."

Robert's father shifted his weight from one foot to the other. "A couple of days, that's all?"

"Not even that, probably. Maybe just for one night."

Robert's father put a hand in his pocket and turned to look at Robert. He rubbed his brow and looked up at the ceiling. Then he mumbled, "To hell with him."

"What?"

"To hell with him!" Robert's father shouted. "We suffered enough from the Germans."

"Then you...*you* are refusing him?"

"The answer is no! You can tell Erwin he should be glad I don't report him to the Americans."

The man clenched his teeth. Robert's father didn't wait for a response. He closed the door and put his arm around Robert's shoulder. "To hell with them all," he said.

In February 1945, Franklin Delano Roosevelt, Winston Churchill, and Joseph Stalin met in the Russian resort of Yalta. Charles De Gaulle was not invited. With the Red Army in control of Poland, Churchill and Roosevelt conceded that the provisional government dominated by the Communist party would govern Poland. Churchill persuaded Roosevelt to give France equal standing when the Big Three occupied Germany, then Roosevelt sold the idea to Stalin. As the meeting drew to a close, Roosevelt sent a message to de Gaulle in Algiers suggesting a meeting during a stopover on his way home. De Gaulle refused. He did not want to give the impression that France endorsed the deal made in Yalta with respect to Poland.[125]

Two days after Yalta, British and American bombers pulverized the fairy-tale city of Dresden. In a quiet city of ornate spires and cobblestone streets having no military significance, 175,000 homes were destroyed and 135,000 people perished. It was the worst firestorm of the war.[126]

By March 15, all the villages around Sarreguemines were cleared of German soldiers. The Sarre Territory was in Allied hands a week later.

As the weeks passed, news trickled in about family and friends. Jules Frank had died in a concentration camp two years after he drove Léonie and the children to Lutzelbourg. All of Robert's relatives returned home, except for Léonie's brother Emile, who was missing in Poland.

A government agency required all residents to report any plunder abandoned by the fleeing Germans. Robert's parents reported the intricate Czechoslovakian furniture left behind by Karl Beitz. The agency set a price, the Mullers bought the furniture, and the money was deposited in a government account.

Robert read the newspaper at night after dinner in the kitchen. Léonie rarely glanced at it. She was content to bring the house back to order, hunt for fresh produce and fruit at the market, and cook an occasional fish.

"Why do you hold the paper like that?" she asked him.

"Like what?"

"Like you might devour it at any minute."

"I'm looking for signs that we will have peace someday."

"Hitler is dead and the Germans are finished. What more do you expect?"

"I read about a meeting in San Francisco, where they drafted a charter for the United Nations."

"We had the League of Nations and look how much good that did," his mother said, her voice suddenly harsh.

"But the Americans are in favor of the UN," Robert said.

"The League of Nations was President Wilson's idea."

"Maybe the Americans learned from Wilson's mistake."

"There is always hope," Robert's father said, "and then there is always war. They take turns, but our job is to live."

"In the first World War, ten million people were killed," Robert said. "This time, it could be over fifty million—more than all the people who live in France. Next time we have a world war, we could destroy every person on Earth. It has to stop somewhere."

"All right," Robert's father said, "if you want to make peace, that's fine. You can make peace *and* make hats."

"I don't know, Papa. I saw something in Paris when I was coming home. The women were getting their hair curled with chemicals—they called it a 'permanent.' They won't want to cover their hair with a hat and squish it down."

"Stop wearing hats because of a chemical?" his father laughed. "I don't believe it, but I can tell you this! There's no future in peace!"

"There's no future in hats!"

"Nonsense."

"I have made my decision. I am going be a lawyer."

"Do you want to know what will happen?" Robert's father said. "You will starve! How do you expect to raise a family if you're a poor lawyer? You will have to marry some rich girl just to put food on the table!"

Robert's father looked helplessly at Léonie. She sat down

and took his hand.

"Four generations of hatmakers..." he said.

Her eyes were filled with tears, but there was no regret.

The year 1945 was not a banner year for lawyers in France. Over 10,000 French people were accused of collaborating with the enemy and executed without any legal proceedings during "The Purge."[127] Trials could be chillingly swift, as in the case of Paul Ferdonnet, the radio announcer known as the "traitor of Stuttgart." Ferdonnet was tried, convicted, and sentenced to death in a trial lasting only ten minutes. Trials could also be painfully slow, as in the matter of Henri Philippe Pétain.

Huge headlines announced the start of Pétain's trial on July 23, 1945, before the High Court in the First Chamber of the Court of Appeal in the Palace of Justice. The prisoner and his wife were housed in the judges' cloakroom, where two hospital beds had been installed. The President of the High Court of Justice wore a heavy black and red cloak trimmed with squirrel fur for the opening day, despite the suffocating heat. He looked down at his former commander and said, "Accused, stand up."

Pétain turned pale as he rose, holding himself erect as he faced the three familiar faces on the bench.

"State your surname, Christian name, age, occupation."

"Pétain, Philippe, Marshal of France," he said. They knew he was 88.

The clerk read the indictment. Pétain "had committed crimes against the internal security of the state," and "had dealings with the enemy with a view to promoting their enterprises in conjunction with his own."[128]

Marshal Pétain, fallen savior, was charged with treason.

Robert kept a wary eye on the trial from Strasbourg, where he had moved at the beginning of summer so that he would not miss the first opportunity to get into law school when classes resumed.

Robert's uncle, Alphonse Lechner, was an accountant at Radio Strasbourg, the biggest radio station in Alsace-Lorraine. Robert got a job as his assistant. The sound booths for the entertainment shows were in the same building as the business offices, so the halls were teeming with characters. Announcers and guests were always coming and going, but the news department was located with the engineers in a separate building outside of the city, so Robert had no contact with reporters covering the trial.

Pétain was a symbol of the French nation. Throughout Robert's life, the Marshal's distinguished face had appeared in newspapers. He had ruled Vichy France with popular support. The presiding judge at Pétain's trial had enforced the laws of Vichy without raising objections during the Occupation. The judge sitting on his right was an old family friend of the Pétains, and the judge on his left had sworn an oath of loyalty to the accused.

Robert read a lyric description of Pétain's expression in the *France-Soir: a sort of abstract sorrow not addressed to mankind, and bound up with glory, fate and country, the great symbols whose weight this old man bears.*

It seemed to Robert that the trial was a sad reenactment of an old French melodrama. The trial was the ritual beheading of a King.

Robert discussed the trial with his cousin Eugene when they got together to trade stories about the war. Eugene Schneider had been attending German engineering school when he was drafted into the German army. Wounded in Stalingrad, he was evacuated on the last plane to get out before the Nazis were defeated there in 1943.

"Is Pétain's trial supposed to purge France from its pent-up disappointment and guilt?" Robert asked.

"They have to blame somebody," Eugene said.

"The Armistice allowed millions of refugees to go home," Robert said. "It gave the Resistance time to organize. I was with the Resistance in Vichy and we were very active. Both the U.S. and the Soviets had embassies there; England maintained diplomatic relations with Vichy.[129] It was not a renegade government."

"I was in Stalingrad, Robert. Hitler sent a million men there. If the Russians had decided not to fight us, Hitler would have won the war. The Russians lost 100,000 men in Stalingrad, but they didn't give up. The Germans lost three times that many. I'm lucky I wasn't one of them."[130]

"Pétain accepted defeat, but he prevented annihilation. I guess it may be important that he was never really chosen by the people. Even Hitler won an election when he first came into power. Pétain was more of a king than an elected official."

"I don't see why you are concerned about Pétain anyway. I thought you were with de Gaulle."

"Yes, I'm in favor of de Gaulle," Robert said. "It's an interesting name, de Gaulle, don't you think—*of Gaul*. This fighting goes all the way back to Gaul, doesn't it—ever since the Romans. We have to stop these wars before it's too late."

"You have big ideas. I just want to get on with my life."

Churchill, Stalin, and Harry Truman met in Potsdam in the final week of July, again without inviting de Gaulle to the table. Truman found himself in treacherous and unfamiliar diplomatic waters on his first major summit since the death of FDR. While Truman and Churchill wrestled with Stalin, the Conservative Party in Great Britain lost an election to the Labour Party, a surprising upset that left Churchill stripped of his authority as Prime Minister. Before the Potsdam Conference ended on August 2, 1945, it was decided that Europe would be divided into two spheres, and the Russians were free to rule Eastern Europe as they saw fit.[131]

Robert's conversations with Eugene about Pétain ended abruptly on August 7. The final week of Pétain's trial was eclipsed by news of two blinding flashes in Hiroshima and Nagasaki, explosions which would claim more lives—most of them women and children—than the Battle of Verdun.[132]

The verdict in the trial of Marshal Pétain was read by the President of the High Court and broadcast over radio on August 15, 1945. The number of listeners was no greater than the small audience who heard Charles de Gaulle's first statement on 18 June 1940, owing to the hour of the verdict—4:21 a.m.

The Potsdam Conference was President Harry Truman's first encounter with Joseph Stalin. Prime Minister Churchill was voted out of office at home during Potsdam. Stalin returned to Moscow with a grand prize—Eastern Europe.

Robert heard the verdict when it was rebroadcast later in the day:

> In conclusion, there is no doubt that (Pétain) had dealings with Germany, a power at war with France, in order to cooperate with the enemy, crimes punishable under Articles 75 and 87 of the Penal Code. On these grounds, the High Court of Justice sentences Pétain to the death penalty, national indignity, and the confiscation of his property.
>
> In view of the great age of the accused, the High Court of Justice recommends that the death sentence not be carried out.
>
> Guards, take the prisoner away. [133]

Robert listened as reporters surrounded the Marshall.

"What, is it all over?" Pétain asked his lawyer.

Pétain's lawyer helped him to his feet. The Marshal looked pale and haggard with his eyes half closed in a blaze of flashbulbs, and for a moment he seemed to stagger. Then Pétain's lawyer shouted in one ear that the death penalty would not be carried out.

"That's kind of them," Pétain said.

A few minutes later, Pétain boarded General de Gaulle's private plane and was flown to the fortress of Le Portalet located high on a rocky crest between two sheer walls of granite on Île d'Yeu, where he was placed in Cell No. 5.

De Gaulle immediately commuted the sentence to life imprisonment. [134] Newspapers that day ran huge headlines, but the top story was not about the fall of a French monarch. August 15 was V-J Day—Victory in Japan.

Henri-Philippe Pétain died on Île d'Yeu six years later.

In the mind-numbing aftermath of the stunning finale to World War II, Robert Muller settled into the quiet routine of school. He soon realized that law school was not the place to find answers to the questions hounding him. Law was a minefield of issues, where squabbles sometimes ripened into cases, and the worst cases matured into precedents on which the law was founded. Lawyers kept the peace by providing a mechanism for the orderly resolution of disputes, but if it were not for conflicts, there would not be any work for lawyers. When Robert entered law school, he enlisted in basic training for an army of paper warriors.

Robert visited his mother's relatives in Strasbourg on the weekends. He had the most in common with his cousin, Simon Hermann. Simon was from the little farming village of Kilstett north of Strasbourg. He had been working for the railroad when he escaped to France in a train engine, like Robert. He joined the First French Army in North Africa and marched through Lyon on the same day Robert and Gregory Trifonof waited for their *Maquis* unit at the Wilson Bridge.

Simon's parents were farmers. They were not deported after Simon disappeared because Hitler needed peasants to till the land, but Simon's younger brother Eugene enlisted to protect them. Eugene was wounded in Normandy by hand grenades and machine gun fire. An American ambulance picked him up and shipped him to England. Surgeons operated on his legs eight times—in London, Heidelberg, and Strasbourg. He regained partial use of his legs and eventually learned to walk with a limp.

"It's funny Robert," Simon said one day, "the Americans found me dying in the dirt and carried me back to England. The Brits sowed me back together and flew me to Germany in a prisoner exchange. The Germans operated on me again and sent me home to Strasbourg. Then the Americans and the Brits loaded up their planes with bombs and flew all the way to Germany to kill civilians in Dresden. I must be lucky, because I don't see any logic to it."

Robert's grandfather completed the restoration of his living quarters at the Panama hat factory and invited the family to a reunion in Sarralbe. With all of his children and grandchildren gathered around, Laurent announced that all his efforts during the war had been aimed at getting his family back together. A week later, Robert was called back to Sarralbe, where he held vigil by his grandfather's bedside until he died peacefully on December 1, 1945.

Robert's Uncle Emile was the only member of the family who hadn't come home. After he was missing a year, his wife started wearing black mourning clothes. When Emile finally returned and knocked on the front door, his wife almost fainted. The family rushed to Strasbourg to hear his story.

Emile had been traveling through the woods in Poland with a fellow German soldier from Saarbrücken when a Russian tank lumbered across their path. The German surrendered with his hands held high and was immediately shot. Emile hid under a haystack at a remote farm. A German farmer protected him and employed him as a laborer for a year while the war wound down and the Russians took over Poland. Finally the farmer gave him a ride to the French embassy in Warsaw in the back of his wagon, hidden under a pile of potato sacks, and the embassy arranged to send Emile home.

When Robert mentioned to Emile that he wanted to be a peacemaker, Emile shook his head. "I don't know, Robert. You should have seen those Russian tanks. They're never going to leave Poland. I don't see how you can have peace with all those tanks there."

"It may take time, but there must be a way," Robert said.

The United Nations General Assembly met for the first time in London on January 10, 1946. One of their first tasks was to select a Secretary General. There was no discussion about who would do the best job. They wanted someone who would not rock the boat. After the delegates went down a list of respected leaders that included Lester Pearson, Anthony Eden, and Dwight Eisenhower, U.S. representative Edward Stettinius walked over to Brian Urquhart's table and asked him to identify Mr. Trygve Lie, whose name he mispronounced. Urquhart was in charge of the speakers' list—he was about to start a distinguished career as a top political advisor to four Secretaries General. In his memoirs, Urquhart wrote:

> I pointed out the substantial figure of the Foreign Minister of Norway, and shortly thereafter listened with some skepticism as Stettinius, in his nominating speech, referred to Lie as a household word, a figure

known to all the world, a leader in the Allied struggle for freedom, etc. I was still unused to international political rhetoric and felt an indignant pang of anxiety for the future.[135]

Trygve Lie (pronounced trig vo lee) became the UN's first Secretary General on February 1, 1946. A Norwegian labor leader who was raised in an apartment behind a bar on the docks of Oslo, he was out of his league from the start.

In April 1947, Robert was searching for a thesis topic to earn his Doctorate of Law when Charles de Gaulle arrived in Strasbourg to make an announcement. After watching the Fourth Republic flounder for an entire year without the benefit of his leadership, de Gaulle decided to step into the political arena and put the nation back on track. The people of Strasbourg gave him a hero's welcome.

"The time has come to form and organize the rally of the French people," de Gaulle said while the crowd chanted: "Put de Gaulle in power." He promised "common salvation and the profound reform of the State." The *Rassemblement du Peuple Français* (RPF), the Rally of the French People, was launched the next day—a new political party to rid France of the party system. Almost a million people joined during the first month.[136]

The RPF appeared to give Robert an opportunity to get involved in politics. He asked to meet with Charles de Gaulle. As a law student and a veteran of the *Group 18th of June*, he had no difficulty getting in.

Standing six foot five, de Gaulle towered over Robert by a full nine inches. It seemed as if the others in the room disappeared when the General spoke, so strong was his personal magnetism.

"What is your background?" de Gaulle asked.

"I studied economics before joining the *Group 18th of June*. I am studying law here in Strasbourg."

"First you must finish your studies," de Gaulle said. "Then you might consider working with the RPF."

"I'm looking for a subject for my thesis," Robert said.

"I think the Sarre Territory might be an interesting topic. I am in favor of a greater degree of cooperation between France and the Sarre Territory," de Gaulle said. "I think we should move towards an economic union between the Sarre Territory and France, if not a political union. Why don't you write about that?"

Robert got permission to write a thesis on the economic attachment of the Sarre Territory to France. He stayed with his parents in Sarreguemines whenever he had to conduct research in Saarbrücken, the capital of the Sarre Territory. One night, as he hurried out of the law school to catch an early train home, Robert picked up a leaflet announcing a writing competition. When he boarded the train, he realized he had no books to read on the long ride home. It was a slow ride because the tracks had not been replaced since the war. As the train pulled out, he read the leaflet, an invitation for students to write an essay, "What are your opinions about a world government?" As the train crawled through the countryside late into the night, Robert jotted down ideas. The next day he typed up his notes and mailed them to the sponsor of the contest, the French Universities Union:

> It must be comprised of all organs characteristic of government—legislative, executive, and judicial. It must have all humans as subjects. World government is very different from international government, which has been a bankruptcy, unable to provide humans with peace. There are needs that are common to all humanity.
>
> World government must not be a slave. It must be the master, and the State its servant. The notion of an army must be reduced to its true meaning, that of a police. Only this world police would be allowed to intervene and impose the sanctions of world rules.
>
> Many voices have been raised and have grown over the past 50 years, proof that the challenge is not utopian.

Of everyone Robert knew, only one friend from high school showed any interest in his determination to bring an end to war. René Lejeune visited Robert in the summer of 1947.

"You might enjoy getting involved in the local elections," Lejeune said to Robert. "Robert Schuman could use your help in October, and it would be a good first step if you might want to go into politics after you graduate."

Lejeune had joined the Christian Democratic Party, popularly known as the *Mouvement Républicain Populaire* (MRP), after the war. His first assignment was to recruit a candidate to run for parliament from Lorraine. He knew the best man was Robert Schuman, but Schuman didn't want the job. He wanted to stay home and practice law in Metz, having served for twenty years in France's parliament, plus two years in German prison. Lejeune wouldn't give up. He insisted it was Schuman's duty to run for office because he was the only man who could prevent another war between France and Germany. Schuman reluctantly gave in and was re-elected to the French parliament in 1946.

"Schuman is well respected in Lorraine," Robert said, "but I have no feeling for the Christian Democrats."

"You would like Schuman," Lejeune said. "He is a modest man and he lives a simple life. He wanted to be a monk, so he never married, and he's dedicated to public service."

"I am a de Gaulle fighter. It's my duty to be on his side."

"De Gaulle is a general, Robert."

"The Catholics have caused some trouble, too," Robert said, "and were it not for de Gaulle, France might still be an occupied country. But I'll think it over."

Robert's answer came a few days later. A letter arrived from the French Universities Union. He had tied for first place in the writing contest and was invited to participate as an intern at a meeting of the World Federation of United Nations Associations in Geneva.

When Robert sat in the front row of the meeting room at the former headquarters of the League of Nations, he was filled with excitement. James Orrick, Public Information Officer for the UN in New York, welcomed the interns to Geneva.

Orrick spoke with pride about the drafting of the UN

Charter. Then he said, "I realize that some of you may be skeptical. The League of Nations didn't prevent World War II, so why should the UN fare any better? Let's take some questions."

Jean-Pierre Martin, a thin, angular man sitting next to Robert, was the first to speak. "Why do you suppose the League of Nations failed?"

"That question was raised once before in this room," Orrick said. "There was a lot of soul-searching during the final session of the League of Nations. Lord Cecil of England said the League failed because the member states did not genuinely accept their obligations to support it, and he admitted the official opinion in England was either neutral or hostile. Mr. Paul-Boncour of France agreed that it was not the principles of the League that failed, but rather it was the nations who neglected it. The League of Nations succeeded as long as governments put their faith in it and animated it and fortified it with their will." [137]

Robert was next. "The League had no representatives chosen by the people. Everyone was government appointed. Isn't that also true for the United Nations?"

"Maybe on the political side of the UN," Orrick said, "but there is one exception on the social and economic side. Non-governmental organizations can attend meetings of the Economic and Social Council and submit papers. So that may be where we will see the most interesting progress.

"Why should it be any different this time?" Orrick asked. "Let me remind you of something Franklin Roosevelt said: 'The only limit to our realization of tomorrow will be our doubts of today.'

"Now let's hear from Brock Chisholm, Deputy Minister of National Health in Canada and Chairman of the Drafting Committee that is working on a structure for the World Health Organization."

"During the war," Chisholm said, "it occurred to me that people were going to be moving around more after the war. We now have airplanes that fly people across the ocean in one day. With mobility like this, what are the chances that epidemics will spread from one continent to another? I urged the European nations to form an international health organization, and they refused. Then an epidemic in the

Middle East threatened to spread to Europe. Suddenly, the World Health Organization seemed like a pretty good idea, and since we had a United Nations, they wasted no time getting together.

"What other ideas are sprouting in the human imagination that will find fertile soil in this organization?"

"How many of you have considered devoting your lives to peace?" Orrick asked.

To Robert's surprise, many of the interns were smiling and raising their hands.

"The UN doesn't have a lot of money and we're working out of a factory in New York, so I don't want to pretend we have it easy. This is just the beginning of a difficult mission. But what are the chances if we don't try, eh? Where will the world go without the UN?"

Robert felt relieved to be with others who thought about peace. Sitting next to him, Jean-Pierre was smiling.

Almost as soon as he returned home, Robert received an invitation to a UN meeting in Czechoslovakia. While working on his thesis, he wrestled with feelings of insignificance. He had done nothing important in his life. He had stayed in school, avoided the army, made hats, joined the Resistance, and gone back to school.

Now he was trying to finish his thesis, and it wasn't going well. The Sarre basin seemed to have an invisible wall. Something was missing.

"I can't even finish my thesis," his mother heard him say.

"You are not yourself these days," she said.

"Why do people on this side of the river never get along with people on that side of the river?"

"They're Prussians," she shrugged. "Why worry about something you cannot change?"

"It's just a river. The people in this region should be working together, but something drives them apart."

"They're different," she said, shaking her head.

"De Gaulle is right. This is one geographic region and it could prosper as one economy. Alsace-Lorraine has iron ore and plenty of food. The Sarre the coalmines. They are a perfect fit. I can't figure this out."

Robert felt discouraged when he arrived in Prague for the UN meeting. Jean-Pierre tried to cheer him up by taking him for a ride through the Czech countryside in his new sports car. The terror was distracting. He never slowed down, not even on blind curves or on the narrow streets in small towns.

"Jean-Pierre. You drive like a madman!" Robert shouted.

"It sharpens my thinking."

"What if you will find something in the road you can't control, like a child running into the street?"

"You're upset about your thesis," he laughed.

As they waited in the elaborately decorated meeting room, Robert noticed that the interns were a sullen group. Jean-Pierre was more vivacious than the others, but even he had a general weariness about him—when he was not flirting with death—that was typical of Europeans who had come of age during the war. Robert thought of himself as quiet, rather than gloomy, but he wondered if he was being honest with himself. They had been through so much.

James Orrick introduced the featured speaker, Jan Masaryk, Czechoslovakia's Foreign Minister. "Our speaker Jan Masaryk is the son of the late Tomas Masaryk, the founder of Czechoslovakia. Jan could barely wait until he turned 21 to get out from under the shadow of his famous father and go see the United States."

Masaryk laughed when he heard this. He looked relaxed next to Orrick as he studied his audience. A stocky man about sixty years old with a big smile, he wore a wrinkled white shirt and tie with no jacket, as if his desk were down the hall and he had just dropped in for an impromptu visit.

"When Czechoslovakia gained its independence in 1918 and his father became its first president, Jan Masaryk served in Washington for three years as chargé d'affaires, then went to London as Czechoslovakia's ambassador to Britain until his homeland was taken over by Germany in 1939. He joined the Czech government-in-exile, and that is when we got to know each other in London. Jan is one of the most positive, good natured, and patient human beings I have ever met. He rallied his people from London during the war with a series of radio broadcasts on BBC while he worked tirelessly to get Jews out of Europe through Czechoslovakia. He will soon go to New York for the General Assembly. Let's welcome Jan Masaryk, Czechoslovakia's Foreign Minister."

"What Jim didn't mention," Masaryk said casually, "is that it was prohibited to listen to a radio in Czechoslovakia under Hitler, so I was an outlaw. Every radio came with a label saying that listening to foreign broadcasts was punishable by death. You can imagine how that affected my self-confidence as a radio announcer. I knew that if I said anything funny and it made people laugh out loud, it could have catastrophic consequences. So I went hunting all over London for the world's worst jokes—not as difficult a task as people in London might think—and that's where I met Jim Orrick.

"We all worked together to end Nazi oppression, but now we face new challenges. Last year, we had an election here in Czechoslovakia. I was surprised and disappointed when the Communists won, but we continue to work together. The dialog goes on.

"I want to mention the work of the UN Human Rights Commission headed by Eleanor Roosevelt. Her husband, President Franklin Roosevelt, insisted there be a reference to human rights in the UN Charter.[138] Nothing was ever said about human rights in the Covenant of the League of Nations, but in the UN Charter you can find human rights from the beginning to the end. In the Preamble, members of the UN reaffirm their faith in fundamental human rights, in the dignity and worth of the human person, in the equal rights of men and women. Is that a miracle? Some day we may take all this for granted, but this is an historic step.

"Article 1 says one of the aims of the UN is 'the respect for self-determination of peoples, for human rights and for fundamental freedoms without distinction as to race, sex, language or religion.' Then Article 56 says that all member nations will promote human rights and freedoms, and it assigns responsibility for promoting human rights to the Economic and Social Council. Isn't it astonishing that all 50

Robert Muller and Jean-Pierre Martin wore suits and sat in the front row when they attended a meeting of UN interns in Prague in September 1947.

Jan Masaryk, below, Czechoslovakia's Foreign Minister, spoke about the UN's pioneering work in drafting an international declaration of human rights.

nations, including our colleagues in Russia, signed this charter in San Francisco on June 26, 1945?

"So the commission is now drafting a declaration of human rights for the Economic and Social Council, which they will pass on to the General Assembly. They have on the commission Peng-chun Chang, a Chinese playwright, René Cassin, a French lawyer, and Charles Malik, an Arab philosopher from Lebanon. Try to imagine the challenges of writing one bill of human rights for the entire human species, working with Hindus, Moslems, Christians, Buddhists, Arabs, Jews, and Marxists."

Robert tried to picture representatives of all the people on Earth meeting to talk about common values. It filled him with hope. He had been stirred by Masaryk's optimism and gentle humor. At a reception following Masaryk's remarks, Robert spoke with an American army officer.

"Are you from around here?" the colonel asked.

"I'm from Sarreguemines," Robert said.

"I'm from Colorado. I was in the Seventh Army when we came through Sarreguemines. Were you there during the war?"

"I joined the Resistance in southern France."

"My hat is off to you fellows. I was with General Patch. We got a message from one of your outfits that helped us out. Hell, it probably shortened the war by a day or two."

"What was the message?" Robert asked.

"That the Germans abandoned Lyon! That freed us up to go straight to Belfort without stopping in Lyon."

"I found that message in a wallet. As soon as I showed it to Commandant Marey, he radioed the Americans."

"Marey, that was his name! You found it? No kidding!"

Robert felt elated that he might have saved lives, perhaps even in Sarreguemines. He soon found himself talking to Jan Masaryk.

"Jim Orrick said you were in Washington D.C.," Robert said. "Maybe you could explain to me why the United States Congress is supporting the UN, when it was so strongly opposed to the League of Nations."

"President Roosevelt chose people from both parties to represent the United States during the negotiations in San Francisco," Masaryk said. "He picked Harold Stassen, John

Foster Dulles, Arthur Vandenberg. They were all prominent Republicans who became involved in drafting the charter."

Robert said, "If I may I ask one more question, India and Pakistan split in two last month, the UN is leaning towards partitioning Palestine, which will probably lead to war, the civil war in China is turning in favor of the Communists, and Russia has abolished all the opposition parties in Eastern Europe, including here in Czechoslovakia. Do you think we are heading towards another world war?"

"New lines are being drawn," Masaryk said gravely, "but they are based on ideology now, rather than racial hatred. We always will be faced with new challenges. In July, the United States offered financial aid to Czechoslovakia with the Marshall Plan, and the Soviets objected. I said to our Prime Minister, 'What is this? The Russians are now setting our foreign policy in Czechoslovakia?' So the Prime Minister and I went to Moscow to negotiate. I left here as a minister of a sovereign state, but I came back as Stalin's lackey."

"And yet you don't seem discouraged."

"People must be free; it's our God-given right. Be patient. Human nature always wins in the end."

France's municipal elections in October 1947 gave a landslide victory to Charles de Gaulle and the Rally of the French People. RPF candidates captured 40% of the vote and won control of municipal councils in most major cities, including Paris.

General de Gaulle issued a bold demand to dissolve the National Assembly and hold national elections. The Radical Party offered to join forces with the RPF and form a coalition, but he rejected their offer. De Gaulle thought he had enough votes and refused to make any deals.

The Radicals turned around and united with *Mouvement Républicain Populaire* (MRP) and the Socialists to form a coalition, which they called The Third Force. Members of The Third Force had three things in common: they were against the Communists, they were fed up with Charles de Gaulle, and they had enough votes to form a new government without holding an election. They also agreed on a new Prime Minister for France—Robert Schuman.

On November 29, 1947, the UN General Assembly voted to partition Palestine into two separate states over the strong objections of Arab nations, who wanted a single democratic state. The vote required a two-thirds majority because the delegates decided that it was an *important question*. It was one of the few confrontations in the UN where Russia and the United States agreed on the outcome.

Robert felt a chill on his 25th birthday when he read that Jan Masaryk had been found dead in the courtyard outside his apartment at the Foreign Ministry in Prague. His death occurred only two weeks after the Communist takeover of the Czech government. There were conflicting theories that Masaryk was thrown from the balcony or leaped to his death. He landed on his feet—his head was not injured—seven feet from the building, after falling 45 feet from a third story window. Only an athlete could have leapt seven feet. Robert was certain that Masaryk did not kill himself.

When Robert saw de Gaulle at a meeting in Paris, the General wanted to know how his thesis was going.

"There's something that doesn't fit," Robert said. "The people along the Sarre have never been able to get along."

"When they see the benefits of an economic union," de Gaulle said, "they will be happy with the arrangement. But your title is not right. It is not *attachement* we propose. We are proposing a *rattachement*. This is not something new. There has been an economic link between the regions since 1919."

The more data Robert collected in his research, the more it did not fit his hypothesis. One day a clerk was bringing him a file from the Municipal Archives of Saarbrücken when he said a word Robert didn't recognize.

"*Ich gehe nach hause,*" he said to a coworker. I will go home soon.

"Why do you use the word *hause?*" Robert asked.

"It is how we say *home* in Plattdeutsch," he said. "You would say "*Ich geh heim,*" because you speak Hochdeutsch."

"Why does everybody here speak Plattdeutsch?"

"It's just how we talk."

"When did your family move here?"

"My grandfather came from Berlin when he was a boy."

Robert finally saw the pattern. A migration had occurred between 1870 and 1890. Record after record showed a gift of real property to a retired military officer—Sergeants, Captains, Lieutenants. Bismarck had induced his officers to retire to the frontier Saarland, offering them good pensions and a grant of land so that he could build a human bulwark to shield Germany from the French. Saarländers spoke the dialect of Berlin, while Germans farther east in the Rhineland spoke Plattdeutsch, like the people in Lorraine.

"Saarländers will never vote to be a part of France," he told his mother that night. "They are all Prussians."

"Yes, of course," she said.

As summer approached, Robert revised his thesis. "De Gaulle will be amazed when he sees this," he said to his parents, who were amused that their college student son could find so much satisfaction in anything so obvious.

With the extra work of rewriting a thesis on top of his classroom studies, Robert did not have time to help his father.

"How many pages do you still have to write?" he asked.

"Quite a few more," Robert said.

"Why can't you copy a few pages out of the newspaper and get it over with?"

"Because I would not graduate," Robert said.

"Well, hurry up, because we have to paint the balconies."

"As soon as I finish my thesis," Robert said.

In June 1948, Robert submitted his thesis, *Le Rattachement Economique de la Sarre à la France*. He sent copies to de Gaulle and Prime Minister Robert Schuman. On the day of Robert's graduation, he invited his parents to accompany him to Strasbourg to watch him defend his thesis and receive his Doctorate of Law.

"I couldn't care less about that," his father said. "I have work to do." His mother said she preferred to stay home.

Robert traveled alone to Strasbourg, where he sat in a wood paneled room and succinctly answered the questions posed by the faculty. In a medieval ceremony, he added another white stripe of ermine to his black and red jurist's robe. He regretted that his parents had not come as he rode back to Sarreguemines and walked up Rue de la Montagne. His father was still up when he arrived home.

"Are you finally a doctor?" his father asked.

"Yes, and I received the title *summa cum laude.*"

"I do not understand Latin, son. The important thing is that starting tomorrow, we will repaint the balconies."

The iron railings on the balconies needed heavy sanding and three coats of paint. Robert's back was aching and his arms were tired when he cleaned up for lunch a few days later and joined his family in the kitchen.

"You have a letter," his mother said. "It's in the living room."

Robert got up with a groan to get the letter. When he walked back into the kitchen, he was reading. Then he stopped in the doorway. His face was frozen.

"What is it?" Léonie said.

Robert's lips moved slightly, but there was no sound. His eyes grew wider.

"Is there something wrong?" his father asked.

"Robert!" Marcelle yelled.

"What?" he said, blinking, his mouth wide open.

"Say something!"

His eyes filled with tears. The letter drifted to the floor.

"I'm going to the United Nations."

Chapter 11 – Lake Success

Marcelle didn't want to talk about it. His father couldn't understand it, why anybody would accept a job in a factory half a world away. Robert's mother worried about the plane.

"Airplanes fall out of the sky, son. Don't you think a steamship would be safer?"

"Those planes you saw falling out of the sky were shot down, Mama, and they don't do that anymore."

"If the UN is meeting in Paris in September," his father reasoned, "why don't you stay here a few more weeks, take the train to Paris, and save yourself all that trouble?"

"The General Assembly is meeting in Paris, but I'm an intern with the Secretariat in New York. It's a different job."

"It wouldn't hurt to ask."

Robert could think of no one in his family, or in his school, or even in his town, who had ever ventured out of France, except in uniform. When friends and neighbors talked about his journey, they seemed to pull back a little, as if he were not someone they could trust anymore, like he had broken some unspoken taboo. With strangers, Robert felt like he had stepped into a spotlight and people wanted him to perform.

An item appeared in the *Courier de la Sarre* on July 18:

Our local compatriot, whose successes at the

University of Strasbourg were previously reported, will respond at the end of July to an invitation by the United Nations to go for two months to the United States.

Robert's mother bought an extra copy of the newspaper. She seemed indifferent when she handed one to Robert, but she had read it aloud so many times even Robert's father could recite it by heart.

At the train station, his father and sister were subdued.

"It's only for two months," Robert said cheerfully.

Léonie handed him the splinter of wood he had pried from the bed frame in the Metz prison. His words were still legible in pencil: "August 21, 1943. Gestapo, Metz, thirst, heat, lying on the floor, no air."

Robert's eyes watered.

"Never forget what you and your father went through," she said. "Remember your origins, and always try to be a good man."

It might have been the vibration of the engines, or perhaps it was the feeling of soaring between the old world and the new that kept Robert awake. His heart lingered in France while his mind soared ahead to the United States and the United Nations. Ever since Geneva he had felt divided, as if his childhood had been a still mountain lake and now it was seeping out. The future was rushing up to meet him as he flew away from his familiar world at 300 miles per hour.

Robert studied Air France's colorful 8-page foldout brochure with detailed diagrams describing the Lockheed Constellation. It crossed the Atlantic Ocean in 12 hours, including fuel stops in Shannon and Gander. The return flight was only half as long, due to prevailing winds. Cabin air was renewed every 90 seconds. The 44 armchairs converted into 22 bunks, with privacy curtains, reading lamps, and mirrors. He asked the stewardess, a blonde woman from Alsace, for permission to keep the brochure for his records.

He carried with him a book describing Lake Success on

Long Island, where the UN offices were located. The Matinecock Indians had called it *Sukut,* but Dutch settlers could not pronounce the word correctly, so they called it Lake Success. The name had a distinctly American ring to it. Robert had only started to get his feet wet in the nuances of American English, but there was something about calling a "kettle-hole lake" *Success* that exuded confidence. There was no beating around the bush about it. Boom-boom! Two syllables, chock full of enthusiasm. Success!

Robert read about "robber barons" who transformed the north shore of Long Island from rural farmland into the "Gold Coast" at the turn of the century. In 1902, William K. Vanderbilt II, under the alias of Mr. Smith, bought 600 acres on Lake Success from an unsuspecting farmer and built a summer home, which he named "Deepdale." He then built the nation's first parkway from Queens to Suffolk County so he could race cars across Long Island back and forth from Deepdale. America's richest men built vacation palaces on the North Shore during the next few years—J. P. Morgan, William Randolph Hearst, Marshall Field, Henry Ford, Thomas Edison.[139] Mansions sprang up around Lake Success with names like The Cove, Sunshine, Martin Hall, and Nirvana.[140] Publishing tycoon Frank Doubleday built a huge estate in Mill Neck; F. Scott Fitzgerald used Great Neck as the setting for *The Great Gatsby* after living there in the 1920's—he called it West Egg—exposing the sheltered souls of the Nouveau Riche to anyone who could read.

Sperry Gyroscope Corporation shattered the tranquility of Lake Success in 1941 when it cleared 93 acres to build an arms factory the length of four football fields in each direction—1.5-million-square-feet. Residents vowed to fight the industrial intrusion—after all, the war hadn't even started yet—but Gold Coast opposition faded as American isolationism melted.

Five years later, the United Nations came calling. New York City Mayor William O'Dwyer offered an ice skating rink to the UN at the World's Fair grounds in Flushing Meadows for meetings of the General Assembly, and lined up the Sperry factory in Lake Success for the Secretariat and the Security Council. Local residents rose up again in opposition to the United Nations. Some were afraid of losing their homes and others feared a reduction in Sperry's property taxes. Mayor Schuyler Van Bloem rallied the citizens of Lake Success to welcome the United Nations and all its varied visitors to its temporary home, lest intolerance tarnish the town's reputation.[141] As the number of visitors grew, the Gold Coast started calling the UN "the bottleneck between Great Neck and Little Neck."

Robert asked the stewardess where she thought he might find a Matinecock Indian village on Long Island.

"Don't get your hopes up," the stewardess said. "Long Island is not like Alsace-Lorraine, but they might still have a few Indians there."

She was a slender blonde in her twenties from Alsace, and they knew many of the same places in Strasbourg, but she yawned more than once while they talked—Air France had assigned only one attendant to the long flight. Robert convinced her to lie down and sleep on a sofa behind the women's restroom in the back of the plane while he served food and beverages to the passengers. His legs felt heavy and he slept soundly after his shift.

Robert felt great admiration for Americans and how they had rolled across France and Belgium and fought their way to Berlin to defeat the Nazis, then insisted on including human rights in the UN Charter, then created the Marshall Plan to put Europe back on its feet. Truman stood up to Stalin over Berlin when the Soviets blocked every route into the city. American and British planes were airlifting food and supplies over Soviet-controlled territory to Berlin 24 hours a day at a rate of one planeload every three and a half minutes. The tremendous strength, courage, and generosity of the American people prepared Robert for something more elaborate than the monotonous prefabricated houses he saw on Long Island. They looked like barracks. Robert wondered how the richest country on Earth could tolerate its citizens moving into settlements that had no character. Even the peasants didn't live like that in Europe.

The Sperry factory was not anything like the beautiful

buildings where the interns had met in Geneva and Prague. It was a flat, plain, rectangular, 3-story brick structure with three wide horizontal stripes of double-hung windows. A curved driveway with 55 flagpoles led to the UN offices, passing a wide front lawn dotted with young pine trees. Sperry had employed 20,000 workers there to make airplanes and parts for warships during the war, including the famous Sperry gyroscope, which made it possible for bombers to find their targets and submarines to move forward without spinning. Half of the Sperry factory was still producing weapons, and Robert wrestled with the idea that the UN was starting off in a gyroscope factory to steer the world towards peace while an arms manufacturer with a bigger budget prepared for war under the same roof.

At Jim Orrick's first meeting, Robert counted 52 interns in the room, and not just Europeans. Every region of the world was represented. Robert saw so many styles of dress and heard so many languages spoken that he imagined he had slipped into a cocoon where young people were weaving the new strands of a better world. The brutality of war was etched on many of their faces, but they seemed alert and hopeful. The only one he recognized was Jean-Pierre Martin.

"No car yet?" Robert asked.

"Not just for two months. Let's see how things turn out." Jean-Pierre said. "What a dreary excuse for an office this is. You can tell they fixed this place up in a hurry."

"My father warned me that there is no money in peace," Robert said. "But the people here are so bright! I worked in a war factory for two summers, and this is more like it."

Robert Muller, Jean-Pierre, and Albert Thebault—all French interns—rented rooms from a European woman in a house by the last stop on the railroad line. The house was a pleasant two-story house on a tree-lined street. During his daily ride to Lake Success, Robert missed the simple beauty of the individually crafted houses in Alsace-Lorraine, where every home showed some mark of character. He missed his family more than he expected. All of their correspondence could not satisfy the gnawing feeling of loneliness that grew stronger as the weeks passed.

Robert was assigned to the Department of Economic and

*Three interns outside the UN's temporary headquarters
at Lake Success in 1948—Tommy Koh, Malcolm
Templeton and Robert Muller.*

Social Affairs, where he was given the task of indexing boxes filled with documents from the League of Nations. His desk was in a cubbyhole lined with metal shelves full of old files from the League of Nations. The work was tedious, but he looked forward to lunch in the cafeteria, where the whole world seemed to come together and almost everyone was eager to strike up a conversation.

A man sat down next to Robert during the first week. "I'm Georges Schmidt," he said. "Where are you from?"

"My name is Robert Muller, and I'm from—"

"You're from Lorraine. I could tell that right away. I'm from Strasbourg, myself. Why did you come to the UN?"

"I made a promise during the war that I would work for peace. What about you?"

"I am a linguist and I'm here to set the world's record for fluency in languages. I work in the Languages Division."

A graceful woman with dark hair walked by them and sat down two tables away.

"Who's that?" Robert asked.

"Margarita Gallo—she's from Chile. I heard she got the highest grades in the history of her university when she was earning her doctorate in Santiago."

"She is so beautiful!"

"And she has a photographic memory. Smart girl."

"Well, she's too much for me," Robert said. "I wonder if she is seeing anyone."

"I've noticed her with Chris Maersk, who's not such a bad looking fellow. I'm told that he might be a real Danish prince. Have you met anyone?"

"A nice girl from Canada, Suzanne Barriére. Her father is on the city council. She told me the Quebec Provincial flag was designed in her home. You've probably seen her. Suzanne has a beautiful face and a bright smile, and we both speak French. How about you?"

"I only date women who speak a language I haven't yet learned.

"Then how do you have a conversation?" Robert asked.

"Who needs to talk?" Schmidt joked.

"I need to practice that language," Robert said.

· · ·

While the interns worked at Lake Success, UN delegates traveled to Paris for the opening of the third session of the General Assembly on September 21. There were rumors the delegates picked Paris for their meeting so that they could conduct their business at a safe distance from the razzle-dazzle of a U.S. Presidential election. New York Governor Thomas E. Dewey defeated former Minnesota Governor Harold Stassen for the Republican nomination. A few weeks later in the same Philadelphia convention hall, President Harry Truman walked onto the stage to deliver his acceptance speech to the Democratic Party at two o'clock in the morning. Frank Kelly, Truman's speechwriter, described the incumbent President's unforgettable grand entrance:

> Flocks of doves and pigeons were released into the air to symbolize the Party's commitment to peace. The dazed birds flew in all directions, hitting the spotlights, fluttering toward the balcony, and showering wet droppings on spectators and delegates.

Truman revived the bleary-eyed delegates as he told the world that isolationism would not freeze American foreign policy while he was President: "The United States has to accept its full responsibility for leadership in international affairs. We have been the backers and the people who organized and started the United Nations—first started under the great Democratic president, Woodrow Wilson, as the League of Nations. The League was sabotaged by the Republicans in 1920. We must see that the United Nations continues a strong and growing body so we can have everlasting peace in the world." [142]

On September 17, four men in an army jeep dressed as Israeli soldiers stopped a three-car convoy in Jerusalem carrying the UN Mediator, Count Folke Bernadotte of Sweden. The men were members of an underground Zionist group headed by Yitzhak Shamir. One of the assailants stuck a machine gun through the window and shot Bernadotte and Colonel Andre Serot, a UN observer who was sitting next to him.[143] Bernadotte's assassination sent a chilling reminder to UN workers at Lake Success, especially those in political affairs, that their lives might be on the line. Four other military observers on Count Bernadotte's staff had been killed in Israel during his four-month term as the UN Mediator.[144] Ralph Bunche, from the United States, the grandson of an American slave, was appointed to take his place.

Suzanne Barriére and Robert met for dinner the night after the assassination. "I needed to talk to someone about Bernadotte," she said. "I don't understand, Robert. Israel's identity as a nation was first recognized by the UN. When Israel declared its independence in May and a war broke out, Bernadotte negotiated a cease-fire within a month. Now the Jews have killed him. It doesn't make any sense to me."

"I don't know much about it," Robert said. "Bernadotte was starting to question the wisdom of the partition vote. The people who killed him were a militant group and they probably don't represent the Jewish people."

"But to kill the UN Mediator for raising a question?"

"There is always the risk that an extreme group will fan the flames. I don't think we should assume that Shamir has the support of the Israeli people."

"I don't think I want a permanent job here at the UN, do you? It's such a thankless job."

"I don't mind Economic and Social Affairs," Robert said. "We're allowed, in fact we're encouraged to have ideas. In political affairs you have to keep your head down."

"The president of the American Bar Association warned that the Declaration of Human Rights is a plot to establish state socialism, if not communism, all over the world.[145] Doesn't that put a little pressure on Economic and Social Affairs?"

"The Declaration elevates our thinking and gives people hope. A few crackpots can't stop that from happening. I think Eleanor. Roosevelt can put that lawyer in his place."

While political affairs struggled to make peace between warring nations and received most of the publicity, the economic and social side of the UN enjoyed an early period of freedom from criticism and public scrutiny. Robert worked for Henry Bloch, Director of the Fiscal and Financial

Branch of the Department of Economic and Social Affairs. Bloch had emigrated from Alsace to the United States before the war and joined the Roosevelt administration. He brought his New Deal enthusiasm to the UN. As political affairs circled its wagons, economic and social affairs sailed into uncharted waters where new social responsibilities and economic relationships were shaping a different world.

Robert was surprised by the idealism expressed in some of the reports generated by the League of Nations. "We are not starting out from scratch," he told Bloch. "There were good ideas and programs being considered, but I see one shortcoming. The League did not invite direct participation by the people. It was only for governments. I think that non-governmental organizations should be encouraged to participate in Economic and Social Affairs."

Eleanor Roosevelt continued to write her weekly column, "My Day," for U.S. newspapers while she lobbied for the Universal Declaration of Human Rights and attended meetings of the General Assembly. Her description of a Parisian woman stirred Robert's feelings about home:

> Most of the people you see look tired and listless...the older people uniformly look badly...One woman, speaking of what she had been through, said she had seen the French army routed, with officers picking up their wives and children and fleeing through Paris to any place where they might find temporary safety. She said rather sadly, "It takes a long time to restore the soul of a conquered country. You are free, but you know that you have been beaten. You cringe because you have known the conqueror's touch.[146]

The Universal Declaration of Human Rights was debated in the General Assembly on December 9, 1948.[147] Many delegates had concerns. The Soviets were concerned about freedom of travel and the loss of national sovereignty. There were fourteen million displaced persons living in refugee camps who had fled from Eastern European countries, and the Declaration said that everyone had the right to change their nationality and to leave any country, including their own. Saudi Arabia was concerned about freedom of religion, since the Declaration affirmed that everyone had the right to freedom of thought, conscience, and religion, including the freedom to change their religion. In answer to Saudi Arabia, Pakistan's Foreign Minister quoted the Koran: "Let him who chooses to believe, believe, and him who chooses to disbelieve, disbelieve."

Charles Malik, a tall, striking Lebanese Ambassador who was Chairman of the Economic and Social Council, introduced the Universal Declaration. It was 11:30 a.m. in Lake Success, where Robert listened by short-wave radio.

Every member of the UN had pledged to respect human rights when it signed the Charter, Malik began, "but precisely what these rights are, we were never told, either in the Charter or in any other international instrument. This is the first time the principles of human rights and fundamental freedoms are spelled out authoritatively and in precise detail."

Malik acknowledged that thousands of minds had helped to draft the Universal Declaration. India stood for the principle of nondiscrimination; the United States and the United Kingdom advocated political and civil liberties; the Soviet Union championed social and economic rights; China Greece, and Latin America stressed that rights entail duties and responsibilities.

Eleanor Roosevelt spoke near the end of the discussion. "This Declaration may well become the international Magna Charta of all men everywhere."

As Robert followed the discussion, he felt an incessant energy that seemed to emanate from the proceedings in Paris, as if history was generating a current that could be felt overseas. Hernán Santa Cruz, Chile's UN Ambassador wrote that there was "great solemnity, full of emotion" as speakers took turns contributing to a discussion "characterized by sincerity and a sober eloquence free of bombast...as to the supreme value of the human person."

When the roll was called, all six members of the Soviet bloc abstained—Czechoslovakia, Poland, Byelorussia, the Ukraine, Yugoslavia and the USSR—plus South Africa and

Saudi Arabia. Every other member voted *yes*. When all the votes were counted and the Universal Declaration was adopted with 48 in favor, 8 abstentions, and none opposed, the General Assembly rose to give Eleanor Roosevelt a standing ovation. As Robert applauded at his desk, he heard others clapping over the partitions.[148]

"What's the big deal?" Jean-Pierre asked on their way home. "The Declaration has no teeth in it. It is just talk."

"It says that all people are entitled to be free from want," Robert said. "Not even the French Declaration or the American Bill of Rights made that statement. It says human rights are universal, which means they exist in every country, and are not subject to the whim of any state. And the rights are recognized, rather than conferred, so human rights are no longer dependent upon the state granting them. They are implicit to life."

"The Soviets let the Declaration go through because they know it can't be enforced."

"Over time, I believe these rights will mature," Robert said. "The world will change because we have come to a new understanding of what it means to be human. It's a big deal."

"You are more optimistic than I am," Jean-Pierre said.

"No, because I also think we will have another world war within twenty years. But I also can see some progress."

"All right, so you're more pessimistic. We should be having more fun if everything is going to hell. I need a car."

Robert wanted to see an Indian reservation. A local librarian gave him directions, but when he found the address with the help of Jean-Pierre and Suzanne, all they could see was a fenced-off compound with a few junk cars and some dilapidated shacks. A group of men were passing around a bottle across the street. Robert pressed Jean-Pierre and Suzanne to take a short walk. The men followed them, but when Robert approached them to ask a question, they turned their backs.

"They don't look like Indians to me," Suzanne whispered.

"Let's go," Jean-Pierre said. "I didn't bring any ammo."

Robert started reading books about local Indian history. The Matinecocks were a band of Algonquians that had lived on the north shore of Long Island. Matinecock meant "at the hilly land," referring to the land they occupied from Astoria, in Queens, to Port Jefferson. The south side was home to the Massapequa, Merrick and Rockaway tribes. The Matinecocks taught Europeans to grow corn and harvest shellfish, but when Dutch settlers turned against them and attacked their villages in 1643, they fled to Staten Island, then to New Jersey, then Pennsylvania and Ohio, always trying to avoid the white invaders. After migrating west for 150 years, they were given refuge in 1792 by Moravian missionaries in Ontario, Canada. A handful of Matinecocks still spoke the Munsee Delaware language at the Moraviantown reservation, but every other indigenous language spoken on the Eastern seaboard for thousands of years had disappeared.

"We still have Indians in Canada," Suzanne said. "Why don't you come up and visit us in Montreal when our internship is over?"

Robert eagerly agreed. Then Henry Bloch dropped by Robert's office. "How would you like to meet Norman Mailer?"

"I haven't read his book," Robert admitted, "but I've heard he is a good writer. It would be interesting to meet him. I think he's becoming quite famous."

"There is a party for him in Manhattan in a couple of weeks. I thought you might like to come with me and meet him since you two have something in common. You were both in combat."

"Two weeks? No, that's after I return home."

"I want you to consider staying with us for a whole year, Robert. I'm very impressed with your work and so is Carl Lachman. We could use your help here."

"Is anybody else staying?"

"Jean-Pierre Martin, a couple of others. We can only pay you $300 a month, but it would be great if you stayed."

"Indexing boxes does not seem very important."

"You could do well here, Robert. This might turn out to be a great career for someone like you."

"Or the whole thing could fall apart in five years."

"You never know, but it feels better when you try. FDR left a handwritten speech in a drawer when he died. He was going to deliver it at the UN meeting in San Francisco. He wrote, 'If civilization is to survive, we must cultivate the science of human relationships—the ability of all peoples, of all kinds, to live together and work together in the same world, at peace. The only limit to our realization of tomorrow will be our doubts of today.' [149]

"Franklin and Eleanor Roosevelt—they were quite a team," Robert said.

"I know things are a little disorganized around here, and we don't have much to show for our efforts yet, but this is the laboratory where the science of human relationships is being developed. This is where peace will grow, and I'm not talking about putting out fires. We're building something here."

"My father wouldn't understand, and my sister might never speak to me again."

"Do you want to think it over?"

"I don't really care for New York, but I'm willing to stay."

"Good, so we can go to the party together!"

When the interns said their farewells, Robert promised Suzanne he would come to Montreal, but he regretted that Margarita Gallo was returning to Chile. They had said no more than a few words in conversation, but she lit up every room she entered.

Norman Mailer had appeared on the New York social scene the previous May with the publication of his first novel, *The Naked and the Dead*. By October, he was regarded as symbol of First Amendment free speech due to the language used by his characters. Robert stood near the window, where he could watch the New York elite without being noticed. He thumbed through a copy of Mailer's book, a fictional account of his combat experiences in the South Pacific. Two pages from the end, Robert stopped to read a few lines about a group of Americans who were escorting three wounded Japanese prisoners back to camp. It was getting dark: *The platoon leader looked at his watch at last and sighed. "We're going to have to dump them," he said.*

Robert set the book down. He had seen enough of war.

"Hi, where are you from?" a man asked.

"A small town in Alsace-Lorraine."

"Really? What's it called?"

"Sarreguemines...but you probably have heard of Metz."

"Oh God, do I remember Sarreguemines! I was one of the pilots who bombed your city."

"Before or after Normandy?"

"Before."

"I was there," Robert said.

"The man covered his mouth for a moment and shook his head. "We were making a raid on Saarbrücken, but the flak was too heavy and we couldn't get through, so we had to turn back, but we couldn't get home with all that weight, so we dumped everything on the next town. We tried to hit the railroad station, but you're always going to miss a few."

"You missed quite a few," Robert said quietly.

"I hope you didn't lose anyone...close."

"There was a young German woman who lived across the street with her baby, and the fish merchant lost his family, but I didn't really know the others."

"I want you to know how sorry I am. With the German towns, I didn't mind so much at first. But when we hit Sarreguemines, that was it for me."

"You were risking your lives for us."

"It was stupid—"

"War is a stupid condition," Robert said.

"—but we couldn't get back to England with that weight."

"Just think," Robert said, "what were the chances that you and I would ever meet?"

Robert's thesis may have been the reason he got the important assignment. Bloch never explained it, but he chose Robert to write a detailed report describing the work accomplished by the League of Nations in fiscal matters and suggesting unfinished business that needed to be resumed. Robert worked on it through the Christmas holidays.

On January 15, 1949, Robert presented his research to

Robert Muller worked through the Christmas holidays in 1948 to complete his first major report to UN delegates serving on the Fiscal Commission.

the Fiscal Commission of the Economic and Social Council. Jacques Woulbroun from Belgium congratulated Robert for writing an excellent document that had great historic value and recommended that it be published in Spanish. The Cuban delegate, Perez Cubillas, added his congratulations and asked for 2,000 copies in Spanish. Mr. Bartelt from the United States added his praise for the thoroughness and clarity of the report. Robert was beaming when he wrote home and described the meeting.

Robert was assigned to Carl Lachman, director of the International Taxation Section of the Fiscal and Financial Branch, which collected and published international tax agreements. Lachman was another veteran of the Roosevelt administration. Robert assembled tax codes from countries around the world and hunted for loopholes and tax havens that might point to a need for new agreements between nations. In the next room, economists in the Budget Section compiled national budgets so that they could put together a combined budget for the world showing total expenditures for the military, education, health, and so on. While the diplomatic side of the UN butted up against the political obstacles to making peace, the economic and social side explored new ideas. The U.S. delegate even proposed that individual tax returns be made public so that they could be published in the newspapers.

In June 1950, Robert volunteered to attend a meeting of the International Chamber of Commerce in Quebec City. As he rode north on the train, he saw little villages nestled among the trees lining the Hudson River. He vowed that if he ever decided to stay in the United States, he would live in the Hudson Valley.

After meetings in Quebec City and Ottawa, Robert traveled to Montreal to meet Suzanne Barriére and her family. They all greeted him in Indian costumes, apologizing that they had not found any Indian reservations. Robert asked them to keep looking, and they found something—a Caughnawaga reservation across St. Lawrence River from Montreal. They crossed the river in the afternoon and stopped at a gas station to ask for directions. Robert felt excited when he saw a group of men sitting in chairs at the gas station. They were real Indians.

The village museum was closed, so they visited a little church across the street. An old priest answered the door. He said the town had been founded by Jesuits as a refuge for baptized Indians who were persecuted by their tribes when they converted to Christianity. The Caughnawagas were a mixture of tribes, including Iroquois, Mohawks, and Algonquians. The men in the village departed every Monday morning in busloads for New York City, where they built tall skyscrapers—they were not afraid of heights. The only reason the reservation survived was because the residents were tax exempt.

Robert noticed a shrine to a young Indian woman. "Can you tell us about the Indian girl?"

"She's quite famous around here," the priest said. "Kateri Tekakwitha was born almost 300 years ago in the Mohawk Valley in upstate New York. Kateri means *pure* in the Iroquois language and Tekakwitha means *putting things in order*. Her father was a Mohawk warrior, part of the Iroquois Nation, and her mother was an Algonquian who was a devout Christian. When Tekakwitha was four, her parents died in a terrible smallpox epidemic that almost wiped out her tribe.

"Tekakwitha survived and was raised by her uncle, a Mohawk chief in another village. Her face was scarred by smallpox and her eyes were so sensitive to sunlight that she walked with a blanket over her head. She was baptized at the age of nineteen and given the name Kateri.[150] When her uncle told her it was time to marry, she replied that Jesus was her only spouse. She fled by canoe and found refuge here at Caughnawaga. At 23, she became the first North American Indian, so far as we know, to take a vow of chastity. She died here a year later." [151]

"It seems that most of the Indians who survived in North America were Christian converts," Robert said.

"That may be true on the East coast. Perhaps it was different in the west."

The priest directed them to a modest bungalow, where Chief Poking Fire answered the door, a gentle, stocky, middle-aged man. He walked them down to the museum. Chief Poking Fire described the tribal customs associated with each of the artifacts and sat down with them to smoke a peace pipe. He then performed the tribal ceremonies for birth, marriage, and death.

"What is this army helmet doing here?" Robert asked.

"I was a Canadian soldier in France during World War I," the Chief replied proudly.

"I am grateful you came to the aid of my people," Robert said. "In a few days, I will return to my home."

Chief Poking Fire placed a postcard on the counter. On the back, he drew a pictogram showing a man paddling a canoe between two shores. "This means that Chief Poking Fire wishes you a good trip over the ocean to your home," he said as he drew a man on the left shore, waving.

As they drove back to Montreal, Suzanne asked quietly, "Are you going back to France for summer vacation?"

"I didn't expect to be away from home so long. I'm going to look around for a job while I'm there. Henry Bloch is giving me the rest of the year off."

"I didn't like New York either," she said.

"I like the work better than I used to and I feel close to Henry Bloch and Carl Lachman, but Trygve Lie is pretty hotheaded and the UN seems to be floundering. I can't tell whether there is any future for me there. Is it going anywhere? I want to make a difference, Suzanne. I want to be a peacemaker. If the UN isn't going to survive, I would rather be working in my own region."

"You have a lot to offer. I wish we didn't live so far apart."

He touched her hand with a sad smile. They could have been quite a couple.

Robert received an engraved invitation to attend a reception for Albert Schweitzer on July 18, 1949, at 934 5ᵗʰ Avenue. It was one of the few addresses in Manhattan that Robert could recognize.

Robert asked Henry Bloch, "Did you arrange for me to attend a reception at the French Consulate?"

"Yes, I thought you might like to meet Albert Schweitzer,

since he is from Alsace."

"Oh sure, that would be interesting. Thank you."

Robert had never been past the front counter of the French Consulate. The reception in the courtyard was filled with important-looking guests, and Robert wondered why they had come. He had never heard of Albert Schweitzer.

Henry Bloch led Robert across the room. "Robert Muller, it is my great pleasure to introduce Dr. Albert Schweitzer."

Schweitzer had a contagious smile beneath his bushy mustache and enormous eyebrows.

"I am told you're from Alsace," Robert said. "My mother is from Haguenau, and I grew up in Sarreguemines."

"Have you heard the latest joke from Alsace?" Schweitzer said brightly. "There was this Alsatian who wanted to learn to speak French like a Frenchman, so he took every class he could find. One day he was swimming in the Rhine, but he got into trouble and started to drown. *'Helf mir, helf mir!'* the man cried out. An Alsatian happened to be standing on the riverbank, and he yelled back, 'If you had learned how to swim instead of wasting your time studying French, you would not be drowning.' "

They both laughed and Schweitzer moved on. There were no speeches. After two hours everyone drifted off. Robert caught a train home.

Robert turned down a request to speak at Smith College because he was leaving in two days for France. He had asked for the slowest ship, preferably French, and the travel office had booked him on the *de Grasse* for August 23rd. It was a French ship that traveled at half the speed of the *Queen Mary*.

Jean-Pierre chided Robert for making a big mistake. "The girls at Smith are the most beautiful girls in the world, and every one of them is incredibly rich. You should have said *yes*."

"I have too much to do. I still have to finish my work and pack everything."

Jean-Pierre drove him to the pier in Manhattan in his new car. Robert enjoyed the wild ride this time. Everything in New York always seemed to be moving too fast.

On the second night at sea, Robert discovered that a group of beautiful young women sitting at his table were from Smith College. They were on their way to study French at the University of Grenoble, then a year at the Sorbonne.

"I was asked to speak to a group at Smith," he said.

"That was our group!" they giggled.

Suddenly Robert was a celebrity—the bright Frenchman from the United Nations who had declined an opportunity to speak at Smith. His admirers were as beautiful as Jean-Pierre had promised. They asked him about France. Robert suggested they begin by introducing themselves.

One by one, the girls told their stories, alluding to lives of such abundance and privilege that Robert could scarcely believe they weren't making up fairy tales. The last to speak was taller and more striking than the rest.

"Well, I'm the newest member of the group because I just transferred to Smith from Vassar for my junior year. I am twenty years old, five-foot-seven, brown hair, a square face, and eyes so unfortunately far apart it takes three weeks to have glasses made."

"Would you mind telling us your name?" Robert said.

"Oh, *pardonnez moi*. I am Jacqueline Bouvier."

When dinner arrived, Bouvier reached into her handbag, pulled out a bottle of ketchup, and passed it around.

"I don't understand ketchup," Robert said when it was passed to him. He held up the bottle and balanced it on his fingertips. "With all the fine condiments in the world, how is it possible that Americans are so fond of a sauce of tomato paste and vinegar that suppresses every other flavor?"

"Be careful with that," a girl said. "Jackie won't eat a meal without her ketchup."

At that moment, the bottle tipped out of Robert's hand and smashed on the floor, splattering ketchup on the carpet and Robert's trousers. Bouvier was so flustered she left the table and refused to talk to Robert for three days.

"I couldn't dance with her anyway," Robert confessed sheepishly, "She is much taller than I am in her dancing shoes."

• • •

Home did not feel the same. Robert's father seemed annoyed with Robert, as if he had done something wrong. Marcelle barely talked to him. His mother acted as if he had never left.

René dropped by and they went for a walk through town.

"Have you ever heard of Albert Schweitzer?" Robert asked René.

"No, who is he?"

"I have no idea. I met him in New York. They made a big fuss over him and he seemed like a nice man. He told me a joke from Alsace, but he never let on who he is."

"Maybe he has a lot of money," René suggested.

"No, he wasn't like that. Very modest."

Robert asked a Protestant friend the next day.

"Of course I've heard of Albert Schweitzer. He's very famous, you know, and he has spoken here several times."

"In Sarreguemines? Why didn't I see it in the papers?"

"He's a Protestant, Robert. The *Courier* would never print a story about a Protestant."

"So who is he?"

"I don't know. I never went to any of his lectures."

Robert visited André Piettre, his thesis advisor in Strasbourg.

"There is an opening on our faculty, Robert. Your thesis was well received, and I don't see any reason why you shouldn't teach here."

"I'll submit my application today," Robert said.

"I will see to it that you are scheduled for a trial lecture," Piettre said, "and you should publish your thesis. Nothing has been written about the Sarre since you left."

"I'll publish it if you will write the preface," Robert said.

Robert worked hard to prepare a good lecture. Members of the faculty sat in with students to hear his presentation. When he was done, the applause lasted for at least a minute. He started looking for a place to live in Strasbourg. Two days later, the Department Chairman called him in.

"That was a brilliant lecture, Muller. I couldn't have done better myself. But that, you see, is the difficulty. Law school is a structured environment. I'm afraid you would never be able to sustain the brilliance of your lecture for an entire academic year."

"You mean I was too interesting?" Robert asked.

"Not exactly, but you're too good for this place, in my opinion. It would wear you down. A man with your energy needs to be out in the world, not facing the same dour faces day after day."

"I didn't get the teaching job," Robert told his family. "They said I should be out in the world. How do you like that?"

"Anything besides making hats," his father said bitterly.

Robert saw the disappointment in his father's eyes.

"You've taught me everything about living a good life, Papa—how to make something that I'm proud of, how to be happy in my profession. I will always have the profession of my father to fall back on. I will never be afraid of going hungry, thanks to you."

His father clasped his arm with a strong hand.

"I'm giving a talk tomorrow night in the Cultural Center at the Lycée," Robert said. "I hope you will come."

For the first time, Robert's family attended one of his speeches. The room was full, and they sat in the front row.

"I met Jan Masaryk in Prague," Robert began, "a few months before he mysteriously flew out of a forty-foot high window to his death. He taught me in a few short minutes that forgiveness is more powerful that any army or regime."

The *Courier de la Sarre* reported *a great conference with our young and brilliant Robert Muller of the United States. It is not without emotion that we heard Robert Muller mention Jan Masaryk.*

When Robert's family dropped him off at the train station two weeks later, they were sad, rather than angry or bitter. "I'll be back a year from now, in the spring," he said. Then I will decide what's next."

Robert hired a small publisher while he was in Paris to print his thesis. Editions Scientifiques Riber promised to deliver 200 copies to a Paris bookstore that agreed to carry them. Robert flew to New York in January 1950, feeling more discouraged than when he left New York.

. . .

On February 9, 1950, Senator Joe McCarthy asked to be recognized on the floor of the U.S. Senate. He seemed intoxicated to Frank Kelly, who was then serving as an aide to Scott Lucas, Senate majority leader. McCarthy was given the floor and began a tirade that would change American politics for a decade. His thoughts were not organized and he started rambling as he accused one person after another of being Communists or Communist sympathizers. To his Senate audience, it might have seemed like a joke at first, but Kelly saw that reporters in the balcony were listening. He leaned over to the Senate leader.

"You'd better get up and challenge him. Those reporters are writing everything down."

Senator Lucas brushed him off. "I'm not going to get into a pissing contest with a skunk."

The McCarthy era was born that day. Wild accusations were soon leveled against officials in the UN Secretariat, including Gustavo Duran from Spain and America's Ralph Bunche. The Fiscal and Financial Branch was paralyzed when Joe McCarthy accused Henry Bloch and Carl Lachman of being enemy agents.

On May 10, 1950, the top story of the *New York Times* reported that Robert Schuman had announced a proposal to combine coal and steel production in France, Germany, Belgium, the Netherlands, Luxembourg, and Italy. German Chancellor Konrad Adenauer hailed the Schuman Proposal, which was immediately approved by the French Cabinet. It was the outcome Robert had predicted in his thesis. Rather than place Germany's Sarre Territory and its coalmines in French custody, the Schuman Proposal would create an economic partnership between the Sarre and Lorraine so that war between them would be impossible.

Robert's thesis was published the following month. There was no mention of it in any newspaper. Robert Schuman later visited Robert at the UN and told him that his thesis had been Schuman's bible. He kept a copy of it on the nightstand by his bed and read it every night while he was deciding to propose the coal and steel community, which eventually led to the European Union.

When the U.S. petitioned the United Nations to take up arms against North Korea in 1950, the Soviet Union was already boycotting meetings of the Security Council as a protest against the exclusion of Communist China from the UN. It was a tactical error. By failing to exercise its veto in the Security Council, the Soviet Union allowed America's resolution to pass and commit UN troops to Korea. From that day on, the Soviet Union punished Secretary General Trygve Lie by treating him as a non-person. The Soviets even refused to say his name. Meanwhile Senator McCarthy stepped up his attacks from Washington and Lie agreed to provide the FBI with an office at Lake Success to conduct its investigation. Delegates protested that Lie was turning the UN into a police state as it turned into a pawn in the Cold War.

In August 1950 the UN moved its headquarters to Turtle Bay in Manhattan. A few months later, Robert recognized Margarita Gallo in the cafeteria. She had returned to New York as Secretary of the Chilean Delegation. They talked over lunch about their experiences as interns. He explained that he was working in the Fiscal and Financial Branch and said that perhaps, someday, they could have lunch together again. To his surprise, she accepted. A friendship began to blossom as they met from time to time in the UN cafeteria.

In the spring of 1951, Robert addressed a United Nations Association chapter in Manhattan. "I was asked to talk about the importance of the United Nations tonight," he began. "Is it doing a good job? Is it something you should continue to support, or is it not very effective? Most people read about the political issues debated in the UN, where the sovereignty of Israel was decided, for example, and where the decision was made to send troops to Korea.

"I work on the economic and social side of the UN, where we view the world as one entity to see if a new picture might emerge that is more accurate than the picture seen by competing sovereign nations. Our purpose is not to profit from our research and compete in the marketplace, but rather to report our findings for the benefit of all humanity.

"A British delegate recently asked me why I worked at the United Nations. I told him I left my home and family in France to take this job because I did not want my children to see what I saw during the war. The delegate said, 'I'm sorry to hear that because you'll be out of a job in 5 years.'

Margarita Gallo met Robert Muller when she was a UN intern in 1948. She returned to New York in 1951 as a member of Chile's UN delegation.

"Whether he was right or wrong is not up to me, because the United Nations will have the same fate as the League of Nations unless it receives the full support of people like you, the American citizens."

People crowded around Robert to congratulate him after his speech. A beautiful woman waited until they dispersed.

"That was a good speech, Robert," Margarita said.

"Thank you, Margarita. I'm glad you were able to come."

"Maybe we could have dinner sometime."

"Well, sure, but I'm leaving for France in two days."

"That's too bad. How about when you get back?"

"Uh, sure, that would be fine. I'll call you as soon—"

"Oh! I have to go now; my ride is waiting. Call me, okay?"

Robert couldn't tell if his heart was beating so fast because he was excited or embarrassed. Margarita *asked him to go to dinner*—not just lunch in the cafeteria—and she was not only the beautiful woman in the world, she was one of the most intelligent, and she came from a prosperous family in Chile. With that, the words of Robert's father echoed in his ears: "You will have to marry some rich girl."

What Robert didn't get to tell her was that the RPF had persuaded him to run for parliament in France on the de Gaulle ticket. *The whole slate of candidates has to win*, the party official had written in his letter to Robert. *We are up against Schuman's slate in your district, so the chances of getting elected are slim. But if any Gaullist can win for the RPF in Sarreguemines, it's Robert Muller.* Meaning Robert was the only Gaullist from the Resistance who name had appeared in the *Courier de la Sarre*. Robert agreed to run. He thought he might be able to do more good in the French parliament.

Robert flew home with an extra suitcase stuffed with all his possessions and started campaigning for office. His mother hated politicians, but she was happy to have her son home. She followed every step of his progress. Robert even noticed her standing in the back during one of his speeches.

"Did you hear that Ralph Bunche at the United Nations

won the Nobel Peace Prize?" Robert asked his father.

"So what? That's strictly an Anglo-Saxon affair."

Robert's father was impressed that his son could work so hard on anything besides schoolwork. He spoke about a great future for him in the hat business after all the political nonsense subsided. Robert's prestige as a UN official and his skill as a public speaker gave him an edge with the voters. He soared from last place to finish with the highest number of votes in his town, and he got more votes than any other candidate on the RPF ticket.

Robert Schuman and his slate won all the other races in the Moselle. It was a winner-takes-all contest, so Robert did not win a seat in the French parliament. All across France, Charles de Gaulle's party had disappointing results, capturing 21% of the votes and winning only 120 of 626 seats in the Assembly. De Gaulle had expected to win 200. He accepted the defeat with his characteristic distain for parliamentary politics. When a supporter recommended that he compromise and form a coalition with another party, the General snapped, "Never! It will be opposition until the regime collapses."[152]

"You received a letter from Charles de Gaulle," Robert's mother said a few weeks later. He had been moping around the house ever since the election.

Robert opened the letter and read it aloud to his family. "It is dated 18 July 1951. *My dear Muller, your thesis on the economic rattachement of the Sarre to France is a document of great interest. I am very touched by your friendship and dedication.*

"And it is signed, *C de Gaulle.*"

"Well, that is something!" Léonie said. "We should put a copy of that letter on the wall."

Robert was not surprised when he heard from René Lejeune. They hadn't talked during the campaign. Robert had beaten René's candidate in their hometown.

"You should have listened to me," René said. "You could have been on your way to Paris now. Schuman has opened the doors with his Coal and Steel Community."

"I suppose you're right, but I couldn't run against de Gaulle. I'm a *Maquisard*, René, and I owe him a duty."

"If you tried to switch parties now, it wouldn't look right. Tell me, Robert, does Charles de Gaulle treat you as an equal?"

"De Gaulle, no, he never looks directly in your eyes. I wouldn't say that he looks down on me in a condescending manner, but he's a pretty strange character. I don't think he has many friends."

"But is he surrounded by good people?"

"They seem to be mostly yes-men. I don't know for sure, but I don't believe the real thinkers stick around very long."

"So what are you doing with him?"

"I will see him in two days. I'm going to tell him that he should support the Schuman proposal for the Sarre and stop pretending the Saärlanders will vote to join France."

De Gaulle gazed over Robert's head as he talked, as if he were gazing into the future. "There may not be any borders one day, Muller. I may be the last man to lead France as a great nation, but I am the General and I must take sides."

"Right now Germany doesn't have a proper government," Robert said. "But the time will come when Germany will be ready for a testing of power, and the test will be the Sarre Territory."

"Are you saying we should give the Sarre back to the Germans?"

"I explained it in my thesis. The prospects for economic *rattachement* must be weighed against the likelihood of a political renaissance in Germany. Only a powerful German government could start a battle for the Sarre, but whatever its political tendencies, the government of the Fourth Reich will not fail to do it. The Sarre problem will remain a test of power for every German government—forever."

"They have no power. The Germans are finished."

"General, I think you should give the Schuman proposal serious consideration. A coal and steel venture is—"

"Schuman is nothing but a poor German!"

Robert had a sinking feeling when he heard that. If

Schuman was a German in the general's eyes, then so was Robert Muller. They were both from Lorraine.

"We will restore Germany to the old Prussian kingdoms," de Gaulle continued, "so that they will *never again* pose a danger to France. The place to start is the Sarre!"

"But if you have read my thesis, you must appreciate that the people living in the Sarre Territory are Prussians. They will never choose France over Germany, but they can be encouraged to see the benefits of a joint venture."

De Gaulle waved Robert off with an impatient flick of his wrist. "Muller, I have no interest in your ideas. We have different views. You must talk to Grandval." [153]

A few days later, Robert met with Gilbert Grandval, a former General in de Gaulle's First French Army. Since the end of the war, Grandval had served in Saarbrücken as the French High Commissioner of the Sarre Territory.

"Muller, what did de Gaulle tell you about your thesis?"

"He said I should speak to you."

"Your book is prejudicial to the interests of France, not only to the economic union, but also to the eventual political union, if not the independence of the Sarre Territory." Grandval was furious. "You have to change your conclusions."

"I'm not going to change my thesis."

"Why?"

"Because you're wrong! I won't change it because I would look like a complete idiot. In any event, it has already been published."

"I know. I bought every copy I could find. It does not properly represent our vision for the future."

"You bought all two hundred copies?"

"I've seen too many wars, Muller. I will never allow those *Boches* to attack our country again."

"This is much too much," Robert said. He left the room.

Robert sat in the park for a long time that afternoon when

he got back to Sarreguemines. He was late for dinner, but his mother had saved him a plate. They let him eat quietly as they waited.

"I think I'm going back to the United Nations," Robert finally said. "There is nothing I can do here. René was right. I went with the wrong party."

"So change parties, not countries," Robert's father said.

"I would look foolish."

"Is that really what's bothering you, son?" Léonie said.

"I don't really feel like I am a part of any nation, Mama. You gave me a German body and a French heart, but you never showed me any borders. I still don't see them. I don't care for New York, and I miss all of you terribly, but maybe in the UN I will find something to hope for."

Robert's father started wringing his hands.

"I have discovered I am not a politician, Papa. The things I do in New York are not very important, but they might lead to something. I don't see any other way."

Robert's father shrugged helplessly.

Léonie zeroed in on Robert with her piercing blue eyes.

"Then you must go, son. Go there and work for the only other family that matters. Work for the human family."

Robert could not find the answer by applying the Principles of Descartes. How could he use Cartesian logic to answer the most important question of his life when most of the pieces to the puzzle were missing? One minute he was going to New York, the next he was going to practice law in Metz, then Paris, then Lyon. His mind was driving him in circles. There was only one way to make it stop.

Robert walked across the fields at dusk into the Forest of Welferding. His better self always seemed to come out in nature, perhaps because he had come from nature, and that is where he would eventually go.

He felt the cool moisture on his skin. He smelled the musky moss tucked between the stones along the brook. He walked between the trees until he almost forgot why he had come.

It was almost dark when he started home to spend his

last night as a resident of Sarreguemines. The sky was filled with stars. There were no air raid sirens, no distant roar of airplanes, no tinsel foil crinkling under his feet.

In the forest, Robert had caught a glimpse of what the world could be like without war, and it was good.

Appendix - Books by Robert Muller

English

A Planet of Hope, 2nd ed. (New York: World Happiness & Cooperation).

Decide To (Spokane, WA: Adventure Trail Publishing, 1998).

Dialogues of Hope (New York: World Happiness & Cooperation, 1990).

Essays on Education, A Vision for Educators, ed. Joanne Dufour (New York: World Happiness & Cooperation).

First Lady of the World 2nd ed. (New York: World Happiness & Cooperation, 1994).

Most of All, They Taught Me Happiness (New York: Doubleday, 1978), 4th ed. (New York: World Happiness & Cooperation, 1990).

My Testament to the UN (New York: World Happiness & Cooperation, 1992).

New Genesis, Shaping a Global Spirituality, (New York: Doubleday, 1984); 3rd ed. (New York: World Happiness & Cooperation, 1993).

The Desire to Be Human, International essays on Pierre Teilhard de Chardin, ed. Leo Zonneveld (Holland: Mirananda Ed Wassenaar).

What War Taught Me About Peace (New York: Doubleday, 1985).

The World Joke Book, (New York: Amity House, 1988), 2nd ed. (New York: World Happiness & Cooperation).

The World Core Curriculum in the Robert Muller School (Arlington, Texas: Robert Muller School).

Safe Passage into the 21st Century, by Robert Muller and Douglas Roche (New York: Continuum, 1995).

Birth of a Global Civilization (New York: World Happiness & Cooperation, 1991).

5000 Ideas and Dreams for a Better World (Santa Barbara, CA: Media 21, 2002).

German

Ich Lernte zu Leben (*Most of All They Taught Me Happiness*);

Die Geburt einer globalen Zivilisation (*Birth Global Civilization*);

Dialoge der Hoffnung (*Dialogues of Hope*);

Mein Testament an die UNO (*My Testament to the UN*);
All German trans. (Hammelsburg, Germany: Drei Eichen Verlag).

French

Le Rattachement Economique de la Sarre a la France (Paris: Editions Riber, 1950).

Sima mon Amour (Sarreguemines, France: Editions Pierron).

Au Bonheur, a L'Amour, a la Paix (*New Genesis*) (Sarreguemines, France: Editions Pierron).

Italian

Battersi Per La Felicitá (Rome: Editrice Nuova Era).

Nuova Genesi (New Genesis) (Rome: Editrice Nuova Era).

Spanish

La Escuela Robert Muller, Manual del Plan de Educacion Mundial (Costa Rica: Gallo Pinto Press).

El Nacimiento de una Civilizacion Mundial (*Birth of a Global Civilization*) (Costa Rica: Gallo Pinto Press).

Portuguese

O Nascimiento de uma Civilizacao Global (*Birth of a Global Civilization*) (Sao Paulo, Brazil-SP: Editora Aquariana).

Polish

New Genesis (Warsaw: Instytut Wysawniczy PAX).

Japanese

New Genesis (*Japanese ed.*) (Univ of Sacred Heart: Catholic Press)

Dutch

Het Wereld Kern-Curriculum (*trans. World Core Curriculum* and *Birth of a Global Civilization*) (Den Haag: East West Publications).

Bibliography

Baxandall, Rosalyn and Elizabeth Ewen. *Picture Windows—How the Suburbs Happened.* New York: Basic Books, 2000.

Behrens, David. "The World Came to Long Island." *LI History.Com.* www.lihistory.com/7/hs741a.htm. 26 September 2002.

Chateaubriand, François-René. *The Memoirs of Chateaubriand.* Trans. Robert Baldick. New York: Alfred A. Knopf, 1961.

Cole, Hugh. *The Lorraine Campaign.* Washington: US Army, 1950.

Coué, Émile. *Self-Mastery Through Conscious Autosuggestion.* U.S. Trans. New York: American Library Service, 1922.

Deighton, Len. *Blood, Tears, and Folly.* New York: Harper Collins, 1993.

De Gaulle, Charles, *Le Salut.* 1940-1942. Paris. Plon, 1954.

L'Appel. 1942-1944. Paris: Plon, 1956.

L'Unité. 1944-1946. Paris: Plon, 1959.

Lettres: 1905-1918. Paris: Plon, 1980.

Finger, Seymour Maxwell and Arnold A. Saltzman. *Kurt Waldheim and the United Nations.* New York: Praeger, 1990.

Ford, Herbert. *Flee the Captor.* Hagerstown: Review & Herald, 1984.

Glendon, Mary Ann. *A World Made New.* New York: Random House, 2001.

Goethe, Johann Wolfgang. "Primal Words: Orphic." *Poems of Goethe.* Ed. Edwin Zeydel. AMS Press Incorporated. 1966. 77.

"Suleika 2." 87.

"Nature." *Johann Wolfgang Goethe.* Ed. Liselotte Dieckmann. New York: Twayne, 1974. 37.

Hart, Liddell. *A History of the Second World War.* New York: Exeter, 1980.

A History of the World War. Boston: Little, Brown, & Company, 1935.

Heer, Friedrich. *Charlemagne and His World.* New York: Macmillan, 1975.

Irving, David. *The Destruction of Dresden.* New York: Holt, Rineholt and Winston, 1963.

Kelly, Frank. *Harry Truman and the Human Family.* Santa Barbara: Capra Press, 1998.

Kemp, Anthony. *The Maginot Line.* New York: Military Heritage, 1988.

Leckie, Robert. *Delivered from Evil.* New York: Harper & Row, 1987.

Ledwidge, Bernard, *De Gaulle.* New York: St. Marten's, 1982.

Marshall, Brig. Gen. S. L. A. "A March to Oblivion." *Readers Digest Illustrated Story of World War II.* New York: The Reader's Digest Association, 1969. 274-275.

Muller, Robert. *5,000 Ideas and Dreams for a Better World.* Santa Barbara: Media 21, 2002.

Most of All, They Taught Me Happiness. New York: World Happiness and Cooperation, 1990.

What War Taught Me About Peace. New York: Doubleday, 1985.

Paris, Erna. *Unhealed Wounds.* New York: Grove Press, 1985.

"Nixon's China Game." *The American Experience.* PBS. WGBH, Boston. 1999.

Roosevelt, Eleanor. *My Day: The Best of Eleanor Roosevelt's Acclaimed Newspaper Columns, 1936-1962.* Ed. David Emblidge. New York: Da Capo, 2001. 141-142.

Roy, Jules. *The Trial of Marshal Pétain.* New York: Harper & Row, 1966.

Sainte-Beuve, Charles Augustin. "What Is a Classic?" *Literary and Philosophical Essays.* Vol. XXXII. The Harvard Classics. New York: P.F. Collier & Son, 1909–14. Bartleby.com, 2001. www.bartleby.com/32/. 22 Sept. 2002.

Schiller, Friedrich. "On the Aesthetic Education of Man." *Literary and Philosophical Essays.* Vol. XXXII. The Harvard Classics. New York: P.F. Collier & Son, 1909–14; Bartleby.com, 2001. www.bartleby.com/32/. 22 Sept. 2002.

The History of the Thirty Years War. Trans. Rev. A. J. W. Morrison. Champaign: Project Gutenberg, 1966.

Shirer, William. "Hitler's Seizure of Europe," *Readers Digest Illustrated Story of World War II.* New York: The Reader's Digest Association, 1969. 77.

Stokesbury, James L. *A Short History of World War II.* New York: William Morrow & Co., 1980.

Sulzberger, C. L. *World War II.* New York: American Heritage, 1966

Taylor, A. J. P. *Illustrated History of the First World War.* New York: G.P. Putnam's Sons, 1964.

Tournoux, J. R. *Pétain et de Gaulle*, Paris: Plon, 1971.

Urquhart, Brian. *A Life in Peace and War.* New York: Harper & Row, 1987.

Walworth, Arthur. *America's Moment: 1918.* New York: W. W. Norton, 1977.

Index

Source Notes

[1] Seymour Maxwell Finger and Arnold A. Saltzman, *Kurt Waldheim and the United Nations,* (New York: Praeger, 1990), xi.

[2] Robert Muller, unpublished journal, February 4, 1970.

[3] UN Press Release, SG/SM/1236, 11 April 1970. U Thant continues, "The character of the relationship between China and the rest of the world will be a dominant factor in the seventies."

[4] UN Press Release, SG/SM/1286, 26 June 1970.

[5] UN Press Release, SG/SM/1333, 14 September 1970.

[6] UN Press Release, SG/SM/1539 24 September 1971. "I believe the People's Republic of China will come to the Organization with the conviction that only unity among nations will lead to world to peace, security and prosperity."

[7] PBS, *The American Experience*, "Nixon's China Game."

[8] Friedrich Schiller, *The History of the Thirty Years' War,* trans. Rev. A. J. W. Morrison (Project Gutenberg), 334. Note: Sweden's General Gustavas Horn conquered Haguenau.

[9] Bosnia and Herzegovina were annexed to Austria in 1908.

[10] Liddell Hart, *A History of the World War* (Boston: Little, Brown, & Company, 1935), 36.

[11] A. J. P. Taylor, *Illustrated History of the First World War* (New York: G.P. Putnam's Sons, 1964), 11; Hart, *A History of the World War*, 37.

[12] Taylor, *Illustrated History of the First World War*, 14.

[13] *New York Times,* Aug. 1, 1914, p. 4.

[14] Taylor, *Illustrated History of the First World War*, 20, 22.

[15] Taylor, *Illustrated History of the First World War*, 109. Germany was not dependant upon imported food before World War I.

[16] Taylor, *Illustrated History of the First World War*, 41.

[17] Anthony Kemp, *The Maginot Line* (New York: Military Heritage, 1988), 16.

[18] Robert Leckie, *Delivered from Evil* (New York: Harper & Row, 1987), 4-5.

[19] Arthur Walworth, *America's Moment:1918* (New York: W. W. Norton, 1977), 11.

[20] Walworth, *America's Moment:1918*, 140.

[21] Treaty of Versailles, Articles 171, 198.

[22] Len Deighton, *Blood, Tears, and Folly* (New York: Harper Collins, 1993), 126-128.

[23] Kemp, *The Maginot Line*, 11-13. The exact ratio was 73% killed, wounded or missing. The number of wounded French soldiers was 4.3 million.

[24] Deighton, *Blood, Tears and Folly*, 129.

[25] Herbert Ford, *Flee the Captor* (Hagerstown MD: Review &Herald, 1984), 70.

[26] Eupen-Malmédy was assigned to Belgium on March 6, 1925. *New York Times,* May 20, 1940, 2.

[27] Robert Muller, *What War Taught Me About Peace*, (New York: Doubleday, 1985), 8.

[28] Muller, *What War Taught Me About Peace*, 18.

[29] Kemp, The Maginot Line, 22.

[30] Robert Muller, *Most of All, They Taught Me Happiness (*New York: World Happiness and Cooperation, 1990), 31.

[31] Muller, *Most of All, They Taught Me Happiness*, 24.

[32] Hart, *A History of the World War*, 18.

[33] Kemp, *The Maginot Line*, 17.

[34] London's Daily Telegraph reported on April 30, 1933: "The French fortifications will, when finished, stretch from the English Channel to the Mediterranean."

[35] Kemp, *The Maginot Line*, 41.

[36] Muller, *What War Taught Me About Peace*, 9.

[37] Taylor, *Illustrated History of the First World War*, 93.

[38] Taylor, *Illustrated History of the First World War*, 103. On July 1, 1916, 13 divisions marched forward in a solid line, with each soldier carrying 66 lb.of equipment, into a steady spray of bullets. It was the heaviest loss in a single day suffered by any army during the war.

[39] Deighton, *Blood, Tears, and Folly*, 125: British casualties soared to 420,000 as the Battle of the Somme continued.

[40] Taylor, *Illustrated History of the First World War*, 135.

[41] in 1915 after destroying a ring of twelve forts around the Belgian city of Liege.

[42] Muller, *What War Taught Me About Peace*, 152.

[43] Kemp, *The Maginot Line*, 46.

[44] Muller, *What War Taught Me About Peace*, 17.

[45] Friedrich Schiller, *On the Aesthetic Education of Man*, XV, 9.

[46] Schiller, *On the Aesthetic Education of Man*, XVIII.

[47] Muller, *What War Taught Me About Peace*, 25.

[48] Johann Wolfgang Goethe, "Nature 1783", reprinted in Liselotte Dieckmann, *Johann Wolfgang Goethe*, (New York, Twayne, 1974) 37.

[49] Liddell Hart, *A History of the Second World War* (New York: Exeter, 1980)*,* 456. "Czechoslovakia has ceased to exist," Hitler said.

[50] Muller, *What War Taught Me About Peace*, 8.

[51] C. L. Sulzberger, *World War II* (American Heritage, 1966), 64.

[52] Deighton, *Blood, Tears and Folly*, 167.

[53] Chateaubriand, François-René, *The Memoirs of Chateaubriand*, trans. by Robert Baldick (New York: Alfred A. Knopf, 1961), 155.

[54] Deighton, *Blood, Tears and Folly*, 165-166.

[55] Muller, *What War Taught Me About Peace*, 20.

[56] Charles Augustin Sainte-Beuve, "What a Classic" (Encylopedia.com), www.bartleby.com/32/202.html.

[57] Leckie, *Delivered from Evil*, 124. The embarrassing defeat of Finland revealed the decrepit state of the French army.

[58] Leckie, *Delivered from Evil*, 159.

[59] *New York Times*, May 12, 1940, 39.

[60] *New York Times*, May 14, 1940, 1.

[61] William Shirer, "Hitler's Seizure of Europe," *Illustrated History of World War II* (Readers Digest, 1969), 77.

[62] *New York Times*, May 11, 1940.

[63] Kemp, *The Maginot Line*, 84.

[64] *New York Times*, May 15, 1940, 2.

[65] Bernard Ledwidge, *De Gaulle* (New York: St. Marten's, 1982), 50-51.

[66] Leckie, *Delivered from Evil*, 162, 166.

[67] Deighton, *Blood, Tears and Folly*, 185.

[68] *New York Times*, May 12, 1940.

[69] Leckie, *Delivered from Evil*, 165.

[70] Deighton, *Blood, Tears and Folly*, 143. France and Britain had more manpower, more tanks, and more planes that Germany.

[71] Leckie, *Delivered from Evil*, 179.

[72] Ledwidge, *De Gaulle*, 32; Leckie, *Delivered from Evil*, 180.

[73] Ledwidge, *De Gaulle*, 23.

[74] Charles de Gaulle, *Lettres 1905-1918*, 336-337.

[75] Ledwidge, *De Gaulle*, 32. De Gaulle was stationed in Mainz

[76] Leckie, *Delivered from Evil*, 178-181.

[77] Ledwidge, *De Gaulle*, 62.

[78] Charles de Gaulle, *L'Appel*, 60.

[79] Hart, *History of the Second World War*, 54.

[80] Ledwidge, *De Gaulle* 63.

[81] Jules Roy, *The Trial of Marshal Pétain* (New York: Harper & Row, 1966), 44-45.

[82] Hart, *History of the Second World War*, 56; Ledwidge, *De Gaulle*, 66.

[83] Muller, *What War Taught Me About Peace*, 128.

[84] *New York Times*, June 18, 1940, p.4.

[85] Sulzberger, *World War II*, 61.

[86] www.charles-de-gaulle.org.

[87] Ledwidge, *De Gaulle*, 68-69.

[88] *New York Times*, June 20, 1940, 7.

[89] *New York Times*, June 20, 1940, 1.

[90] Hart, *History of the Second World War,* 59.

[91] Sulzberger, *World War II,* 182.

[92] Ledwidge, *De Gaulle,* 77.

[93] J.-R. Tournoux, *Pétain et de Gaulle,* 228.

[94] Muller, *What War Taught Me About Peace,* 50.

[95] Muller, *Most of All, They Taught Me Happiness,* 41.

[96] Paris, *Unhealed Wounds,* 40.

[97] Sulzberger, *World War II,* 100.

[98] Muller, *Most of All, They Taught Me Happiness,* 42.

[99] Émile Coué, *Self-Mastery Through Conscious Autosuggestion,* U.S. trans. (New York: American Library Service, 1922), 7-14, 39.

[100] Hart, *History of the Second World War,* 195-198.

[101] Muller, *What War Taught Me About Peace,* 131.

[102] James L. Stokesbury, *A Short History of World War II,* (New York: William Morrow & Co., 1980), 285. Phosphorus bombs were the most cruel of the various incendiary bombs.

[103] Hart, *History of the Second World War,* 269-276.

[104] Émile Coué, *Self-Mastery Through Conscious Autosuggestion,* 37, 40.

[105] Muller, *What War Taught Me About Peace,* 63.

[106] Muller, *What War Taught Me About Peace,* 66-70.

[107] Muller, *What War Taught Me About Peace,* 75.

[108] Muller, *What War Taught Me About Peace,* 52.

[109] Friedrich Heer, *Charlemagne and His World* (New York: Macmillan, 1975), 236-244.

[110] Muller, *Most of All, They Taught Me Happiness,* 53.

[111] Leckie, *Delivered from Evil,* 743.

[112] Leckie, *Delivered from Evil,* 742.

[113] Ledwidge, *De Gaulle,* 172.

[114] Muller, *What War Taught Me About Peace,* 102.

[115] Muller, *What War Taught Me About Peace,* 103-104.

[116] Charles de Gaulle, *L'Unité,* 311; cited in Ledwidge, *De Gaulle,* 181.

[117] *New York Times,* Sept. 5, 1944, p. 3.

[118] *New York Times,* Sept. 16, 1944, 6.

[119] *New York Times,* Sept. 18, 1944, 5.

[120] Ledwidge, *De Gaulle,* 185.

[121] Hugh Cole, *The Lorraine Campaign,* (Washington, DC: U.S. Army, 1950), 598.

[122] Cole, *The Lorraine Campaign,* 528.

[123] Hart, *History of the Second World War,* 461.

[124] Muller, *What War Taught Me About Peace,* 136.

[125] Ledwidge, *De Gaulle,* 194.

[126] See generally, David Irving, *The Destruction of Dresden* (New York: Holt, Rineholt and Winston, 1963); Sulzberger, *World War II*, 420; Hart, *History of the Second World War*, 461.

[127] Ledwidge, *De Gaulle*, 204.

[128] Roy, *The Trial of Marshal Pétain*, 8-14.

[129] Ledwidge, *De Gaulle*, 78.

[130] Brig. Gen. S. L. A. Marshall, "A March to Oblivion," *Illustrated History of World War II* (Reader's Digest, 1969), 274-275.

[131] Ledwidge, *De Gaulle*, 205.

[132] Interview of David Krieger, Nuclear Age Peace Foundation, Santa Barbara, CA. The total number of people who died as a direct result of the two atom bombs dropped on Hiroshima and Nagasaki was 350,000.

[133] Roy, *The Trial of Marshal Pétain*, 248.

[134] De Gaulle, *Le Salut*, 250.

[135] Brian Urquhart, *A Life in Peace and War* (New York: Harper & Row, 1987), 100.

[136] Ledwidge, *De Gaulle*, 212, 215; *New York Times*, April 8, 1947.

[137] Muller, *5,000 Ideas*, Annex.

[138] Mary Ann Glendon, *A World Made New* (New York: Random House, 2001), 9.

[139] Rosalyn Baxandall and Elizabeth Ewen, *Picture Windows—How the Suburbs Happened* (New York: Basic Books, 2000), 4-8.

[140] http://www.nassaulibrary.org/gneck/gnhistory/gestates.html.

[141] David Behrens, "The World Came to Long Island," Long Island Historical Journal, http://www.lihistory.com/7/hs741a.htm.

[142] Frank Kelly, *Harry Truman and the Human Family* (Santa Barbara: Capra Press, 1998), 63-65.

[143] Urquhart, *A Life in Peace and War*, 114-115. Bernadotte was murdered in Jerusalem by the *LEHI* group, headed by Abraham Stern. They were never punished. See also the Jewish Virtual Library at http://www.us-israel.org.

[144] *New York Times*, Sept. 18, 1948, 2.

[145] *New York Times*, Sept. 18, 1948, 4.

[146] Eleanor Roosevelt, *My Day: The Best of Eleanor Roosevelt's Acclaimed Newspaper Columns, 1936-1962*, David Emblidge, ed. (New York: Da Capo, 2001), 141-142.

[147] Glendon, *A World Made New*, 121, 130.

[148] Glendon, A World Made New, 164-170.

[149] Sulzberger, *World War II*, 629; Muller, *5,000 Ideas*, Vol. 2.

[150] Robert Muller, "Tekakuita" (unpublished ms. Short story).

[151] Tekakwitha Conference Center, "Kateri Tekakwitha" (Great Falls, MT: Catholic Information Center, 1996), http://www.cin.org/kat3.html.

[152] Ledwidge, *De Gaulle*, 217.
[153] Robert Muller interview, August 10, 2000.

DECIDE TO BE PEACEFUL

Render others peaceful
Be a model of peace
Irradiate your peace
Love, passionately the peace
    of our beautiful planet
Do not listen to the warmongers,
    hateseeders and powerseekers
Dream always of a peaceful world
Work always for a peaceful world
Switch on and keep on, in yourself
the positive buttons,
    those marked love,
    serenity, happiness, truth,
    kindness, friendliness,
    understanding and tolerance
Pray and thank God every day for peace
Pray for the United Nations
    and all peacemakers
Pray for the leaders of nations
    who hold the peace of the world
    in their hands
Pray God to let our planet at long last
    become the Planet of Peace

And sing in unison with all humanity:

    "Let there be peace on Earth
    And let it begin with me."

—Robert Muller

PO Box 6890, Santa Barbara, CA 93160-6890, USA

www.eastbeach.org

East Beach™ Press Quick Order Form

Online: **www.eastbeach.org**

Email: **orders@eastbeach.org**

Phone: **1-800-942-7617**   Fax: **805-563-9690**

Postal: **East Beach Productions
P.O. Box 6890
Santa Barbara, CA 93160-6890, USA**

Please send the following, books, videos or tapes.
I understand that I may return any item for a full refund.

◆   _____**PROPHET—The Hatmaker's Son** (book) $24.95

◆   _____**PASSION** (Robert Muller audiotape) $9.95

◆   _____**ON THE EDGE** (Award-winning video featuring Mikhail
Gorbachev & other world leaders warning about
the environmental state of the world.) $24.95

Name:_____

Address:_____

City:_____State_____Zip_____

Telephone_____Email_____

Sales tax: Add 7.75% for products shipped to a California address.

Shipping by Priority Mail:
US $4.00 for first item, $2.00 for each additional item.
International: $9.00 for first item, $5.00 for each additional item.

Payment Method: Check or Credit Card

        Visa   MasterCard

Card Number_____

Name on Card _____Exp. Date:_____